Radicals, Rebels
&Establishments

Radicals, Rebels & Establishments

Edited by
PATRICK J. CORISH

HISTORICAL STUDIES XV
Papers read before the Irish
Conference of Historians

MAYNOOTH
16–19 June 1983

CIARAN BRADY
CHRISTOPHER HILL
S. J. CONNOLLY
MARIANNE ELLIOTT
L. M. CULLEN
THOMAS BARTLETT

HUGH GOUGH
JAMES S. DONNELLY JR
PATRICK J. CORISH
MARY CULLEN
MICHAEL LAFFAN
DENIS SMYTH

APPLETREE PRESS

First published and printed in 1985 by
The Appletree Press Ltd
7 James Street South
Belfast BT2 8DL

Ciaran Brady   Hugh Gough
Christopher Hill   James S. Donnelly Jr
S.J. Connolly   Patrick J. Corish
Marianne Elliott   Mary Cullen
L.M. Cullen   Michael Laffan
Thomas Bartlett   Denis Smyth

© 1985

British Library Cataloguing in Publication Data
Radicals, rebels and establishments.—(Historical
   studies, ISSN 0075-0743; 15)
   1. Radicalism—Ireland—History   2. Ireland
   —Politics and government
   I. Corish, Patrick J.   II. Series
   322.4′4′09415   HN400.3.Z9R3

ISBN 0-86281-131-7

Contents

Preface

The Irish Committee of Historical Sciences inaugurated a series of biennial conferences of historians in July 1953. Since then the 'Irish Conference of Historians' has circulated among the Irish universities and university colleges, and the papers read since 1955 have been published as *Historical Studies*. Since 1975 the conferences have been devoted to a single theme, the full list being as follows:

volume	conference	editor	date of publication
I	Trinity College and University College, Dublin, 11–13 July 1955	T. D. Williams	1958
II	The Queen's University of Belfast, 22-23 May 1957	Michael Roberts	1959
III	University College, Cork, 27–29 May 1959	James Hogan	1961
IV	University College, Galway, 25–27 May 1961	G. A. Hayes-McCoy	1963
V	Magee University College, Londonderry, 30 May–1 June 1963	J. L. McCracken	1965
VI	Trinity College, Dublin, 2–5 June 1965	T. W. Moody	1968
VII	The Queen's University of Belfast, 24–27 May 1967	J. C. Beckett	1969
VIII	University College, Dublin, 27–30 May 1969	T. D. Williams	1971
IX	University College, Cork, 29–31 May 1971	J. G. Barry	1974
X	University College, Galway, 23–26 May 1973	G. A. Hayes-McCoy	1977

XI	Trinity College, Dublin, 18–31 May 1975: theme 'Nationality and the pursuit of national independence'	T. W. Moody	1978
XII	The New University of Ulster, Coleraine, 25–28 May 1977: theme 'Minorities in History'	A. C. Hepburn	1978
XIII	The Queen's University of Belfast, 30 May–2 June 1979: theme 'The town in Ireland'	D. W. Harkness & M. O'Dowd	1981
XIV	University College, Dublin, 27–30 May 1981: theme 'Parliament and community'	J. I. McGuire & Art Cosgrove	1983
XV	St Patrick's College, Maynooth 16–19 June 1983: theme 'Radicals, Rebels and Establishments'.	Patrick J. Corish	1985

The sixteenth Irish Conference of Historians, the bulk of the proceedings of which are published in this volume, attracted about a hundred participants. The Irish Committee of Historical Sciences wishes to pay tribute to the hospitality of St Patrick's College, Maynooth, for the provision of services and facilities, including residential facilities.

It also wishes to express its gratitude to the Maynooth Scholastic Trust for a generous grant towards the publication of this volume.

The abbreviations used throughout conform to those recommended in *Rules for Contributors to Irish Historical Studies* (Supplement 1, January 1968).

Introduction

The theme chosen for this Conference was 'Radicals, Rebels and Establishments'. It did seem rather central to what have been appearing to scholars over the last generation or so to represent the real complexities of Irish history, in contrast to the powerful myths this history has generated. Our present discontents in all of this island are an indication that these myths are still powerful.

Every society has its 'establishment', its 'in-people'. It therefore necessarily has its people who are 'out' and who want to get 'in'. The 'rebel' may be defined simply: he wants the complete overthrow of the establishment. The 'radical', on the other hand, wishes to change the composition of the establishment: in practical terms, he wishes to be admitted to it. This results, rather ironically, in a tendency to forget him as a radical if he has been successful, because his success has made him part of the establishment; and if he proves unsuccessful he tends to be remembered as a rebel.

Irish history, by and large, has traditionally been cast in the mould of rebels and establishments. The central theme of this Conference might be described as a search for the Irish 'radical'. To a certain extent he proved elusive, but there were encouraging traces of his existence, in a wide variety of guises.

Like many of the countries of Europe, Ireland entered the modern world through the gates of the century of the Reformation. Ireland emerged from this century in a unique situation, in that the bulk of the population had committed itself to a religion other than that of its civil ruler. The community of the Pale was of central importance in this development. The adherence of these political conservatives to Counter-reformation Catholicism still remains one of the historical enigmas of the period. Ciaran Brady's paper sets them in the historical context of their political alienation from the royal administation in Dublin.

Exclusion from the 'establishment' led, in the not-so-long run, to confiscation of property. The Irish are sometimes faulted for an inability to forget Oliver Cromwell, but they have good reason to remember him. Christopher Hill's paper helps to elucidate his Irish policy by relating it to English social issues.

Irish society was now left largely without that overall framework provided in pre-industrial England by squire, parish and parson. This is the context of S.J. Connolly's paper. What it reveals of the complexities of Irish society is born out by the three papers, by Marianne Elliott, L. M. Cullen and Thomas Bartlett, dealing with what is more and more coming to be seen as the crucial decade of the 1790s, when this unstable society was rapidly politicised. James S. Donnelly's paper teases out the problems posed by the social composition of some of the secret societies of the early nineteenth century. Here again we are only beginning to appreciate the complexities.

Paul Cardinal Cullen looms large in the history of Ireland in the third quarter of the nineteenth century. Here it is argued that his contribution was, essentially, to leave Ireland without a church established by law, but with two religious groupings, Catholic and Protestant, which were ecclesiastical establishments in fact.

Two papers deal with groups whose interests tended to be overlooked as the nationalist issue came to dominate in a basically conservative society. Mary Cullen deals with the feminist issue, and Michael Laffan with the fortunes—or misfortunes—of organised labour.

Finally, there are two papers on non-Irish topics—Hugh Gough on the radical press in the French Revolution, and Denis Smyth on Soviet policy towards Republican Spain during the Civil War.

It is hoped that the importance of the central theme and the manner in which it was sustained throughout all the papers of the Conference will give this volume a coherence and an interest higher than that normally achieved by collected papers of conferences.

Patrick J. Corish

Conservative subversives: the community of the Pale and the Dublin administration, 1556–86

Ciaran Brady

Albeit there has been in these people a general disposition to popery, as a thing wherein they were misled even from the cradle, yet this general recusancy is but of six years continuance at the most, and began in the second year of Sir John Perrot's government, in the beginning of the parliament holden by him. Before which time I well remember there were not in the Pale the number of twelve recusants, gentlemen of account (Archbishop Loftus to Burghley, 22 September, 1590, P.R.O., S.P. 63/94/37).

The alienation of the community of the Pale from the royal administration in Dublin during the latter half of the sixteenth century remains one of least explained developments of Tudor Ireland. The chronological stages of its advance are, however, generally agreed. Having for long urged the revival of English government in Ireland, the loyal Palesmen achieved their ambition in the 1530s and 1540s with the establishment of a permanent English administration in Dublin and the inauguration of a policy to extend English rule over the whole island under a new constitutional dispensation.[1] Yet in the half century after this success the Palesmen appear to have grown steadily disillusioned with their achievement. Tension between the government and the community first became overt in the late 1550s when a number of serious allegations were made against the regime of the earl of Sussex by one of the most prestigious representatives of the Pale, Archbishop George Dowdall. Under Elizabeth Sussex was again the target of a more systematic campaign which finally brought down his administration. His successor, Sir Henry Sidney, though initially popular in the Pale, encountered rising opposition during his first period in office (1566–71), and in the later 1570s he confronted an even more serious display of resistance which led ultimately to his recall.[2] In the early 1580s relations worsened considerably with the outbreak in rebellion of a leading member of the Pale nobility, Viscount Baltinglass, and the discovery of a conspiracy among some young gentry of the country to overthrow the Dublin government and join with the Desmond rebels in a religious crusade against Queen Elizabeth. Early detection and harsh suppression silenced these tumults. But in the parliament held in the aftermath of the Desmond wars in 1585–6 a vigorous and well orchestrated opposition re-emerged which defied Lord Deputy Perrot's attempts to enforce religious conformity and wrecked his parliamentary programme.

In the wake of their success against Perrot the countrymen as a whole began to display a solid and apparently impenetrable recusancy which readily withstood the government's attempts to enforce religious conformity and which, in spite of emphatic declarations of loyalty to the crown, provided a ready audience for Jesuits and other agents of the Counter-reformation. Thus within little more than half a century the Palesmen had undergone a radical transformation. No longer the vanguard of a revitalised English colony, they appeared isolated within the island, disdaining association both with the English, their former political allies, and the Gaelic Irish, their recent religious confrères.

Until recently attempts to account for this strange reversal tended to take the Palesmen at their own word, to accept, that is, that the source of contention between them and the Dublin government was essentially a matter of conscience. The religious commitments of the majority of Palesmen in the last decade of the century are beyond doubt, and Professor Clarke has argued convincingly that the specific brand of Counter-reformation Catholicism embraced by the Palesmen in the early seventeenth century was the central element in their newly formulated sense of identity.[3] Yet this casts little light on the problem of how religion came to be so important to the Palesmen. After Dr Bradshaw it is no longer possible to argue that they remained secretly loyal to the old religion, accepting the Henrician Reformation only because they were obliged to; and Professor Canny has shown that for at least a generation leading Palesmen remained loyal to the royal supremacy and to the various doctrines taught under its auspices.[4] On the other hand, the crown's acute awareness of the difficulty of pressing innovation upon a conservative provincial gentry prompted a moderate attitude on the part of successive viceroys toward the enforcement of religious conformity. Though the statutory and administrative means of coercion were available in Ireland from the early 1560s, they were not brought into operation in any systematic manner for almost twenty years, while at the same time the chronic neglect of the established church despite numerous attempts at reform allowed a less positive but no less effective form of toleration. In these circumstances the existence of a good deal of religious uncertainty, of a large body of undecided church-papistry surrounded by small pockets of committed Catholicism and Protestantism was as inevitable in the Pale as it was in many parts of contemporary England. Irish bishops like their English colleagues were reasonably confident that the Reformation would eventually take root through the judicious application of inducements and sanctions. The cruel explosion of such modest and well grounded hopes by the sudden and general display of recusancy which occurred in the Pale in the 1580s and 1590s reveals not the churchmen's lack of realism but the radical character of the change which they confronted.

Why the Palesmen independently changed their minds, why they moved, in the absence of significant pressure, from passive church-papistry to active and decisive recusancy remains as yet a mystery. The suggestion that at some point in time the entire community grew sensitive to a whole range of spiritual and doctrinal matters which they had hitherto regarded with indifference is surely inadequate. The concept of a collective crisis of conscience is philosophically dubious; but even if true, it implies some antecedent stimulant which aroused men from their complacency and drove them towards a common commitment. However important it grew to be in the future, religion could not have been the thing at first contended for. That it eventually came to be raises rather than resolves a problem.

In their search for this prevenient determining factor modern scholars have devised a curious secular version of the old religious explanation. It was, it is now suggested, dissatisfaction with the new ideological values and political intentions of Elizabethan administrations that foreshadowed and then provoked the Palesmen's rejection of the official religion. The Palesmen, it seems, were deeply committed both for practical and intellectual reasons to the major attempt at conciliation launched in Ireland in the 1540s. Having for long been convinced that the revival of the Anglo–Norman conquest was neither practicable nor necessary,

politically articulate Palesmen had urged that the gradual assimilation of the Gaelic lordships into a new united polity could be
achieved purely by diplomacy and educational reform. The act for
kingly title of 1541 and the policy of surrender and regrant which
followed from it marked the apogee of the Palesmen's influence in
Tudor politics. But as the optimistic, humanist assumptions which
underlay their arguments gave way before a gloomy Calvinist
assessment of the limits of political reform, so the policy itself lost
credit with English governors who now resorted increasingly to
coercion and repression. Their values and the policies they had
built upon them being thus rejected, the Palesmen realised that
they could have no place in the emerging English colony.
Minerva's owl then took to the skies, and a new and separate sense
of identity dawned upon them in which defiance of a destructive
Protestantism formed a central element.[5]

The strengths of this revised interpretation are considerable. It
accounts for the emergence of opposition in the Pale long before
the religious question had become central. It relates it moreover to
a marked change in the level and the pace of government activity
that became obvious in the latter half of the century. Thus the
complaints against Sussex in 1558–63, and the massive defiance of
Sidney in 1575–7, have been persuasively explained as a desperate
response to the radical change in government ideology which these
men represented. Yet, for all this, the new account retains many of
its predecessor's deficiencies. It is highly idealist, suggesting that
the interrelations of large groups of people over time can be explained in terms of the guiding effects of certain coherent and exclusive systems of thought. Its thrust too is decidedly circular,
since its account of the emergence of religious sectarianism is
premised upon the assumption of prior political commitments
which were no less dogmatic. But most important of all, it fails to
take account of the facts.

The Elizabethan era witnessed no abandonment of the policy of
gradual assimilation but rather an intensification of effort to make
it more effective. The dominant policy of the period is to be found
not in repression or dispossession, but in an ambitious attempt to
stabilise political and social relations within the Gaelic lordships
by standardising and commuting all existing feudal and martial
dues in a process known as composition.[6] It is true that Elizabethan viceroys showed some interest in planting colonies and that
they were fully aware that their diplomatic arrangements with the
native lords needed to be underpinned by the threat and occasional

use of force. But in this they would have met with little disagreement from politically conscious Palesmen. It is possible to extract a tradition of irenic reformism from the Pale's political treatises; but it is possible also to delineate a quite opposite coercive tradition. Yet such an exercise is largely futile, for the majority of political reformers clung to neither extreme exclusively, but advocated conciliation at certain times and places and coercion at others, diplomatic settlements in some areas, colonies in others. This easy eclecticism is the truly dominant theme of Pale political treatises from the writings of Thomas Bathe in the 1520s to those of Rowland White, Patrick Sherlocke and Nicholas Taaffe in the 1570s and 1580s. Thus if any ideological consensus may be discerned in the political attitudes of the Palesmen, it may be seen to lie in a firm commitment to opportunism.[7]

The Palesmen's theoretical pragmatism reflected their material environment. However much they may have desired an accommodation with the Gaelic lords in the long term, they were perfectly aware that no lasting agreement could be ensured unless they were able to defend themselves against those who mistook conciliation for weakness. Centuries of experience had taught them that the ability to support their allies and punish their enemies amongst the Gaelic Irish was essential not simply to progress, but to mere survival. Thus while the peaceful assimilation of the existing Gaelic lordships rather than conquest was generally regarded as the optimum means of bringing peace, it was recognised also that such a policy could be put into effect only if the government exercised sufficient force to sustain its authority within the islands. Amongst the hard-faced men of the Pale, unilateralism was never considered to be a realistic option.

In the light of their common commitment to long-term assimilation, and of their equal willingness to supplement and indeed defend that objective by an occasional resort to violence, any explanation of the Palesmen's estrangement from the government in terms of profound disagreement over matters of high policy may be seen to be wholly inadequate: its case rests entirely upon grand conceptual polarities which have no foundation in fact. That there was a close association between the disillusion of the Palesmen and a significant change in the conduct of the viceroys in the latter half of the century is however undeniable. Yet the change itself, I shall argue, was due not to an early rejection of the Palesmen's political views but, ironically, to a belated appreciation of their very insistence upon the urgency of the Irish problem.

The recall of St Leger in 1556 was prompted not by deliberate repudiation of his stated objectives, but by the gradual realisation that even under his own terms his administration had failed to function effectively. His failure to extend and develop the policy of surrender and regrant through the island coupled with the actual break-down of arrangements he had made in Ulster, Munster and the midlands made it obvious that under St Leger English government was not an effective force. The discovery, moreover, that he had tolerated neglect and corruption within his administration deepened suspicions concerning his commitment to the objectives of 1541. By his self-interested laxity, it appeared, St Leger had discredited the crown in Ireland and allowed the policy launched with such prestige in the 1540s to fall into disrepute.

Sussex and Sidney, the men who replaced St Leger, were determined to restore the reputation of the crown by reviving and enforcing old agreements and by extending the initiatives of the 1540s into as many areas as possible. Yet, conscious of the ease with which St Leger's 'sober drifts and politic ways' had been deflected and exhausted by the native lords, they sought to devise strategies that would enforce the national policy in a progressive and systematic fashion as quickly as possible. And fearful too of the mire of local connection in which St Leger's enthusiasm had foundered, they sought from Westminster an advance endorsement for their objectives which would minimise their dependence upon local *élites*. For all these considerations St Leger's successors set about transforming his sensitive but indefinite process of acclimatisation into a clearly defined and exclusive programme of action whose objects, costs and time of duration could be estimated before the service commenced.[8]

The emergence of this programmatic approach to Irish governance marked no deviation from the principles of Henrician policy: Sussex and Sidney continued to work in their varied ways for the assimilation of the Gaelic lordships under English rule. But the new administrative style carried with it some grave practical implications. It involved a substantial increase in the crown's military and administrative presence in the country and an acceleration in the pace of government activity in every sphere. It implied also a single-minded dedication towards the achievement of select objectives and a consequent insensitivity to secondary issues of local interest. All of this was regarded as a healthy antidote to St Leger's indolence, but in the short term the new approach demanded extraordinary sacrifices from the Pale while offering precious little in return. The Palesmen were now required to support these expensive régimes during their grand national enterprise without raising any distracting issues of their own; and they were expected also to make good any shortfall which bad luck or poor judgement interposed between initial estimations and actual conditions. The new administrative style, that is, required the Palesmen to assume ultimate responsibility for every contingency that might arise from decisions over which they could exert no control. That they should have lost their influence with the Dublin administration at the very point when the viceroys had come to accept their own assessment of the urgency of the Irish problem was a strange predicament indeed. But the Palesmen's first sense of this dilemma was expressed neither in terms of bemused irony, nor of sharp ideological dispute, but in simple outrage at the government's vastly increased demands for supply which they termed contemptuously as 'the cess'.

Asked to explain the term 'cess' by the queen or the privy council, English officials normally proffered a definition of purveyance.[9] Cess was indeed partly purveyance, but it was also a good deal more; for while the prerogative in England had been progressively surrounded by statutory restraints, in Ireland it appeared to be subject to ever wider application. Thus the viceroy claimed the right to have his household and retinue doubly provisioned, both at Kilmainham and during his frequent tours of the country. The country was likewise obliged to support the entire garrison either by victualling the forts or by boarding the soldiers individually. Finally the Palesmen were expected to contribute to the government campaigns in the rest of the country not only by attending upon general hostings, but by supplying horses, corn and cattle to the army in the field. The range of the government's demands upon the country constituted such an extension of the prerogative that even the viceroys hesitated to call it simply purveyance. But for the countrymen themselves the issue was clear: the government's requisitions were unprecedented and wholly illegitimate, and so they accorded to them the same term used indiscriminately to denote the impositions extorted by any great warlord upon his subordinates. They called it the cess.

The composite character of the cess in the early Elizabethan era was largely due to the curious process by which it had evolved. The Palesmen had always acknowledged the conventional military obligations, and it seems too that they yielded some rights under the prerogative to the English monarch's representative in Ireland.

At least from the time of Poynings English soldiers appear to have been billeted on the country occasionally for agreed rates.[10] But until the mid-1550s neither the size of the garrison nor the level of government activity was sufficiently high to be the cause of serious discontent. Yet it was in the relatively dormant period of English government in Ireland in the twenty years or so after the Kildare rebellion that two significant innovations were innocently made. First, St Leger decided to dispense with the 'cators' who previously undertook to provision his household and to assess his demands directly on the country on the basis of the unit of subsidy collection, the ploughland. At the same time he began to convert the country's obligation to attend upon hostings into a cash payment or a payment in kind.[11] Both changes aroused little initial antagonism: in the prevailing peace the governor was arguably relieving the country of tiresome officials and time consuming chores. Yet together the alterations seemed to imply that the supply of the household and the duty to attend upon hostings were no longer simply obligations of circumstance, but positive taxes due to the governor as sources of revenue whose form and content could be altered to accord with his particular needs or desires. In the 1540s, therefore, the precedents for a substantial extension of government power over the community had been clearly laid down, but, except perhaps in the brief viceroyalty of Sir Edward Bellingham, the need for their exploitation did not become evident until the revision of government strategy which occurred after St Leger's recall in 1556.

After 1556 the demands imposed upon the country under the common label of cess increased to such an extent as to constitute a qualitative change in the issue at stake. The garrison itself quadrupled to an average of 2,000 men in the 1560s and 1570s and to over 6,000 in the early 1580s.[12] (These figures, moreover, are exclusive of the wives, mistresses etc., who normally accompanied the garrison and of the two horses and one servant formally allotted to each horseman. So for a real estimation of the numbers dependent upon the country they need to be increased by at least a factor of three.) Thus, given the subsistence nature of the Pale economy, and accepting Professor Canny's estimation of the country's abnormally low yields, these increases constituted a significant demographic problem in themselves.[13] But the garrison posed an acute economic problem also. Though Sussex raised some of the billeting rates by 40 per cent in 1556, they still remained well under market prices. A comparison of the daily proportions issued by professional victuallers to the army in transit with normal market prices and the boarding allowances paid by each soldier reveals that, discounting all forms of extortion and over-indulgence, each soldier was subsidised by the country to the sum of 29 shillings a month.[14]

In addition to this massive increase the viceroys now systematically exploited the household cess as a means of supplementing their income. Both Sussex and Sidney took well over their own needs and re-sold their takings in the market. It is impossible to estimate the exact cost of the household cess to the country in any one year, but the viceroys themselves when pressed to convert their takings into a fixed payment gave perhaps the most dependable contemporary estimate. Lord Grey's auditor estimated that the prerogative was worth about £3,000 annually, while Sir John Perrot offered to surrender the cess in return for an increase of £2,500 to his ordinary salary.[15]

The new viceroys also exploited the commutation of general hostings. We know that general cesses of this kind were summoned every year between 1556 and 1563, in 1566, 1569 and in 1575-6, and there is evidence that similar cesses were made in other years also. The demands made on these occasions were extremely high: Sussex took an annual average of 56,000 pecks of grain and 1300 animals in the early 1560s, and 800 pecks with 2,000 beeves were taken yearly by Sidney in the 1570s.[16] Finally there was the incalculable factor of abuse. The opportunities provided by these several exactions for extortion, fraud and theft were legion. Allegations from the country were endemic, and even the English officials were prepared to admit on occasions that terror was rampant. The total cost of the cess to the country was inevitably a matter of the sharpest dispute. But for the year 1561 where agreed figures are most available I have estimated that it was probably in the region of £20,000. This was admittedly a very bad year, but it is significant that when later governments wished to remind the Palesmen about how oppressive other régimes had been it was this very figure that they recited.[17]

Such a major increase in the country's burden, however, cannot be accounted for simply in terms of the government's disregard of the Palesmen. In the 1560s and 1570s each of the viceroys made successive efforts to reduce the charge through reform. Apart from raising the billeting rates, and enforcing greater discipline in the army, Sussex attempted to shift the burden from the country in general to the lessees of large crown properties. Sidney did likewise, and also sought to reduce the charge of billeting by removing more soldiers from the heartland of the Pale to the borders. Both plans, however, proved unworkable. Later in the decade Sidney attempted to dispense with cess altogether, by victualling the army directly from England. But this plan too went awry, with disastrous consequences for the unfortunate victualler. When Sidney's temporary successor Fitzwilliam attempted to take on the victualling himself the army was reduced to the point of starvation.

The viceroys, then, were clearly sensitive to the Palesmen's plight. Yet their very failure to act effectively on the countrymen's behalf underlines the degree to which their administrations were dependent upon the cess. To men committed in advance to the execution of predetermined objectives, the sufferings of the Palesmen were necessarily of secondary importance and could not be allowed to interfere with the attainment of their principal aims. But the viceroys' attachment to cess was also more positive. For the more their programmes began to founder, the more, that is, the stubborn reality of the Irish problem failed to conform to their initial analysis, the more they were compelled to turn for the discharge of their prior obligations to the most flexible and open-ended expedient available to them. Because it was cheap, because it was reasonably effective, because it was of fixed and estimable cost, the cess made stable that most dangerous of administrative variables, the food supply. More important, because it could be indefinitely extended, the cess offered a means of generating an additional revenue when the money and time allotted in the original calculations were running out. Thus as their administrations began to crumble the viceroys turned compulsively to the cess not merely as an adjunct to their governments but as an essential means of their survival.

The government's fundamental dependence upon cess became starkly explicit in the last viceroyalty of Sir Henry Sidney. In 1575, as his final effort to solve the cess problem, Sidney proposed that all the exactions be abolished in return for a fixed cash payment rated as was the cess upon the ploughland. The terms of this new 'composition' for the Pale were generous enough: the proposed rate of £3.6.8 on each ploughland compared, as Sidney himself asserted, very well with the costs of the actual cess.[18] Yet even by making the proposal Sidney revealed that the government no longer regarded the cess as an assorted collection of temporary though necessary impositions, but rather as an alternative revenue, an annual subsidy which could be levied without parliamentary consent upon the ploughlands of the Pale. While hitherto he and his predecessors had preferred to defend their amalgam of exactions in terms of extraordinary necessity, he now asserted that the entire body of the cess and the composition now proposed were incident to the crown by virtue of the prerogative alone and were not open to negotiation. 'Examine not [the prince's] authority' Sidney roundly assailed the recalcitrant Palesmen, 'neither decipher his power. Compare not your principles with his authority, neither dispute your liberties with his prerogative. For notwithstanding these principles, grants and liberties be great, yet they cannot abate or impugn the least part of your prince's prerogative which is so great as nothing can be greater'.[19]

Sidney's bald offer of a composition and the uncompromising terms in which he presented it made brutally clear to the Palesmen the nature of their dilemma. Loyal subjects of the crown who had repeatedly urged the revival of English government in Ireland, they could continue to support this endeavour only by sacrificing their hallowed rights as Englishmen under English law. Yet they could reject the claims of the English government only at the risk of identifying themselves with their own and the crown's traditional enemies, the Gaelic Irish. It was their consciousness of this acute predicament and their response to it that determined the subsequent evolution of the community of the Pale in the later sixteenth century.

On the basis of this analysis two strategies of defence were ruled out for the Palesmen from the outset. Rebellion, the characteristic response of the Irish, involved an inconceivable reversal of loyalties. Equally, representation, the most natural tactic of loyal subjects with a grievance, was unavailable to them. Though individual Palesmen continued to hold places of influence in the viceroys' councils, the upper limits of that influence were sharply defined. The cess was of such importance to the survival of these administrations that no councillor could argue strongly against and retain his place. Thus men like Cusack and Dillon retained the confidence of several viceroys at the cost of largely ignoring the country's complaints, while men like Nicholas White or Nicholas Nugent who supported the country's case risked losing the confidence of the governor. At best native councillors acted as mediators during times of trouble, but their ability to initiate or suppress country opposition was negligible. Precluded from rebellion and representation, the Palesmen chose a third option: subversion. And there evolved in the 1560s and 1570s an increasingly sophisticated campaign to undermine offending viceroys by civil disobedience at home and political intrigue abroad.

Reflecting the universal character of the burden, opposition to the cess arose in every barony, transcending geographical and factional boundaries, and uniting nobles, gentry and husbandmen in a common refusal to grant the government its demands. In crisis years like the early 1560s and later 1570s this general strike could be startlingly effective: supplies for the viceroy and the forts were grossly deficient, general cesses were left unanswered and clashes between the soldiers and the countrymen multiplied. Strikes like these crippled Sussex's last effort against O'Neill, paralysed Fitz-william's administration and ruined Sidney. Afflicted governors liked to pretend that they were the victims of a sinister manipula-tive conspiracy. But the evidence belied their claims. It is true that Kildare and Ormond individually supported different cess campaigns. It is clear also that leading nobles like Gormanston, Louth and Howth were active organisers of resistance in their own shires and that a small group of lawyers who were clearly aware of the larger constitutional implications of the issue undertook to represent the country's grievances. But the effectiveness of the cess revolt in the face of government suppression and the unity which it sustained in the faction-ridden Pale could not have been generated by the machinations of any small group of political agitators. The leaders of the opposition acquired and maintained their influence in the country for no reason other than the universal grievance of the cess. Extensively and systematically oppressive, the cess rather than matters of religion or high policy produced a groundswell of discontent which the Palesmen themselves labelled 'the country cause'.[20]

The essential ingenuousness of the Palesmen's discontent was most clearly revealed in the second, and apparently more devious, aspect of their strategy of resistance. Debarred from access to the viceroy, the Palesmen sought redress by appealing directly to their sovereign in England. The tactical strengths of such a move were obvious. At court the agents of the Pale were able to exploit the factional struggles of the leading political groupings in their own interests. Their success in manipulating Elizabethan court politics in this manner was considerable: it was largely responsible for the recall of Sussex in 1564, and of Sidney in 1578, and it forced Fitz-william to relent in 1573. Yet the strategy could be defended on sound constitutional grounds alone. Since the Palesmen enjoyed equal legal status with Englishmen as common subjects of the same sovereign, in making their complaints directly to Whitehall it was arguable they were simply affirming their essential loyalty. This was to become the familiar defence of the Pale's agents at court, from the students who made their representation in the early 1560s through the defence of the lawyers Netterville and Burnell for their complaints against Sidney in the 1570s to the case of Gerald Aylmer in the 1580s. But it was more than simply a lawyer's ruse. It was a genuine conviction of the loyal Palesmen expressed in various forms throughout the period from the hastily compiled apologia for the students presented by the nobles and gentry in 1562 to the finely honed phrases of Speaker Walsh in parliament in 1586. It was perhaps most routinely and yet most pithily formulated by Sir Nicholas White. Writing to Burghley at the height of the composition controversy in 1577, White urged his patron to

> make some difference between complaining and disobedience. The gentlemen who now feel themselves aggrieved with the greatness of the cess imagined that to complain was the very gate of obedience through which they must enter with humble petition of redress to their sovereign and prince under whose only will and sentence [the people] and [the viceroy] stand.[21]

Elizabeth's response to such carefully expressed sentiments was characteristic: having at first rebuked the complainants for their impertinence in defying the viceroy, she listened to their case attentively, and then let them have their way. Thus the law students and the agent who succeeded them, William Bermingham, got the full scale commission of inquiry they had sought and Netterville and Burnell not only wrecked Sidney's composition plan, but secured the crown's endorsement for an alternative proposal of their own.[22]

Success at court thus reinforced the Palesmen's communal loyalism as the oppressiveness of the cess had forged their commitment to local subversion. Yet the very repetitiveness of these successes was in itself a sign of their inconclusiveness. The Palesmen, that is, may have succeeded in displacing particularly extortionate governors, but they seemed incapable of removing the potential for extortion by altering the character of the viceroyalty itself. And significantly, the more overtly political their representations were, the less influence they exerted. Thus courtiers like Ormond and Kildare never took a lead in the cess issue, and men like Archbishop Dowdall or the earl of Desmond who attempted to attach the cess to broader political issues were the least effective spokesmen. The limits of the Palesmen's political power were more fully revealed on the few occasions where they actually succeeded in displacing the viceroy. Sir Nicholas Arnold, the commissioner appointed after Bermingham's agency and who eventually displaced Sussex as viceroy in 1564, established an administration that was consciously responsive to the Palesmen's interests. But within a year his government collapsed in the face of increasing demonstrations of defiance and rebellion in Munster, Ulster and even in Leinster itself. In the early 1570s Sir William Fitzwilliam, having determined to do without the cess, also secured the support of the Palesmen, but his administration foundered when he failed to keep the peace in Munster and Ulster. A similar fate awaited the most considered attempt to accommodate the Palesmen's interests in government after Sidney's recall in 1578. Following the advice of Lord Chancellor Gerrard, Sidney's ambitious project of national composition was abandoned and the garrison reduced to 1,200 men. The new administration under Sir William Drury was to concentrate on regenerating the Pale by improving its defences and the administration of law in the shires. The Palesmen's proposal to take over the victualling of the garrison was to be accepted and they were to be encouraged to participate more actively on commissions of peace and array. Gerrard's experiment, which was based upon his own researches into the decay of the old colony, was deliberately designed to restore good relations with Palesmen. But, like Arnold's, it too was to prove short-lived: in less than a year it was engulfed by rebellion in Munster.[23]

For the Palesmen, therefore, the lessons of their activities over the first twenty years of Elizabethan government were profoundly ambiguous. The response of the crown to their grievances had deepened their sense of loyalty while weakening their respect for the authority of the Dublin government. Yet their regular subjection to the demands of helplessly oppressive governors only sharpened their hostility toward a local administration which they had ceased to love but continued to fear.

Thus over the 1560s and 1570s an important but subtle shift began to occur in the political outlook of the Palesmen. At the beginning, it is clear, Palesmen like Dowdall and Bermingham sought for nothing more ambitious than a change of viceroy: they wanted to be rid of Sussex. But gradually, as they began to locate the source of their trouble, not in the conduct of greedy or irresponsible individuals, but in the very character of the viceroyalty, so the nature of their response and the mode in which it was expressed changed. This process of estrangement from the viceroyalty *per se* was a gradual and uncertain one. It emerged first during Sidney's parliament of 1569–71 when even the most neutral and beneficial aspects of the government's parliamentary programme were greeted with a show of suspicion and hostility that quite astounded the deputy.[24] It became even more evident however with the appearance in the early 1570s of a group of self-styled 'commonwealth men' or 'countrymen' who first intimidated Fitzwilliam into inaction and then led the universal and unrelenting opposition to Sidney's offer of commutation.[25] These 'commonwealth men', it is clear, regarded themselves not as politicians, like Desmond or Bermingham, intent upon the replacement of their enemy with an ally of their own, but as a permanent country opposition whose carefully planned apologias underlined their determination to uphold their constitutional rights as Englishmen under English law. Thus the growth of the viceroys' dependence upon the arbitrary cess was paralleled by the advance of the countrymen's opposition from mere economic or physical resentment into a fully articulated, constitutional case. And when Sidney made his defence of the prerogative in blankly absolutist terms in the later 1570s the lines of demarcation in this struggle were clearly drawn. Even then, however, the process of alienation was not altogether irreversible. The new establishment of 1578 was consciously devised to reconstruct good relations between the Pale and the royal administration: had it survived, it might have made good the loss. But in the years following the collapse of that attempt, the pace and direction of the Pale's estrangement changed dramatically.

The Desmond rebellion heralded a return of Sussex's and Sidney's methods with greater intensity than ever. By 1581 the garrison had rocketed to over 6,300 men and the problem of supply had increased accordingly.[26] The arrangements reached with the country by Drury and Gerrard had collapsed almost immediately upon the outbreak of the rebellion. Billeting was reintroduced, general cesses were revived, and in 1580 cess for the viceroy's house was again collected.[27] For the Palesmen, therefore, the new governments of Sir William Pelham and Lord Grey were unprecedentedly oppressive. They were equally unresponsive. Charged with the suppression of the Munster rebellion by the shortest and cheapest means possible, these governors were committed to a programme of stark and brutal simplicity. Issues that had not distracted Sussex or Sidney from their objectives would carry little weight with these men either. The initial reaction of the country to the return of this unresponsive rule was by now automatic. The cesses were left un-answered, soldiers and civilians clashed and preparations were made to despatch yet another representative agency to the Court where the Palesmen knew they would find some relief. Yet before this familiar *modus operandi* was fully activated, an event intervened which wrecked the Palesmen's conservative tactics and fundament-ally altered the nature of their grievance.

The rebellion which killed Gerrard's hopes for the Pale rested upon a far more radical analysis of Ireland's problems than any the Palesmen had hitherto conceived. For James Fitzmaurice and those who followed him in rebellion the cause of the country's con-tinuing conflict with the government was due not to the conduct of individual viceroys, nor even to the character of the viceroyalty itself, but to the essentially aggressive nature of all English mon-archs since their break with Rome and their assertion of an im-perialist, Protestant independence.[28] Even in Anglo–Ireland as a whole, it is clear that Fitzmaurice's views were not widely sup-ported, and in the Pale, where rebellion was regarded as anathema, they had hitherto received little or no support. But among two specific sections of Pale society they had come to acquire increasing appeal. Amongst the most gaelicised of the border lords of the Pale a common awareness of the implications of reform by composition made Fitzmaurice's reaction seem quite appealing. It was attractive too, but for very different reasons, to a small group of young scholars and lawyers who had fallen under the influence of the Counter-reformation in one of its most militant phases during their education on the continent or in the sub-culture of the Inns of Court.[29] On their own it is doubtful whether either of these influ-ences would have been particularly powerful, for there existed suf-ficient countervailing forces on both to contain their effects. But where they combined, as in the cases of James, second Viscount Baltinglass and William Nugent, brother of the Baron Devlin, the result was explosive.

The insurrection planned by Baltinglass and precipitated by the government in June 1580 was a fiasco. Baltinglass's rising collapsed almost immediately, Nugent's belated effort hardly got under way at all. Such fighting as there was, was conducted by the Gaelic septs on the borders of the Pale, while the Pale as a whole remained cold. Yet like another insurrection of poets and intellectuals of more recent times, the Baltinglass–Nugent affair was to be far more important in its consequences than in its origins. The reaction of the viceroy, Lord Grey, was hysterical and ferocious.

Convinced, without foundation as it turned out, that the conspiracy was widespread, he struck out wildly at every level of Pale society. Kildare and Delvin, who had some foreknowledge of the conspirators' intentions but who appear to have tried to forestall them, were arrested, charged with treason and for long seemed on the point of paying the highest penalty.[30] Several of the Nugent kin-group, including Delvin's own family, were arrested and condemned. A number were executed. The sons of leading gentry and legal families in Meath, Kildare and Dublin who were either privy to Nugent's plotting or had merely been told about it were treated with equal despatch.[31] Some were executed simply on the report of a former conspirator who had turned queen's evidence.[32] And while the arrests and executions continued, the lands of Nugents, Eustaces and many more were confiscated and hastily redistributed by Grey to his officers.[33] It was a time too when old scores were settled. Each of the leading commonwealth men was at some point held in danger of his life. Richard Netterville lost two brothers, Barnaby Scurlock lost two sons; Nicholas Nugent, the chief justice of common pleas, who had vigorously defended the countrymen before Sidney on the Irish council in 1577, lost his life.[34] Even the new spokesmen were subjected to intimidation. Patrick Bermingham and Roger Garland were summoned by the governor and warned that their organising activities could be construed as sedition in time of rebellion and treated accordingly.[35]

In the end, however, the amount of blood actually shed in the aftermath of the conspiracy was surprisingly small. Under the extremely courageous urgings of Nicholas White, the English privy council moved to stay Grey's hand after a mere twenty gentlemen of significance had been executed, and by 1584 most of those arrested had been released.[36] But for over three years the community of the Pale had been subject to an onslaught far more deadly than any perpetrated by Sussex or Sidney in their most authoritarian moods, and at the end of this reign of terror their outlook had changed decisively. Though it was fantastic in formulation and foolhardy in execution, Baltinglass's radical interpretation of the relationship of government and society in the Pale had apparently been validated by the government's ruthless reaction to his pathetic demonstration. Young men whose shrill assertions had in the past been treated with wry detachment by their more experienced and complacent elders were now seen to be justified through the loss of their lives, while the constitutional strategies of previous decades appeared helpless in face of unrelenting government repression. This tendency toward a more general reinterpretation of the community's ills was furthered by the disposition of the commonwealth leadership itself. Netterville, Burnell, Scurlock, Bermingham and Aylmer were all committed Catholics. Their victimisation in the years of terror greatly enhanced their status. But even they remained without a focus on which to concentrate the country's fears. Once more it was the government that contributed the final element to this emergent synthesis of politics and religion; and as in the modern instance, the catalyst was provided by the summoning of a parliament.

The suppression of the Desmond rebellion and of a number of related broils elsewhere persuaded the crown to launch one further attempt at a general reform of the whole island. Thus in 1584 the privy council determined upon the appointment of one who had for long urged the acceptance of his plans for government, Sir John Perrot. In essence Perrot's new programme was very close to Sidney's plan to secure a permanent settlement of surrender and regrant by means of general composition, and like Sidney Perrot also planned to include the commutation of the government's cess in the Pale in his national scheme.[37] The new viceroy added, however, two apparently unrelated proposals of his own. First, in order to equalise the burden of the composition, he planned to establish a new uniform unit of assessment which would apply throughout the island, including the Pale. Second, in the light of the previous threats posed by religious dissent, he proposed to enforce religious conformity in every province.[38] And Perrot had one further idea: like St Leger before him, he would institute his new national programme in all its varied aspects by means of a parliament. Thus, unwittingly and with a quite remarkable insensitivity, Perrot at once fused the two converging fears of the Palesmen and provided them with a forum in which to oppose him.

To compound his error, Perrot's chosen strategy for the management of parliament was wholly inept. Though wild rumours had circulated through the country about the extortionate rates to be charged in the new composition, and though he had already begun to act rigorously against religious non-conformity in the Pale, the viceroy approached the assembled parliament with nothing more explicit than a bill to suspend Poynings' Law. The suspension of the law, which was by then conventional, was intended to streamline parliamentary business primarily by granting greater flexibility to the Dublin administration.[39] But in the highly charged atmosphere of the mid-1580s Perrot's action was capable of supporting the most extreme interpretations. Thus the debate over suspension became the focus of all the burgeoning anxieties of the Pale. Leaders of a well-prepared opposition campaign declared that Perrot was intent upon suppressing freedom of conscience just as he was determined to suppress their ancient constitutional liberties by imposing a permanent tax upon the country in lieu of the cess, and their case as urged both in open and in private meetings proved to be immensely persuasive.[40] After much manipulation, Perrot managed to squeeze a narrow majority for suspension in the Lords. But despite intimidation, arrest and a late effort at compromise, the opposition hold in the Commons remained fast. Disgusted, Perrot prorogued parliament, hoping that time would weaken the opposition's influence. The reverse proved to be true. Having deferred the matter of victualling the garrison and his house in the hopes of success in parliament, Perrot's pressing commitments else-where now compelled him to seek supplies rapidly from the country. Inevitably he confronted widespread resistance, and was forced to settle for a mere £1,500 in lieu of all cesses which the Palesmen insisted was to be without prejudice to any further negotiation.[41] During the same period representations from the Pale at court procured a directive restraining him from enforcing the oath of supremacy and ordering him to abandon the proposal to equalise the ploughlands by statute.[42] By the time parliament re-convened, therefore, Perrot's programme was already in tatters. But even then the opposition did not relent: of sixteen bills certified from England, five were defeated, two were substantially amended, and one was withdrawn. Those that remained were either innocu-ous or beneficial.[43] Immediately after parliament the Palesmen readily agreed to the continuance of the composition deal whose formalisation they had so vigorously resisted. But the new arrangement was understood to be yet another temporary expedi-ent, which was to be subject to review by the government and the country at the end of two years.[44]

The Palesmen's victory over this most ambitious of the reformist governors was clear and decisive, and the effect on their morale was immense. In Perrot they had faced a viceroy who had sought to be as materially extortionate and as spiritually repressive as any that might have occurred in Baltinglass's demonology. The protection of the old religion, it was now clear, was not a matter separate from the defence of their ancient constitutional liberties: since both were under siege by an indiscriminately oppressive government, both had to be maintained together. Yet the Palesmen had confronted and defeated Perrot not by Baltinglass's desperate methods, but by the conservative defence strategies that had worked so well against the cess in the past. Once this crucial point was grasped, the fusion of politics and religion was complete. Thus, to the utter dismay of civil and ecclesiastical authorities,[45] recusancy was appropriated as the country cause, not simply as a cover for other underlying discontents, but as an essential element in the Palesmen's new and solidary sense of identity. With their besieged and isolated standing now confirmed, but their traditional strategies of defence now reinforced, the Palesmen faced confidently into the last years of the century. Disdaining all association with the Dublin administration and cultivating a quiet but firm Catholicism, they nonetheless eschewed any dealings with the Gaelic rebels. Instead, they loudly proclaimed their loyalty to their sovereign, and asserted their primacy as defenders of English civility in Ireland, like the anonymous author of a tract of 1598 who urged the crown to delegate the future plantation of Ulster to the Dutch and to the group whom he deliberately and quite self-consciously distinguished as 'the Old English.'[46]

Notes

1. Brendan Bradshaw, *The Irish constitutional revolution of the sixteenth century* (Cambridge, 1979) *passim,* hereafter cited as *Consit. rev.*
2. For the best modern account see N.P. Canny, *The formation of the old English élite*, National University of Ireland, O'Donnell Lecture (Dublin, 1975), hereafter cited as *Formation.*
3. Aidan Clarke, 'Colonial identity in early seventeenth century Ireland' in T.W. Moody (ed.), *Nationality and the pursuit of national independence* (Belfast, 1978), pp 57–71.
4. Brendan Bradshaw, 'The opposition to the ecclesiastical legislation in the Irish reformation parliament' in *I.H.S.*, xvi (1969), pp 285–303; N.P. Canny, 'Why the Reformation failed in Ireland: *une question mal posée*' in *Journal of Ecclesiastical History*, xxx (1979), pp 423–50.
5. See Bradshaw, *Constit. rev.*, Canny, *Formation.* A similar argument has been deployed most persuasively for an individual — and clearly exceptional — case in Colm Lennon, *Richard Stanihursi: the Dubliner* (Dublin, 1981).
6. For a further elaboration of this view see Ciaran Brady, 'The government of Ireland *c.* 1540–1583', (unpublished Ph.D. thesis, University of Dublin, 1980), pp 384–90, hereafter cited as 'Gov. of Ire.,' and for a case study of the government's dealings with a lordship over the sixteenth century, see Ciaran Brady, 'The O'Reillys of east Breifne and the problem of surrender and regrant' in *Breifne,* xxiii (1985), pp 233ff.
7. For Bathe see B.L., Lansdowne MS 159, no. 1; for White, N.P. Canny (ed.), 'Rowland White's "Discors touching the reformation of Ireland" *c.* 1571' in *I.H.S.*, xx (1967), pp 439–65; for Sherlocke, B.L., Cotton MSS, Titus B XII, 15; and for Taaffe, P.R.O., S.P. 63/116/31.

8. See Brady, 'Gov. of Ire.', chs iii–iv.
9. Sidney to privy council, 27 Jan. 1577 (P.R.O., S.P. 63/57/5).
10. Chancellor Gerrard's 'Notes upon Ireland' in *Annal Hib*, ii (1931), pp 93–291; Gerrard to Walsingham, 22 Mar. 1557 (P.R.O., S.P. 63/57/49 and enclosures i–iii); 'Device of how the soldiers may be found with cess' *c*. Feb. 1577, (P.R.O., S.P. 63/57/18 enclosure iii); *Stat. Ire.*, i, 55.
11. 'Device . . .', cit. 'Estimate of St Leger's receipt and expenditures' (P.R.O., S.P. 60/12/54) 'Extracts from the council books' of St Leger and Crofts, (B.L., Add MS 4763, no. 6.).
12. P.R.O., S.P. 63/49/25, 59.
13. Canny, *Formation*, pp 2–10, 35.
14. Irish Council Register in *H.M.C. rep. Haliday MSS*, p. 6; 'Book specifying the miserable estate of the English Pale' and Sussex's 'Reply', Mar. 1562 (P.R.O., S.P. 63/5/51, 57); 'Daily diet notes agreed by victuallers', 1578 (ibid., 64/13); for a detailed estimation see Brady 'Gov. of Ire.', pp 326–8.
15. P.R.O., S.P. 63/106/45; 107/72–3.
16. Secretary Challoner's 'Collection of matters relating to the cess' (P.R.O.I., MS 2753); for 1569, Bodl., Carte MS 58/134; for 1575–6, *H.M.C. De Lisle and Dudley MSS*, pp 425–35.
17. Brady, 'Gov. of Ire., pp 333–6.
18. The actual cess being demanded amounted to a charge of over £9 on the ploughland (P.R.O., S.P. 63/59/23; 54/17; 57/5).
19. 'Annals of Dudley Loftus', Marsh's Library, MS 211, *s.a.* 1575; for similar expressions of Sidney's view see B.L., Cotton MSS, Titus B X 61, *H.M.C. De Lisle and Dudley MSS*, ii, 55–6.
20. The phrase occurs in Wallop to Burghley, 15 Jan. 1583 (P.R.O., S.P. 63/99/25) but it is evident from its use there that it was already widely current in the Pale.
21. White to Burghley, 13 June 1577 (Hatfield House, Cecil MSS, 60/130–32.)
22. Burnell's 'Device', *c*. Nov. 1577 (Lambeth Palace, Carew MSS, 628/147); Resolution of the privy council (P.R.O., S.P. 63/39/45).
23. 'Instructions to Sir William Drury' 29 May 1578 and 'Orders to be observed by the lord justice and council', 31 Mar. 1579 (P.R.O., S.P. 63/66/17); 'Instructions by Lord Chancellor Gerrard', Jan. 1579 (ibid., 65/26); 'Gerrard Papers' ed. C. MacNeill in *Anal. Hib.* ii (1931), 117–27.
24. See his concluding speech as reported by Campion in his *Historie*, ed. A. Vossen (The Hague, 1963), pp 145–51.
25. The label 'commonwealth-man' is to be found in Sidney's 'Memoirs of government' in *U.J.A.*, 1st series, iii (1885), p. 83, but Sidney there indicates that it was commonly applied by contemporaries; for similar use, see John Symcott to Burghley, 3 Dec. 1574, 10 Mar. 1575, (P.R.O., S.P. 63/48/17, 50/7); see also Canny, *Formation*, pp 24–6.
26. 'Book . . . of the garrison', 20 Jan. 1581; 'Schedule of 300 men sent to supply the bands', 25 June 1581 (P.R.O., S.P. 63/80/25 enclosure ii and 84/6 enclosure ii).
27. Lord deputy and council to Elizabeth, 9 May 1582 (P.R.O., S.P. 63/92/20 and enclosures).
28. Ciaran Brady, 'Faction and the origins of the Desmond rebellion of 1579' in *I.H.S.*, xxii (1981), pp 289–312.
29. Lennon, *Richard Stanihurst*, pp 35–44; some light is cast on the proceedings

and outlook in the letters collected by Gerrard in Feb. 1581 (P.R.O., S.P. 63/80/60 enclosures i–viii).

30. See P.R.O., S.P. 63/79/27–30; 'Matters to charge the Baron Delvin' (ibid., 79/30; 93/50).

31. 'Traitors' lands within the Pale', 26 Apr. 1581 (P.R.O., S.P. 63/82/54 enclosure ii); 'Schedule of those apprehended... for the conspiracy of William Nugent' (ibid., 86/30 enclosure i); Confessions of conspirators, Oct. 1581 (ibid., 86/19 enclosures i–iv).

32. 'Confessions of John Cusacke', Jan., Mar. 1582 (P.R.O., S.P. 63/88/47 enclosure i and 90/58 enclosure ii).

33. For memoranda and correspondence on the topic see P.R.O., S.P. 63/87/72, enclosure i; 98/86–7; 88/14; 88/39).

34. See P.R.O., S.P. 63/86/19–70, 102/121); 'The trial and execution of Justice Nicholas Nugent' (T.C.D., MS 842).

35. P.R.O., S.P. 63/92/25, 35, 52.

36. White to Walsingham, 9 Dec. 1581, and to Burghley 9, 23, Dec. (P.R.O., S.P. 63/77/24, 22, 55); for lists of attainders and executions in 1581–2 see P.R.O., S.P. 63/76/79, 80 enclosure i; 90/59; 102/131).

37. For general statement of his objectives see Lambeth Palace, Carew MS 621, pp 97–115; P.R.O., S.P. 63/106/43; 107/73, 108/87).

38. For his religious objectives see ibid., 107/173, 108/87, 116/56, 119/13, 112/45); 'Order for... the oaths of supremacy', June 1585 (ibid., 119/32 enclosure i); Walsingham to Archbishop Long, Dec. 1585 (ibid., 121/50).

39. For contemporary accounts of the first session of parliament see P.R.O., S.P. 63/116/19, 56, 24, 69; 117/37, 39.

40. On the opposition's tactics see P.R.O., S.P. 63/117/11, 62.

41. Perrot to Burghley, 24 Sept. 1585 (P.R.O., S.P. 63/119/32 and enclosed agreement concerning the cess, nos iv–viii); 'Book of objections... against Sir John Perrot' (ibid., 119/10).

42. Viscount Gormanston and others to Elizabeth, 10 Dec. 1585 (P.R.O., S.P. 63/121/35); Walsingham to Archbishop Long, Dec. (ibid., 50); Walsingham to Perrot, Feb. (ibid., 94).

43. Compare 'Note of English statutes to be found in Ireland' (25 items, P.R.O., S.P. 63/112/36) with 'Acts to be found', 'Acts found and dashed', 14 May 1586 (ibid., 124/18, 19, 22) with the eleven statutes as printed in *Stat. Ire.* and the Shaw Mason collation of statues (T.C.D., MS 1739).

44. 'Act of composition', 15 May 1586 (P.R.O., S.P. 63/124/25); Fenton to Burghley, Sept. 1587 (ibid., 131/5 enclosures i, ii); 'Composition arrears', 15 May 1588 (ibid., 134/6 enclosure ii).

45. Fitzwilliam and Loftus to Burghley, 26 Feb. 1590 (P.R.O., S.P. 63/150/74); Fitzwilliam to Walsingham, 29 Apr. 1589 (ibid., 143/46; Loftus to Burghley, 22 Sept. 1590, ibid., 154/37); and to Whitgift, 12 Mar. 1591 (ibid., 157/35).

46. 'A discourse [on]... the planting of colonies' [1598] (P.R.O., S.P. 63/102 pt 4/75); the author further argues, 'the extract of the English nation there [in Ireland] ought not to be excepted unto but rather employed against the Irish' and complains that 'the descent of the English, to their great grief are here [in England] called and counted Irish though there are reputed and called English'.

Seventeenth-century English radicals and Ireland

Christopher Hill

England's Irish problem in its modern form dates from the seventeenth-century English revolution. It is an old and wry observation that whenever Englishmen are most successfully establishing liberty at home they are most ruthlessly denying it to the Irish. This was never more true than of the seventeenth century. My subject is the attitude of radical groups in the English revolution to Ireland. Why did they not do more to oppose the brutal subjugation of Ireland under Oliver Cromwell?

We must start from the Reformation, which an American historian called Henry VIII's Declaration of Independence from the papacy. Throughout the rest of the sixteenth century England felt itself to be a beleaguered isle,[1] isolated in a world dominated by the great Catholic powers of Spain, Austria and France. These powers were, it was feared, liable at any time to combine to conquer England and restore the old religion — and monastic lands. In these circumstances Protestantism and patriotism came to be closely interwoven, not only in government propaganda but also in educated public opinion. John Foxe's best-selling *Book of Martyrs* popularised a view of history as a continuing struggle between the forces of good and evil, with God's Englishmen foremost in the battle against Antichrist, the pope.

Popery was associated with treachery and cruelty. Starting with the burnings under Mary, plenty of evidence was produced to support the allegation—Alva's Council of Blood in the Netherlands in the 1560s, the massacre of St Bartholomew's Day in 1572, the Gunpowder Plot in 1605, Spanish cruelty to the Indians in South

America (though, as Professor Canny has suggested, English colonisers in Ireland and North America may have learnt a thing or two from Spanish practice).[2] The Spanish Armada, defeated in 1588 when God blew with his winds and scattered them, was believed to have been filled with racks, whips and other instruments of torture to be used in the reconversion of England.

Ireland's place in this cosmic drama was that of back door for a foreign invasion of England. In the reign of Henry VII the pretenders Lambert Simnel and Perkin Warbeck had both invaded by way of Ireland. Spaniards landed there in 1601, James II with French troops in the 1690s. English rulers rightly assumed that almost any army that was not English would be welcomed in Ireland.

The English had been in Ireland since the twelfth century. Over the centuries the original settlers had adapted themselves to Irish customs. No serious attempt had been made to extend English law to the whole island, and English rule had been indirect. But things began to change in the later sixteenth century. Pressure of relative over-population in England led to emigration to Ireland—initially sponsored by private enterprise. This meant seizures of Irish land, removals of population, local fighting and periodic massacres.[3] Ireland was easily accessible from south-western England, Wales or Scotland, and it has been suggested that in the seventeenth century there was more British emigration to Ireland than to any trans-Atlantic colony.[4]

From the 1580s onwards English governments began to be alarmed by the infiltration of Counter-reformation priests aiming at the reconversion of England, just when the long-postponed war with Spain was seen to have become inevitable. This and the possibility of disputes over the succession when the ageing Elizabeth should die raised sharply the strategic issue. It combined with increased pressure from the New English settlers in Ireland for outright military conquest and the enforcement of English law on Ireland.

For some Englishmen in Ireland the motives behind this were not wholly discreditable. Once the Irish aristocracy was removed, it was argued, the two populations could merge; the Irish would enjoy the advantages of regular and disciplined labour, and improved agriculture would in the long run be to the advantage of the Irish common people themselves. Men like the first earl of Cork, Professor Canny has told us, believed that profits for him could be combined with benefits to the Irish.[5] But all such ideas presumed military conquest first. They totally disregarded Irish habits and traditions in the interests of economic progress, whose main advantages would go to Englishmen. It is the classic colonial situation, looking forward to all those well-intentioned colonial civil servants in nineteenth-century India and Africa.

Even relatively liberal thinkers *assumed* the total inferiority of the Irish and their culture. The gentle Edmund Spenser spoke of 'their savage brutishness and loathsome filthiness which is not to be named'. He was referring especially to the clothes they wore, their sexual habits, and their lack of any fixed abode.[6] Spenser's account was based on a historical analysis and explanation already familiar to Englishmen. He made a similar point about the ancient Britons in *The Faerie Queene*:—

> They held this land, and with their filthiness
> Polluted this same gentle soil long time,

until Brutus came, representative of a higher civilization, 'and them of their unjust possession deprived'. People who fail to make full economic use of the land have no right to it: the same argument was to be used against the American Indians.[7] Spenser therefore wanted to 'reduce things into order of English law'. Everybody must be drawn into labour, so that the old attitudes could be transformed. This must be preceded by thorough military conquest, and removal of most of the Irish from areas to be occupied by the English. Until the military power of the lords had been broken, as it had in England, those Irish who remain must be cut off from their old connections. For 'all the rebellions that you see from time to time in Ireland are not begun by the common people, but by the lords and captains of countries'.[8]

That other sensitive poet Sir John Davies in 1612 shared this attitude. The nature of Irish customs is such that 'the people which doth use them must of necessity be rebels to all good government, destroy the commonwealth wherein they live, and bring barbarism and desolation upon the richest and most fertile land of the world'. 'To make a commonweal in Ireland', he said, necessitated 'settling of all the estates and possessions' by English law, establishing 'lawful matrimony to the end they might have lawful heirs', and insisting that 'every man shall have a certain home', so that he could manure his lands and provide for posterity. Only the English could 'make a commonweal in Ireland'.[9]

There were various reasons for looking down on the Irish. Their religious practices seemed to English settlers to be as much pagan as Christian. It had always been possible to compare the seminomadic Irish with masterless vagabonds in England, or with right-less American Indians. The wild Irish and the Indians do not much differ, declared Hugh Peter, just back from New England, in 1646.[10] Inculcation of religious hatred and contempt had long been used to discourage the fraternisation with the Irish to which some masterless English colonists were regrettably prone. Professor Canny has shown that the same problems and the same answers arose in New England.[11] However unattractive we may find it, there is a consistent philosophy behind the denial of rights in the land to those who had for so long occupied it undisturbed.

After the peaceful succession of James I in 1603, the ending of the Anglo–Spanish war and the termination of O'Neill's rebellion, English panic about Ireland diminished. The main concern of English rulers of Ireland was to keep costs down after this ruinous war. But Thomas Wentworth as lord deputy in the 1630s pursued a more active policy, an experiment in direct rather than indirect colonial rule. He tried to persuade the Old English to pay for his taking the New English off their backs, but he was still balancing the two interests, papists against Protestants, and was trusted by neither.

Meanwhile in England Protestant anxieties had been roused by James I's policy of appeasing Spain whilst the Thirty Years War seemed to be threatening Protestantism all over Europe. Charles caused even greater alarm by his devotion to his Catholic wife, by receiving a papal nuncio in London for the first time since the reign of Bloody Mary, by supporting Archbishop Laud's cere-monial innovations which struck Protestants as a reversion to popery, and supporting the enforcement of Laudianism on Scot-land by military means. As Catholic power advanced on the con-tinent, the English government seemed to be at best half-hearted in opposing it, if not indeed positively co-operating with it. Alarm was intensified by the fact that Wentworth was building up an army in Ireland whose soldiers were not subject to the customary religious tests. When the lord deputy—now earl of Strafford—promised that this army was ready for use against 'this kingdom', it seemed to alarmed Protestants to matter little whether 'this king-dom' was England, or in the first instance Scotland.

The collapse of Charles I's government with the assembly of par-liament in November 1640, followed by the trial and execution of Strafford in May 1641, led to the breakdown of English authority in Ireland and to the revolt of 1641—the catalyst which forced civil war in England because neither king nor parliament would trust the other with command of the army which all agreed must be sent to restore English power in Ireland. The Irish revolt and alleged massacres of Protestants became one of the great myths of history. Nobody knows exactly how many English and Scottish Protestants were killed — probably quite a lot, some of them unpleasantly. But English propaganda exaggerated this beyond all bounds. John Cook, the lawyer who was to prosecute the king at his trial in 1649, said that 154,000 people had been 'barbarously murdered in one province of Ireland'—more than the total of English and Scots settlers.[12] The grotesque exaggerations of propagandists were accepted by perfectly rational and balanced Englishmen, including John Milton. Richard Baxter, a middle-of-the-road man, believed that religion had been the main cause of the civil war in England.[13] There had been an international Catholic conspiracy against England with which Charles I had connived. 'Arise, O Lord and scatter the Irish rebels', cried Edmund Calamy in a sermon preached to the House of Commons in December 1641: 'arise, O Lord and confound Antichrist'.[14] The second prayer merely repeated the first. Towards the end of the civil war the king did empower the earl of Glamorgan to negotiate with the Irish. The discussions came to nothing, but Charles, with typical ineptitude, allowed his correspondence to be captured after his final defeat at Naseby in 1645, and his participation in the international Catholic conspiracy seemed to be established.

Further confirmation of the antichristian conspiracy was not lacking. The pope sent money to the Irish rebels. Non-participant Catholics were excommunicated.[15] From 1645 to 1649 effective command of the revolt was taken over by Archbishop Rinuccini, the papal nuncio. The earl of Glamorgan, who was regarded as Charles I's lord lieutenant, swore submission to the nuncio. Such facts were used to assert *national* responsibility for the Irish rebellion and for all the unpleasantness which resulted from it.

Meanwhile money for the reconquest of Ireland had been subscribed by a group of London adventurers, who no doubt promised themselves ultimate handsome returns on their investment. It may be noted that again private enterprise rather than the government was looking after English interests in Ireland. But the adventurers' money was diverted to pay for the civil war against Charles I. Hence after the king's defeat increased pressure from the City was added to the strategic reasons for reconquest.

Parliament debated the matter at length in 1646–7, urged on by Puritan preachers of Fast Sermons calling for help to be sent to poor Ireland.[16] The final decision neatly linked the Irish problem with the problem of getting rid of the increasingly radical New Model Army. Parliament voted that part of the army should be sent to Ireland and the remainder disbanded. Unfortunately they failed to provide for payment of wages — and the army's pay was many months in arrears. Mutiny resulted, which soon acquired political overtones. The rank and file took the lead, chasing non-co-operative officers out of the army, electing 'agitators' to represent their views, linking up with the London democratic party, the Levellers, and forcibly taking the imprisoned Charles I away from the custody of parliament's commissioners. Cromwell and the generals put themselves at the head of the mutiny. Officers wanted to be paid their arrears too, and the generals were well aware of the suspicion with which parliament viewed them. Conniving at mutiny was risky; attempting to smash it would have been even riskier, and would have left the generals—and the cause of religious toleration—at the mercy of a hostile parliament. The reunited army advanced on London, and parliament submitted.

Then came the second civil war. Charles escaped from captivity, a Scottish army invaded England in his support, and former parliamentarians in Wales, Kent, East Anglia and elsewhere joined in support. When the royalists were finally defeated, feeling in the army was so intense that the generals again had to act. Parliament was purged, Charles tried and executed, monarchy and House of Lords abolished, and a republic proclaimed. Having co-operated with the Levellers and their allies in London and the army for these purposes, the now all-powerful generals turned on them, provoked and suppressed mutinies in the army, and by May 1649 were in supreme control.

One stimulus to these drastic actions was concern about Ireland. Unlike the French and Russian revolutions, the English revolution had known none of the foreign intervention which so embittered the later conflicts. The main reason for this was that throughout the 1640s the major European powers had all been involved in the Thirty Years War. But in October 1648 this was ended by the Treaty of Westphalia. France and Spain remained at war, but in Germany many professional troops were suddenly forced to look for employment. What more natural than to use some of them to restore the English monarchy *via* Ireland? Negotiations did in fact take place between royalists and the duke of Lorraine, one of the *condottieri* leaders; newsbooks of the time reveal that alarm in England was great. It was therefore essential to finish with Ireland quickly and finally, to shut the wide-open back door. This is the background to the Cromwellian campaign that began in 1649. 'Send all the pack of Babylonish trash' back from Ireland, 'to Rome, after the nuncio', William Cooper urged parliament in a sermon of August 1649.[17]

So the year 1649 saw attitudes towards Ireland hardening in England. The military government was very conscious of its unpopularity. But it commanded vast resources from confiscated church, crown and royalists' lands, and had a powerful army at its disposal, which might again become dangerously radical if it was not used. The solution was obvious. As early as 1575 Lord Deputy Sir Henry Sidney had pointed out that the military subjugation of Ireland was 'no subject's enterprise: a prince's purse and power must do it'.[18] But neither Elizabeth, James nor Charles had the resources for such a conquest, though English settlers repeatedly called for it. But now conquest had become not only possible but necessary, and the demand was reinforced by pressure from the City to milk Ireland to pay the debts outstanding to the adventurers. Confiscations of Irish land could also be used to make the army self-supporting. Public opinion had for nine years been nurtured in anti-popery: the time seemed ripe for going over to the offensive against the international forces of Antichrist before they should strike through Ireland. The legend of Irish national responsibility for the exaggerated horrors of 1641 had intensified the feelings of religious and cultural contempt for the Irish, which had long been fostered. After the conquest and total overthrow of traditional stability in Ireland, the routed Irish looked more like vagabonds than ever.

All this may help to explain the acquiescence in, indeed enthusiasm for, the conquest of Ireland among radical supporters of the Revolution. They were trapped in the assumptions of their age. If Levellers and Diggers were alive to-day we could hold a rational discussion with them about politics and economics; we could argue about sex with Ranters. Pym, Cromwell and Ireton would be old-fashioned by any modern standards; we must always set them in a historical context if we are to be fair to their ideas. But on Ireland we no longer have the illusory sense that the radicals are our contemporaries; they too have to be understood historically. The object of the preceding background sketch was to suggest how the Irish came to be cast for the role of supporters of Antichrist, the enemy of all that the revolutionaries stood for.

The radicals were the most fiercely anti-Catholic, the most

anxious to defend the Revolution against what they saw as the forces of reaction. Their strength depended on the army, which many of them believed was God's instrument for the final overthrow of Antichrist. So, for a whole variety of reasons, most of the radicals accepted the necessity of conquest. Vavasor Powell, in a Fast Sermon of February 1649, hailed 'the concurrence of God's Providence in effecting those great things which you have undertaken, both in this land and in Ireland' as evidence that the Lord had smiled on parliament 'since you have appeared and acted for Him of late so impartially and courageously'.[19] Powell was a Fifth Monarchist, relatively very radical. So was Christopher Feake, who in 1659 spoke of 'the work of justice in Ireland ... prospering under the standard of the interest of Christ'.[20] Quakers too (not pacifists before 1661): Francis Howgil and Edward Burrough after their visit to Ireland in 1656 declared 'to the natives of that nation': 'You are shut up in blindness and covered with darkness which may be felt, and you ... are become wild and brutish as the beasts of the field. ... The indignation of God is against you. ... Cease from your filthy, nasty, polluted ways of idolatry'.[21] The Quaker George Bishop praised the army's conquest of Ireland 'with wonderful success and hard service'; he thought 'insufficient thanks had been rendered to God for that deliverance.'[22] There were many Quakers in the army in Ireland.

So, many of the most radical supporters of parliament applauded the conquest. Colonel Axtell, just before his execution as a regicide in 1660, gloried in his share. 'When I consider their bloody cruelty in murdering so many thousands of Protestants and innocent souls that word was much upon my heart, "Give her blood to drink for she is worthy"; and sometimes we neither gave nor took quarter'.[23] National responsibility again.

It is remarkable that any voices were raised on the other side, but some were. By 1646 men were asking whether it was lawful to fight in Ireland. A colonel said the Irish did but fight for religion and liberty of conscience and for their lands and estates. Some sectaries even justified the rebellion of 1641, Thomas Edwards tells us; others argued against and hindered the sending of help to Ireland.[24]

The Leveller William Walwyn, according to Edwards, said 'the Irish did no more but what we would have done ourselves if it had been our case'. 'What had the English to do in their kingdom?', he asked: 'why should not they enjoy the liberty of their consciences?'.[25] The charge is repeated in the anonymous *Walwins*

Wiles (April 1649) where he was alleged to have said that English troops had been sent to Ireland in 'an unlawful war, a cruel and bloody work to go to destroy the Irish natives for their consciences... and to drive them from their proper natural and native rights'. The author spoke of Walwyn's 'constant endeavour to hinder the relief of Ireland, ... arguing that the cause of the Irish natives in seeking their just freedoms, immunities and liberties, was the very same with our cause here, in endeavouring our own rescue and freedom from the power of oppressors'.[26] Walwyn never committed himself to such views in print. But he never repudiated them. His son-in-law Humphrey Brooke and he himself replied at great length to *Walwins Wiles*, but both ignored the charges about Ireland.[27]

The Levellers as a group did not take up Walwyn's generous position. This and Walwyn's public silence may indicate how unpopular and dangerous it might be to speak up on behalf of the Irish in the 1640s. *Walwins Wiles* suggested that Lilburne and Prince, two of the Leveller leaders, would not 'be persuaded to hinder the relief of Ireland': by implication the charge of being pro-Irish was limited to Walwyn and Richard Overton.[28] Overton had argued in 1645 that persecution had caused the Irish rebellion of 1641,[29] but I am not aware that he otherwise committed himself on Irish questions. Prince did express views on Ireland, but they are less radical than those attributed to Walwyn. In June 1649 he urged a moderate settlement and conscientious government by 'faithful men' who would not try to enforce 'their own domination, a taste whereof, you know is exercised in England'. Then 'there would be some hopes .... that the Irish would soon be reduced, as being willing to change their condition of bondage for freedom'. But apart from that pious aspiration he gave no indication of what exactly the Irish would get in return. Prince is really more concerned to make propaganda against the English government: 'For keeping out of rebels I am not only against any that shall invade the land from abroad, but I am against all that any ways invade our liberties within the nation'.[30]

A Leveller pamphlet of December 1648, *Several Proposals for Peace and Freedom by an Agreement of the People*, proposed merely that Irishmen who had not been 'beginners and fomentors of the war' should be allowed to compound for their delinquency on the same terms as English royalists.[31] The rights and wrongs of sending English troops to Ireland caused running controversy throughout 1649. *The English Souldiers Standard* tried to persuade English soldiers not to fight in Ireland: 'it will be no satisfaction to God's justice, to plead that you murdered men in obedience to your general'; but it entered into no discussion of Irish rights and liberties.[32] *The Levellers Vindicated* (August 1649), signed by six troopers who had been involved in the mutiny which was crushed at Burford, said they had been 'designed by lot to be . . . sent over into Ireland, . . . in order to the peace and safety of this commonwealth, which we think necessary to be performed'.[33] So they actually accepted the necessity of re-conquest.

So far then we have no attempt to look seriously at the Irish point of view apart from words attributed to Walwyn by Edwards: for it is highly likely that *Walwins Wiles* derived from *Gangraena*. Now Edwards, though a virulently hostile witness, took pains to be accurate in his facts. Walwyn's failure to declare himself in public must be due to strong pressures of public opinion on the other side. But in August 1649 an anonymous pamphlet, *Tyranipocrit Discovered*, sometimes attributed to Walwyn, was more radical and more generalising. It denounced the robbery, killing and enslaving of 'the poor Indians' by English merchants, as well as national wars in which 'we will send our slaves to kill some of their slaves', and all sorts of persecution - of the Waldensians by the French, of the Moors and the Dutch by Spaniards, of Dutch Arminians by Dutch Calvinists, and 'how the English hunted the poor Irish'.[34] Three months earlier *The Soldiers Demand* had been published in Bristol, written presumably by a soldier on his way to Ireland. 'What have we to do in Ireland', he asked, 'to fight and murder a people and nation . . . . which have done us no harm? . . . We have waded too far in that crimson stream already of innocent and Christian blood'.[35]

Most significant of all was a Leveller leaflet of April 1649, which has not survived but which can be reconstructed from a reply in the government newspaper, *The Moderate Intelligencer*, extending over six numbers in May and June. Much more intellectually satisfying than any other Leveller statement, it called in question the right of Englishmen 'to deprive a people of the land God and nature has given them and impose laws without their consent'. It is 'as unjust to take laws and liberties from our neighbours as to take goods one from another of the same nation'. A conquered people cannot 'be accounted rebels, if at any time they seek to free themselves and recover their own'. It was therefore 'the duty of every honest man' to oppose Cromwell's expedition to Ireland. This stands in very remarkable contrast to the assumption which had prevailed since Spenser and Davies, that a people has no right to land which they have not fully developed in private ownership.

But the leaflet went even further, insisting that the English government should 'proclaim Ireland a free state, repenting of all the evil themselves have acted and intended and that our kings have formerly acted against that nation'. The two nations should join in a 'mutual league as friends', though England should retain 'some considerable seaports or towns for security and bond to tie the Irish to performance of covenants' and as a strategic guarantee. Brailsford, who first drew attention to the significance of this leaflet, commented that its approach to international relations was in advance even of Grotius. Brailsford stressed no less the hardheaded practicality of the policy outlined. Many Irishmen had no love for the Stuarts as such, and might have been prepared to accept a neutral status in return for English withdrawal under guarantees. The leaflet was perhaps less realistic in ignoring the economic reasons for the presence of Englishmen in Ireland.[36]

If the Levellers were half-hearted in their public utterances about Ireland, their enemies did not fail to attribute pro-Irish sentiments to them. John Owen, preaching to parliament on 28 February 1649, referred to 'some mountains of opposition that lie in the way against any success' in Ireland. He denounced 'the strivings and strugglings of... people... totally obstructing... any deliverance for Ireland', and especially 'that mighty mountain (which some misnamed a level) that thought at once to have locked an everlasting door upon that expedition'.[37] Just over three months later, preaching to parliament to celebrate the defeat of the mutineers at Burford, Owen rejoiced not only 'that our necks are yet kept from the yoke of lawless lust, fury and tyranny' of the Levellers, but also in the 'hope that a poor distressed handful in Ireland may yet be relieved'.[38] This sermon was preached just before Owen left for Ireland with Cromwell.

Cromwell accepted the Irish command on 29 March 1649, the day after the arrest of Lilburne, Walwyn, Overton and Prince signified the end of the Leveller movement. His preparations were remarkably careful and thorough, and he did not leave for Ireland until 13 August, nearly five months later. On arrival he announced to the Irish 'We come (by the assistance of God) to hold forth and maintain the lustre and glory of English liberty in a nation where we have an undoubted right to it'.[39] There is a significant dualism in his attitude towards the conquest of Ireland. On the one hand, holding all Irish Catholics responsible for the rebellion of 1641, Cromwell saw the slaughter and repression both as strategically necessary and as part of a religious war against Antichrist. In his thinking Rinuccini and the duke of Lorraine contributed to the massacre of Drogheda. On the other hand the conquest was also a commercial operation. 'If we should proceed by the rules of other states', he told the Speaker, getting towns to surrender 'would cost you more money than this army hath had since we came over. I hope, through the blessing of God, they will come cheaper to you'.[40] He had told the Irish that the English government would hardly spend five or six million pounds 'merely to procure purchasers of confiscated Irish lands to be invested in that for which they did disburse little above a quarter million'—though he hoped and believed the adventurers would receive reasonable satisfaction.[41] The commercial attitude recalls—perhaps symbolically—words which Lilburne said he had heard Cromwell use to the council of state in April 1649, that if the Levellers were not broken in pieces 'they will break you; and bring all the guilt of the blood and treasure shed and spent in this kingdom upon your heads and shoulders, and frustrate and make void all that work that with so many years' industry, toil and pains you have done'.[42] The defeat of the Levellers was necessary to realise returns on this investment — in Ireland as in England.

Not until 1655, after massacres, transportation and emigration, did an English settler in Ireland, Vincent Gookin, reject the concept of national guilt and show some compassion for the Irish common people. He argued that only landlords and priests should be transplanted; then the Irish, an industrious people, would soon adapt to English rule and English customs.[43] This revival of Spenserian policies was wildly optimistic; and by then it was much too late.

Ireland indeed was vitally important for England as a source of plundered wealth: the first English colony. The vast land fund at the disposal of the state after expropriating Irish landlords was used to pay not only the English adventurers but also the army. Leveller-led mutinies in England in 1647 had been fomented in large part by arrears of pay: there was no danger of that happening again.

The Elizabethan and Jacobean settlements in Ireland had been financed by private enterprise, just as colonial trade and the colonisation of North America and the West Indies were, just as the navy which defeated the Spanish Armada was. What was new from the 1650s was the central role of the state. As Spenser, Davies and others saw, only the state could finance a thorough conquest, just as only the state could finance the war against the Netherlands which guaranteed English merchants' monopoly of trade with the colonies promised by the Navigation Act, and only the state could produce the naval force which seized Jamaica and guaranteed English naval pre-eminence in the Caribbean as well as in the Mediterranean. But when we say 'the state' it must be borne in mind that it was a new state, the product of the Revolution, with vastly greater financial resources at its disposal; the governments of the old régime could never have undertaken any of these activities.

Marx in 1869 said that the English republic met shipwreck in Ireland. When he said 'the English reaction in England had its roots . . . in the subjugation of Ireland',[44] he meant, I take it, that Ireland split the radicals on the religious issue, and so ended any possibility of united opposition to the dominance of Cromwell and the generals. Seeing the Irish as part of the international forces of Antichrist united a section of the radicals with the commercial interests and isolated those who thought, like Walwyn and the authors of the lost leaflet of April 1649, that the Irish people might become allies of the English people against their mutual oppressors.

What is difficult for us to grasp is the crucial role of the army in so dividing the radicals. Without the army religious toleration could never have been established, and so the radical minority would have been unable to organise and propagandise freely. Without the army Charles I would never have been brought to trial, nor the republic proclaimed, nor the House of Lords abolished. The Levellers, more prescient than most, foresaw that military dictatorship would lead back to the supremacy of the propertied class and ultimately to a restoration of monarchy. But once the Leveller challenge to the generals had been defeated, and the social basis of the republic correspondingly narrowed, other radicals saw that the army, with all its faults, stood between them and a return of intolerance and unfreedom. In particular the occupation of Ireland was a guarantee against a restoration of monarchy by foreign papist arms. That is why millenarians, Quakers and Baptists, and Milton, Erbery and Sedgwick, saw the army as the lesser evil even while it was being converted from a collection of liberty-loving citizens with arms in their hands into a police force for the men of property. There was no way out of their impasse. In consequence Cromwell and the conservative wing, in alliance with the City of London, got the upper hand in England, where the plunder of Ireland helped to finance the stabilisation of the regime. When monarchy was finally restored in 1660 to preside over the victory of the propertied revolutionaries, the Cromwellian policy for the military subjugation and colonial exploitation of Ireland was taken over. It was worse than that. Under the protectorate Ireland had been incorporated within the English economic system, and so might have expected to get the benefits of the Navigation Act and increasing British prosperity. But after 1660 Ireland was excluded from these advantages, with all the consequences that we know so well. Irish industries which competed with English were deliberately destroyed; export of sheep, cattle, butter and cheese to England was prohibited. Absentee landlords took most of what agrarian profit there was. Repeated famines anticipated that of the 1840s.

Looking back with Marx's dictum in mind we can see that even the relatively good intentions of some English rulers of Ireland were bedevilled by the strategic problem which raised its head again in World War II and remains unsolved to this day. In the early 1650s Colonel John Jones, one of four parliamentary commissioners for governing Ireland, hoped (like Gookin) that in Ireland 'all men of estates' would 'be banished, and the Irish ploughman and the labourer admitted to the same immunities with the English'. Then the two peoples would 'cohabit peaceably'. But he accepted that this was a policy of 'doing the people good though against their wills'.[45]

From Spenser through Jones and Gookin to Maria Edgeworth in *Castle Rackrent*, there were English men and women who hoped by a judicious combination of coercion and education to force the Irish people to be free in the sense of accepting the work ethic and all that goes with it. Jones had had a similar policy for Scotland - 'to break the interest of the great men . . . and to settle the interests of the common people upon a different foot from the interest of their lords and masters; . . . . to propound freedom to the people and relief' against the 'tyranny' of 'the great men'.[46] In Scotland this policy worked. The brutal Cromwellian conquest of the 1650s, followed by the corrupt union of 1707, did in fact work to Scotland's ultimate economic advantage, if not to the advantage of all Scots. Maria Edgeworth and others like her hoped that the defeat of the rebellion of 1798 corresponded to Culloden in 1746, and that the union of 1800 would be accepted as final and advantageous to the Irish. But all Irish history, and particularly the events of the seventeenth century, were against these hopes.

So I have attempted, I hope not altogether unconvincingly, to suggest that the Irish problem of the seventeenth century can be seen as a once-off problem: the Irish people, through no fault of their own, found themselves on the wrong side in an international war between England and Antichrist. What is disturbing for an Englishman is that this once-off situation helped to confirm an attitude of mind among most ordinary Englishmen which disposed them to put lesser breeds—including all non-Protestant Christians—without the law. Given also the survival of Calvinist predestinarianism, against which the radicals had protested, this contributed to John Bull's national arrogance and to a racialism which is no less a problem for England today than is Ulster. The gods are just, and of our once-off vices make instruments to plague us.

In principle the only solution—in the seventeenth century as today—would have involved taking full account of the Irish people in trying to solve England's Irish problem, difficult and complex though that would have been even then. Some Levellers grasped the point, but not even the Leveller movement as a whole ever made alliance with the people of Ireland a main point of its platform. Presumably the Levellers knew the society of which they were part, and believed that it would have been hopeless to try to overcome the passionately-held association of English patriotism with Protestantism. But some of them at least had more realistic as well as more humane ideas than most politicians who have failed to solve the problem over the past three centuries. Walwyn and the author of the lost leaflet of April 1649 deserve to be remembered, both by Irishmen and by English radicals.

Notes

1. Cf. Carol Z. Wiener, 'The beleaguered isle' in *Past & Present*, no. 51 (1971), pp 27–62.
2. Nicholas P. Canny, *The Elizabethan conquest of Ireland: a pattern established 1565–76* (hereafter cited as Canny, *Elizabethan conquest*), (Hassocks, Harvester Press, 1976), p. 103; 'The ideology of English colonisation: from England to America' in *William and Mary Quarterly*, series 3, xxx (1973), pp 593–4.
3. Canny, *Elizabethan conquest*, especially chapter IV; and cf. Donald Jackson, 'Violence and assimilation in Tudor Ireland' in Eoin O'Brien (ed.), *Essays in honour of J.D.H. Widdess* (Dublin, 1978), pp 113–26.
4. Nicholas P. Canny, 'The Anglo–American colonial experience' in *Hist. Jn.*, xxiv (1981), p. 489.
5. Nicholas P. Canny, *The upstart earl: a study of the social and mental world of Richard Boyle, first earl of Cork* (Cambridge, 1982), *passim*.
6. Spenser, *View*, in *Works* (Globe edn.), p. 632.
7. Spenser, *The Faerie Queene*, bk II, canto x, stanza 9; and cf. Canny, *Eliza-*

bethan Conquet, pp 160–63; 'The ideology of English colonisation...', cit., pp 588–9, 595.

8. Spenser, *View*, cit., pp 672–4, 677. See also a paper presented to James I in 1615 which advocated strict segregation until the Irish had been freed from the tyranny of their lords and then re-educated (Nicholas P. Canny, 'Edmund Spenser and the development of an Anglo–Irish identity' in *The Year-Book of English Studies,* xiii (1983), pp 16-17).

9. Davies, *Discovery*, in Morley, *Ireland under Elizabeth and James I*, pp 290, 336, 379, 385–6.

10. *Mr Peter's last report of the English warres* (1646), p. 5.

11. Canny, *Elizabethan conquest*, chapters VI and VIII; 'The ideology of English colonisation...', cit., *passim*.

12. John Cook, *Monarchy no creature of God's making* (1652), p. 96.

13. W.M. Lamont, *Richard Baxter and the millennium: Protestant imperialism and the English Revolution* (New Jersey, 1979) pp 29, 80–81, 292.

14. Edmund Calamy, *England's Looking-glasse* (1642), p. 10.

15. Patrick J. Corish, in *N.H.I.*, chapters XI, XII, especially pp 298, 321–4.

16. At least six such appeals were made in Fast Sermons preached between July 1646 and November 1647, by Samuel Bolton, William Bridge, Thomas Horton, Matthew Newcomen, Simeon Ash and Richard Kentish.

17. *Jerusalem fatall to her assailants* (1649), p. 30.

18. Canny, *Elizabethan conquest*, p. 90; 'Edmund Spenser and the development of an Anglo–Irish identity', cit., p. 17.

19. *Christ exalted above all creatures* (1651), pp 87–8.

20. *A beame of light shining in the midst of much darkness* (1659), p. 30.

21. *The visitation of the rebellious nation of Ireland* (1656), pp 37–8.

22. *Mene Tekel: or, the council of officers of the army against the declarations &c. of the army* (1659), p. 37.

23. [Anon.], *A complete collection of the lives and speeches of those persons lately executed* (1660), p. 83.

24. *Gangraena* (1646), iii, 23, 239–40.

25. Ibid., ii, 27.

26. Op. cit., in W. Haller and G. Davies (ed.), *The Leveller Tracts, 1647–1653* (New York, 1944), pp 288–9, 310; and cf. p. 315.

27. Humphrey Brooke, *The Charity of Church-Men* (May 1649) and *Walwyn's Just Defence* (June 1649) in Haller and Davies, op. cit., pp. 329–49, 350–98. Walwyn likewise ignored the accusation that he had spoken against communism, which Brooke tried to brush aside (ibid., pp 332–3).

28. Ibid., pp 314–15.

29. *The Araignement of Mr Persecution,* in W. Haller (ed.), *Tracts on liberty in the Puritan Revolution* (New York, 1933), iii, 222; and cf. p. 238.

30. *The silken Independents snare broken* (June 1649), pp 6–7.

31. In D.M. Wolfe, *The Leveller manifestoes of the Puritan Revolution* (New York, 1944) p. 318. Cf. George Wither's *Prosopopeia Britannica*, which a month or two earlier had called for mercy to all of the Irish who had not been 'murderous rebels' (in *Miscellaneous Works* (Spenser Society, 1875), iv, 92).

32. In A.L. Morton (ed.), *Freedom in arms: a selection of Levellers writings* (London, 1975). H. N. Brailsford, in *The Levellers and the English Revolution* (London, 1961), attributed this pamphlet to Walwyn, but Morton thinks that all four leaders had a hand in it.

33. In Morton, op. cit., p. 305.

34. In G. Orwell and R. Reynolds, (ed.), *British Pamphleteers:* i, *From the sixteenth century to the French Revolution* (1948), 90–91, 105.
35. Quoted in Brailsford, op. cit., pp 508–9.
36. Ibid., pp 501–5.
37. W.H. Goold (ed.), *The Works of John Owen* (London, 1850–55), viii, 231.
38. Ibid., ix., 216.
39. Cromwell, *Writings*, ed. Abbott, ii, 205.
40. Ibid., ii, 234.
41. Ibid., ii, 204. In fact, perhaps three quarters of a million pounds rather than five or six millions had been spent when he wrote, though of course more bills were to come in.
42. Lilburne, Prince and Overton, *The picture of the council of state* (1649) in Haller and Davies, op. cit., p. 204.
43. *The great case of transplantation in Ireland discussed* (1655).
44. Dona Torr, *Karl Marx and Friedrich Engels: Correspondence, 1846–1895: a selection* (London, 1934), pp 279, 281; and cf. p. 264.
45. A.H. Dodd, *Studies in Stuart Wales* (Cardiff, University of Wales Press, 1952), pp 104–6.
46. J. Mayer (ed.), 'Inedited letters of Cromwell, Colonel Jones, Bradshaw and other regicides' in *Transactions of the Historical Society of Lancashire and Cheshire*, new series, i, 192.

Law, order and popular protest in early eighteenth-century Ireland: the case of the Houghers

S. J. Connolly

Problems of law and order occupy a justly prominent place in the thoughts of social historians. Their main attraction as a subject of study is inevitably that they offer one of the rare occasions on which the lower classes of a society, the 'anonymous and undocumented' majority,[1] move to the centre of a picture otherwise dominated by their betters. Episodes of popular protest and rebellion not only tend to be more fully recorded than other aspects of life at the bottom of the social scale; they also break down barriers of silence, bringing into the open attitudes and resentments which on other occasions remain either latent or prudently unexpressed. At the same time this concern with the popular side of social disorders should not lead to a neglect of the response to such disorders by the privileged and powerful few. If open social conflict permits us to observe the common people saying what they would not otherwise have said, or at least what would not otherwise have been recorded, the way in which their words and actions were received by their superiors can also tell us much about the character of social relationships, and the normally unspoken assumptions which determined them. This paper will examine the light thrown on the character of Irish society in the early eighteenth century by the response to one particular outbreak of popular protest, the Hougher movement of 1711–12.

The wave of agrarian crime associated with a group known as 'the Houghers' first appeared around October 1711 in Iar Connacht, the area of west Co. Galway made up of the baronies of Moycullen and Ballynahinch, and the half-barony of Ross.[2] By

January 1712 the disorders had spread from Co. Galway into Mayo, and by the end of February outrages had also been reported in the counties of Sligo, Leitrim, Roscommon, Fermanagh and Clare. The main cause of these disturbances appears to have been a recent expansion of pasture at the expense of tillage, leading to the displacement of large numbers of small occupiers. According to William King, the Church of Ireland archbishop of Dublin, 'lands of late have been raised mightily in their rates, and the poor people not being able to pay when demanded are turned out of their farms, and one man stocks as many as ten, twenty, or perhaps an hundred inhabited'. The result, King went on, was that 'these poor people are turned to stock-slaying or starve ... and they every where endeavour to destroy whole stocks of cattle, that they may get land to plough at the former rate'.[3] A notice posted in the town of Galway in December 1711, signed with the name of Ever Joyce, the mythical leader of the Houghers, spoke of the grievances of 'many poor, distressed and banished people, who were destroyed and banished by several covetous, cruel landlords and farmers, to establish dairies to sell milk, which ought to be given to the poor, as also abundance of sheep, which took up all the lands, so that there is no room left for Christians to live'.[4] Other proclamations issued by the Houghers set out in detail the amount of land which any farmer was to hold, or any gentleman to retain in his own hands, as well as the number of livestock they were permitted to maintain on these holdings. All other lands in their possession were to be let 'to poor people, according to the former rates'.[5] These demands were backed up by widespread attacks on sheep and cattle, the instruments of the dispossession complained of, which were either killed outright or else fatally injured by the cutting of their hamstrings. By the middle of February 1712, according to Archbishop King, 'several thousand sheep and bullocks' had been destroyed in this way.[6] In Co. Mayo the Church of Ireland archbishop of Tuam, John Vesey, reported on 22 January that nearly 300 cows and bullocks had been killed within the past week, almost half of them belonging to one of his tenants.[7] In Co. Clare three individuals were said to have lost between them a total of 1,400 sheep.[8] In some cases at least the men who carried out these attacks were on horseback and carried arms.[9] All in all there seems little doubt that the Houghers' campaign represented the most formidable single manifestation of popular discontent in the period between the end of the Williamite war and the first appearance of the Whiteboys in Co. Tipperary in 1761.

The first response by the government to this crisis in the west was to issue a proclamation, on 30 November 1711. This began by restating the provisions of an act of the Irish parliament (9 Anne, c. 11) passed in the previous year, apparently in response to an earlier outbreak of cattle maiming in Iar Connacht. These were, first, that compensation for cattle destroyed in any of the three baronies of Iar Connacht should in future be levied on the inhabitants of that barony, rather than on the county as a whole, and secondly that from September 1710 the maiming of cattle, sheep and horses would be adjudged a felony, and so become punishable by death. The proclamation went on to call on magistrates and other officers to be diligent in putting the act of 1710 into operation, and in addition offered a reward of £10 for the discovery of those responsible for the recent outbreak of houghing, along with a pardon if the informant had himself been a party to the offences.[10] As the disorders became more widespread, the rewards on offer were increased. A second proclamation, on 13 December 1711, noted that those responsible for the maiming of cattle had also forced their way, armed and disguised, into houses in order to levy money on the occupants, and offered an additional reward of £20 for the apprehension or discovery of any Hougher to be convicted of such burglary. In January Archbishop Vesey reported that some magistrates in Co. Mayo had suggested that a reward of £100 should be offered for the first discovery of any one of those responsible for the houghing, 'and hope the government will encourage them to make this promise which in the mean time they were resolved to make by voluntary subscription'. The lords justices approved the scheme, undertaking to reimburse the county for any rewards so paid, and a proclamation of 8 February made this offer of a £100 reward a general one.[11] In July 1712, after the outrages had apparently subsided, the judges of assize for the Connacht circuit were asked to decide between the competing candidates for the reward thus promised to the first discoverer, as well as advising on what persons were entitled to the other rewards which had been offered.[12]

In addition to offering or underwriting rewards in this manner, the government called on local authorities to take direct action against the Houghers. On 15 December 1711 Joshua Dawson, secretary to the lords justices, wrote to John Carter, a magistrate living near Headford, calling on him, in the name of the lords justices, to use his best endeavours to have some of the Houghers taken and brought to trial. To aid him in this task he was to be permitted to call on the assistance of up to fifty soldiers from the garrison at Galway.[13] As the disorders spread to other areas, Dawson entered into correspondence with a steadily wider circle of sheriffs, magistrates and others in the affected counties, encouraging effort, reproving inactivity and suggesting measures to be taken. What the government called for was a general tightening of security in the areas where the Houghers had been active. Its first recommendation, and one on which the lords justices clearly placed particular emphasis, was for the setting of night-time watches. The proclamation of 13 December called on judges, magistrates and other officers to 'take effectual care, that watch and ward be set and kept nightly, in all proper and convenient places, by such numbers and in such manner, as the nature of the case shall require, and the laws of the land do appoint and permit'. The same advice was repeated in letters to individuals, and when Carter reported in January 1712 that a band of mounted men which had appeared on two successive nights to hough certain cattle had each time retired on finding a watch set, this was seized on as proof that 'the country have been very remiss in not keeping nightly watches [by] which might have been prevented a great deal of the mischief that has happened'.[14] In addition the government called for searches of suspected houses and places for arms. The proclamation of 13 December enjoined this as a duty on all sheriffs and magistrates, while Dawson suggested to both Carter and Vesey that they should 'send out privately by night a number of stout fellows, well armed under a bold leader', to search the houses of suspected persons and arrest any who were found to be in possession of arms.[15] Finally it was suggested that the authorities in the disturbed areas should 'take up all idle and loose persons who cannot give a good account of themselves and commit them to gaol'.[16]

To back up the local authorities in these efforts, the government provided a certain amount of military aid. Carter, as already mentioned, was authorised to draw on the assistance of soldiers from the garrison at Galway. At the request of Archbishop Vesey soldiers were ordered to quarter at Ballinrobe, Castlebar and Tuam, and later another company was sent from Galway to Foxford, Hollymount and Kilmaine.[17] At the beginning of March a foot company from Limerick was ordered to march to two stations in Co. Roscommon, while two other companies were sent to the barracks at Carrick-on-Shannon and Jamestown.[18] Orders were sent to these forces, as well as to others already stationed at Loughrea, Roscommon and Headford, to act under the direction of specified local gentlemen in tracking down and apprehending those involved in the houghing of cattle.[19] As well as these regular soldiers, the government provided arms for the use of local forces. On 9 February Sir Arthur Gore was authorised to draw 40 muskets, with half a barrel of powder and a proportionate quantity of ball, for the use of his militia troop in Mayo. In Co. Galway Sir George St George was allocated 20 muskets with half a barrel of powder and ball. In Roscommon Gilbert Ormsby was allocated 30 muskets and two other gentlemen half a barrel of powder with ball, while another half barrel of powder plus ball was to be divided between the counties of Sligo and Leitrim.[20]

A further response to the disturbances in Connacht was to call for action against the Catholic clergy. The decision came at a time when this body had enjoyed more than two years of relative freedom from harassment. In 1708 news of a projected Jacobite invasion had led government to issue a proclamation calling for the arrest of all Catholic priests, and priests in a number of counties were in fact detained.[21] This was followed in 1709 by an act requiring all priests to take the oath of abjuration, renouncing the claim of the exiled Stuarts to the thrones of Great Britain and Ireland. But here the authorities seem to have gone beyond what they had the ability or the will to enforce. The vast majority of priests refused to take the oath and the government, faced with defiance on such a scale, made no real attempt to compel them to do so. At the beginning of 1710 Irish bishops were still expressing serious alarm at the likely effects of the oath of abjuration, but the formation of a Tory ministry in August gave them greater confidence, and by October it was reported that Catholic chapels were reopening.[22] The outbreak of houghing in late 1711, however, led to new charges being levelled against the priests. Vesey forwarded to government a letter from a correspondent who claimed that none of the Catholic clergy he had spoken to had condemned the houghing, that a priest ordered by the Houghers to preach a sermon 'exhorting the rich and stock masters to reduce their flocks and set the lands to the poor people' had done so with apparent enthusiasm, and that an Augustinian friar had 'openly prayed for Eaver and his friends' good success'.[23] Gilbert Ormsby, the Co. Roscommon magistrate, was even more emphatic: 'all our unhappiness and misfortunes proceed from the priests to whom the greater men communicate their designs and they stir up the common people to execute them'. Safety and quiet, he went on, would never be restored, 'till a wolf's head and a priest's be at the same rate. Such a time I remember, and then there was not a quieter populace in the world.'[24] The government did not go so far as to gratify Ormsby's desire to see the return of better days, but they nevertheless seem to have agreed that action of some kind was called for. On 19 February Dawson announced that it had been decided to arrest all those priests in Connacht who had not taken the oath of abjuration, 'on suspicion that they are encouragers of this mischief'.[25] On 26 February he announced that the order had been extended to 'all the priests without distinction'.[26] A formal proclamation was issued on 20 March, announcing that the Catholic clergy 'have not only neglected to acquaint the people under their direction with the heinousness of the aforesaid crimes, and their duty to discover the offenders, but on the contrary have encouraged them to commit the same, and to abet, assist, receive and conceal the malefactors'. All priests in the counties of Galway, Mayo, Roscommon, Sligo, Leitrim, Clare and Fermanagh were ordered to surrender themselves to the authorities by 28 March, and all who did not so surrender were to be apprehended.

These instructions were enforced with varying degrees of success. No arrests of priests were recorded in Sligo or Fermanagh, while in Galway and Mayo searches yielded one priest in each case. In Leitrim one priest gave himself up to the high sheriff.[27] In Clare the sheriff was initially slow to move against the priests of the county, but a sharp letter from Dawson spurred him into highly effective action, in the form of an announcement that the securities given for the good behaviour of the registered priests of the county would be forfeited unless they gave themselves up. This threat led to the voluntary surrender of twenty-four registered priests in Clare, while three unregistered priests were also apprehended.[28] In Roscommon eight priests were confined, although these too claimed in a petition to government that they had surrendered voluntarily.[29] Thanks to a false report that the houghing had spread into Donegal, the county was included in the instructions sent out on 26 February, though not in the proclamation of 20 March. The sheriff reported that he had taken steps to secure the priests, beginning with the baronies nearest to Connacht, but there is no evidence of whether any arrests were made.[30] The failure of local authorities to carry out the government's instructions more effectively is understandable, for arresting priests was a hazardous undertaking. The night after Lord Mayo had apprehended a priest, men gathered menacingly outside his house, while the man who arrested a regular clergyman near Loughrea claimed that only the presence of soldiers saved him from being stoned to death by a mob of between 200 and 300 Catholics.[31] This attempted round-up of Catholic clergy in the areas affected by the houghing may have helped to prepare the way for the nation-wide drive against un-registered and non-juring priests which began in the autumn of 1712, following the receipt of information concerning the activities of regular clergy and persons exercising ecclesiastical jurisdiction contrary to the provisions of the Banishment Act of 1697.[32]

Two other counter-measures adopted by the government may be briefly mentioned. In January 1712 the lords justices heard from Carter that, whenever any sheep were houghed, 'great numbers of the poorer sort of people flock to the place and buy the carcasses at very low rates vizt one shilling apiece which he [Carter] apprehends is an encouragement to those who are concerned in that villainous practice and also gives opportunity at those great meetings to such persons to concert and contrive the further prosecutions of that mischief'. Accordingly the county authorities in Mayo and Galway were instructed to buy up the carcasses of all animals that had been houghed, 'at the rates they are commonly sold at', and to have them burnt, 'that the country people may not hope for any support from thence'.[33] In February two army sergeants, Pue and Ridley, both under sentence of death for mutiny, were offered pardons if they would agree to go to Connacht and attempt to infiltrate the ranks of the Houghers. The two men were sent to Colonel Sandford in Co. Roscommon, who was asked to advise them on the best method of getting into the company of the Houghers, 'and likewise to concert with them the properest way of giving you intelligence of the Houghers' motions, and of a method to surprise and appre-hend them'. They were furnished with an advertisement, 'printed on purpose', stating that they had broken gaol in order to escape execution, and ordering that they should be apprehended.[34]

The effectiveness of these different counter measures is impos-sible to assess precisely. Dawson, writing on 19 February, made clear that up to that point there had been little progress. The lord justice, he reported, 'is surprised at the strong confederacy and combination of the commonalty, that no discovery has all this time been made of the actors in that wicked practice, and that neither the rewards promised nor the punishments threatened have been able to prevail on any of them'.[35] Pue and Ridley, in their role as fugitives from justice, were apparently well received in the district they went to, but they returned with no satisfactory information concerning the Houghers.[36] The next month, however, matters improved. On 11 March Archbishop King expressed the hope that 'the knot of Houghers that have done so much mischief is broke, several being taken', and a newspaper report a few days later confirmed that several men had been captured and sent from Headford to Galway.[37] Four prisoners were tried and convicted at the Galway spring assizes in April 1712, and a further two at a special commission held in early June.[38] The last recorded houghing incident was in late March 1712,[39] and a falling off in the frequency of references to the topic suggests that the maiming of cattle must have ceased at some time in the spring or early summer of 1712. Certainly by the end of the year the houghing had come to an end.[40] However there is nothing to indicate why this had happened. It is possible that the houghers had suspended their campaign because of the arrest and execution of some of their number. But they may equally well have done so because they had expended their energies, or because the circumstances which had originally moved them to protest had somehow changed.

Even if the effectiveness of the government's counter measures remains unclear, however, its response to the challenge presented by the Houghers illuminates from several angles the nature of law and order, and of social relationships generally, in early eighteenth-century Ireland. The first point to emerge is the lack of resources available to government for coping with an outbreak of this kind. Dawson's correspondence with magistrates and others in the disturbed areas makes clear that the government expected the main burden of dealing with the Houghers to be met from local resources: the sheriffs, magistrates and other officers were to organise nightly watches, send out parties to search the houses of suspected persons, if necessary raise a posse to pursue offenders. The government was willing to provide troops to aid local authorities, and the Houghers arrested in Iar Connacht were in fact taken by a party of dragoons.[41] At the same time it is clear that soldiers were made available only on request, and in limited numbers. This may have reflected a desire to ensure that local officials did not simply pass over to the army duties they should have carried out themselves. But it also appears that the quartering of troops away from their normal stations gave rise to practical difficulties. By March 1713 the inhabitants of Co. Mayo were complaining of the need to provide the troops quartered at Ballinrobe with fuel and candles, and Dawson wrote to assure Lord Mayo that the soldiers would soon return to Galway.[42] Further evidence of the strain which extraordinary measures imposed on the resources of government was provided at the end of 1712, when Justice Coote was informed that it would not be possible to send a special commission to try some robbers recently taken in Co. Monaghan, because all the money available for such purposes had already been spent, 'especially in Connacht, against the Houghers'.[43] Most surprising of all, perhaps, were the problems encountered in attempting to provide weapons for the use of local forces. When Sir Arthur Gore was allocated 40 muskets with ammunition in February 1712, he was told that he would have to send for them to Dublin, as there were no serviceable arms in any nearer store. A few days later 100 muskets with powder and ball were sent from Dublin to Athlone, so that they could be more readily available if needed in Connacht, but this was an emergency measure.[44] Such details provide a useful corrective to the still-common image of post-Williamite Ireland as a country held down by force. Already, only twenty years after the close of the Jacobite war, it is clear that this was not in fact a society geared to the frequent or widespread deployment of the machinery of repression.

Lack of resources was not, however, the only factor which reduced the ability of the government to respond effectively to the problem of the Houghers. The correspondence of the lords justices makes clear that they were also far from satisfied with the zeal and efficiency of their local representatives. The failure of the measures so far adopted to put an end to the houghing, Dawson wrote on 19 February, 'in a great measure is attributed to the inactivity of the gentlemen of the country'. The lord justice, he told another correspondent on the same day, 'wishes the gentlemen of the country would exert themselves more vigorously than they seem to have done on so extraordinary [an] occasion'.[45] This type of recrimination was probably inevitable at a time when little progress was being made in coping with a serious problem. At the same time the government also had specific charges to make. In February Dawson wrote to Sir George St George pointing out that, although he was governor of both the city and county of Galway, he had not once set foot in the county in the four months since the disturbances had begun.[46] There were also complaints concerning the absence from his post of the governor of Co. Mayo, Sir Henry Bingham, while on 1 March Dawson sent a sharp rebuke to the high sheriff of Co. Roscommon for his failure to take steps to apprehend the persons responsible for a notice, 'a great piece of insolence', which had been posted up in the area under his jurisdiction.[47]

This failure of local authorities to respond to the Hougher outbreak as effectively as their superiors in Dublin would have liked was not due solely to idleness or incompetence. There was also reason to believe that some individuals were in fact protecting the persons responsible for the houghing of livestock. The involvement of members of the landed class both as protectors of the Houghers and as actual participants in attacks on livestock was one of the most distinctive features of the movement, setting it clearly apart from the later agitations of the Whiteboys and similar groups. In most cases those so involved were members of the surviving Catholic landed class, motivated by a combination of paternalism, self-interest and possibly a general hostility to the new political order.[48] But in at least two cases accusations of connivance in the proceedings of the Houghers were also levelled at members of the local magistracy. In a second letter to St George, Dawson pointed out that in 1709 informations had been sworn against a certain John Joyce and others, concerning their plans to hough cattle in County Galway. However St George had granted this Joyce his protection, 'which was the occasion of making his escape, and never being called to an account for it, and that if he had been prosecuted for that fact in all probability that great mischief of houghing which has since happened might have been prevented'.[49] In May there were complaints that a magistrate, Charles Morgan, had abused the witnesses against certain persons accused of houghing the cattle of a Mr Shaw, and had sought to discourage them from giving evidence.[50] The precise background to these allegations remains uncertain. But there was clearly reason to believe that some of the individuals on whom the government was forced to rely for the maintenance of law and order at local level had become at least partially integrated into a network of local loyalties which ran counter to their duty to the state.

The significance of all this, of course, depends very much on whether the areas affected by the houghing outbreak were in any way representative of early eighteenth-century Ireland generally, or whether their problems were in fact unique. There is little doubt that Iar Connacht, the main centre of the Houghers' operations, was a district which presented particular problems of law enforcement. Samuel Molyneux, who visited the district in 1709, summed up its reputation in a famous passage:

> nothing appeared but stones and sea, nor could I conceive an inhabited country so destitute of all signs of people and art as this is. Yet here, I hear, live multitudes of barbarous, uncivilised Irish after their old

fashions, who are here one and all in the defence of any of their own or even other rogues that fly to them, against the laws of Ireland, so that here is the asylum, here are committed the most barbarous murders after shipwrecks, and all manner of rogueries protected, that the sheriffs of this county scarce dare appear on the west side of Galway bridge, which, though Ireland is now generally esteemed wholly civilised, may well be called the end of the English pale . . .[51]

Fifty years later Edward Willes, chief baron of the Irish exchequer, writing in the aftermath of another outbreak of agrarian trouble in Iar Connacht, described it as an area inhabited by 'the ancient Irish, who never yet have been made amenable to the laws'.[52] Nevertheless, the problems encountered in Iar Connacht, though extreme, were not unique. The south west, and in particular Co. Kerry, was also recognised as a region in which the normal operation of the law could not be taken for granted, and where the control of central government over its local agents was at best a limited one. As late as 1714 it was complained that some 'heads of Irish clans' in the area around Glenflesk 'have gained the ascendant over the civil power by their insolence and number, so that the ordinary course of the laws cannot be put in force against them, without hazard to the lives of such as go about to do it'.[53] If magistrates in Co. Galway apparently connived in the operations of the Houghers, magistrates in Co. Kerry twenty years earlier were alleged to have sold protections to the bands of tories who terrorised the region, in some cases charging a fee of £50 for each protection.[54] A few years later the joint agent of the Shelburne estates, also a magistrate, was reported to have developed such close links with local Gaelic notables that he had used his authority to enforce their completely illegal demands for rents arising out of the short-lived Jacobite land settlement.[55] Nor was this kind of official delinquency entirely unheard of elsewhere. In 1700, for example, the creditor of a certain Mr Jones found himself unable to recover a long-standing debt because Jones 'being a great magistrate in Athlone he was so powerful there that he could not get the law to proceed against him'. When Jones was eventually arrested for the debt, he was 'violently rescued'.[56] As late as 1738, when an English army officer was killed by a group of local minor gentry after a quarrel in a public house in Roscrea, both his relatives and the government expressed concern—with apparent justification—that the sheriff and magistrates of the county would attempt to protect those responsible.[57]

Such evidence of magistrates and other officials, not only in Iar

Connacht but also in less remote and backward regions, being prepared to bend or break the law in a variety of ways, stands in sharp contrast to a further feature of the government's response to the Hougher outbreak. This is the extent to which persons suspected of involvement in attacks on livestock were treated with strict regard to due processes of law. Archbishop King, writing in March 1712, complained that the local authorities had in fact been too scrupulous in this respect:

> The business might have been done sooner, if the punctilios of law, and the timorousness of the gentlemen in the country, who between you and me seemed to suspect that advantages would be taken against them if they did not observe forms, had not lain in the way, for which jealousy to be sure there was no reason, but so it seems to be, for they would not stir but by order of council, and perhaps it was not convenient for the council to order some things, that were fit and necessary to be done.[58]

The archbishop's complaint is at least partly borne out by two letters from Dawson to separate magistrates in Co. Roscommon in February 1712. One of these men had apparently enquired about whether he should search papist houses for arms, while the other had asked whether he should raise a posse in pursuit of suspected persons. In both cases Dawson had to reply pointing out that the procedures they mentioned were perfectly legal, and should in fact have been adopted as standard practice.[59] His tone in each case was somewhat impatient. But despite this, and despite King's sinister reference to things 'fit and necessary' which it might nevertheless not be 'convenient' to order directly, there is no evidence that the government encouraged or sanctioned arbitrary measures. When there were complaints that a Mr Dominic Martin, one of those arrested for the houghing of Shaw's cattle, had been injured, and his wife abused, the judges of assize were directed to enquire into the allegations, 'and to give such orders therein as your lordships shall see convenient and according to law'.[60] Priests and other persons alleged to have been involved in the outrages were arrested and detained, but it is clear that there was no question of anyone being convicted on mere suspicion. At the end of March 1712 Dawson wrote to the judges of assize concerning several individuals who had been committed to gaol on 'very strong suspicions' of having been involved in houghing, but against whom there was 'no positive proof... which may be sufficient to convict them'. Accordingly he requested that they should be continued in gaol until the next assizes or general gaol delivery.[61] It is perhaps signi-

S. J. Connolly

ficant that the four men sentenced at the spring assizes were convicted on the evidence of their own leader, who had presumably been granted immunity for himself in exchange for his testimony.[62]

The efforts of the government to deal with this outbreak of agrarian crime in west Connacht thus highlight several issues of broader relevance: the limited resources available for the repression of disorders of this kind; the lack of control by central government over its local representatives, reflected both in inertia on the part of those whose duty it was to take action, and in connivance in illegality by those whose duty it was to suppress it; the extent to which both central and local authorities accepted the limitations imposed on them by the law. These points in turn contribute to an understanding of the way in which the government chose to respond to the challenge presented by the houghers. Dawson's correspondence in the early months of 1712 leaves little doubt that he and his superiors were anxious to see some of those responsible for the houghing taken and punished, and the first men against whom a case could be proved were in fact severely dealt with: of the four convicted in April 1712, one man is known to have been hanged and quartered and the other three were also sentenced to death, while the two men convicted in June were also hanged and quartered.[63] However, these represent the only sentences known to have arisen out of the houghing outbreak. Attempts to track down others who had been involved in the attacks continued for some time longer. Throughout the summer of 1712 a magistrate named Robert Miller was engaged, with the approval and support of the government, in collecting information against suspected persons, while as late as November there is a reference to a prisoner awaiting trial on a charge of houghing.[64] By the beginning of 1713, however, the government had clearly decided to put an end to the whole affair. On 13 January Dawson informed the mayor of Galway that the lords justices were considering a proclamation 'that may quiet the minds of the inhabitants that have been concerned in that barbarous practice [of houghing] and may be apprehensive of their being prosecuted for the same'.[65] The proclamation, issued on 4 February, offered a pardon to any person who had been involved in the houghing of cattle in the province of Connacht, with the exception of two ringleaders, provided that they surrendered themselves to a justice of the peace before the last day of March, and gave security for their future good behaviour.[66] The grant of such a general amnesty, to 'quiet the minds' of the persons responsible for a major wave of agrarian crime, might at first sight seem a surprising gesture, especially in a period generally thought of as characterised by a harsh and repressive criminal law. But harsh laws are of little value without the means to enforce them effectively. For a government which did not have those means a policy of controlled severity—the making of a few dreadful examples, followed by an offer of pardon to other offenders—represented a sound strategy, if not indeed the only practical course available.

The picture which thus emerges of the maintenance of law and order in early eighteenth-century Ireland has obvious parallels with that which has been built up in certain recent studies of eighteenth-century England. According to this analysis, the English landed classes, influenced by fears of the possible development of an over-powerful central executive on continental lines, chose to govern without the backing of an effective machinery for law enforcement. From this there developed the apparent paradox of extremely bloodthirsty laws applied with what has been described as 'delicacy and circumspection'.[67] The law provided for the regular use of judicial terror, but this was never indiscriminately applied. Instead, terror and mercy, ruthless retribution and discretionary pardon, were carefully balanced in a manner intended both to encourage general acceptance of the laws and to distract attention from their inability to punish more than a minority of offenders. In addition, it has been argued, the notorious formalism of the English legal system, and the consequent high rate of acquittals, often on trifling grounds, were not in any sense a defect or irrationality. On the contrary, these advertisements for the scrupulous impartiality of the justice dispensed by the courts gave an indispensable legitimacy to laws which in practice served mainly to protect the property of the rich from the depredations of the poor, while at the same time being upheld by consent rather than coercion.[68] None of these points, of course, can be applied without qualification to eighteenth-century Ireland. The comments of contemporary observers suggest that relations between social groups had a sharper edge in Ireland than in England, with straightforward power playing a more prominent role and the reciprocities of paternalism and deference a correspondingly lesser one.[69] Certain notorious episodes—for example, the execution of the Jacobite Sir James Cotter in 1720, and the trial of prominent Co. Tipperary Catholics in 1765–7 for their alleged involvement with the Whiteboys— make clear that a scrupulous regard for legal procedures did not always carry over from England into Ireland.[70] The use of the army to maintain public order—although this is a topic which has yet to be properly investigated—appears to have been more common in Ireland. At the same time the evidence of events in Connacht in 1711-2 suggests that these contrasts should not be overstated. Even in the early eighteenth century Ireland was not, on the basis of the evidence presented here, a society ruled by naked coercion or arbitrary power. Instead, it seems likely, the main basis of social order must be sought in some variation on the themes of deference and hegemony already familiar to students of eighteenth-century England.[71]

One further element is essential to a full understanding of the reaction to the houghing outbreak. This concerns the government's perception of the Houghers and the threat they posed. Some local observers saw the outbreak, not as a simple agrarian protest, but as the beginnings of another papist rising. Archbishop Vesey maintained that these 'oppressions' 'are the beginnings of a rebellion, and the common Irish hope will follow for they are grown very saucy and uppish in their countenances of late'.[72] According to the sheriff of Co. Galway 'it is a general rumour that there are several men with scarlet cloaks and that speak French go up and down the country by night', and a similar tale seems to have been current in Co. Roscommon.[73] There were also reports that the Whig opposition sought to make political capital out of the outbreak, and that they too suggested 'that the pretender is at the bottom'.[74] However there is nothing to indicate that the government in Dublin ever shared this view of the Houghers as a threat to the state. Instead they appear throughout to have seen the outbreak in perspective: as a serious problem, but one to be dealt with out of local resources, judiciously supplemented by limited amounts of military assistance. This absence of panic or over-reaction once again helps to explain what might otherwise seem the surprising mildness of the government's response to the Houghers. But the point also has a wider significance. The Protestant *élite* in eighteenth-century Ireland is often seen as a threatened and insecure group. And no doubt the members of that *élite* did have a sense that their position was a precarious one. But the evidence of the Hougher movement would suggest that, at the centre of government at least, there was a quite clear perception of where the danger lay. An invasion from abroad might bring back the exiled Stuarts, just as an invasion had ousted them, and threats of such an occurrence were always taken seriously. But faced with a purely domestic challenge, even one as apparently formidable as that posed by the Houghers, the rulers of early eighteenth-century Ireland appear to have had few fears concerning the security of their position.

Notes

1. The phrase is taken from E.J. Hobsbawm and George Rudé, *Captain Swing* (Harmondsworth, 1973), p. xviii.
2. The account that follows is based mainly on the out-letter book of the secretary to the lords justices of Ireland, covering the period July 1711 to September 1713 (Bodl., MS Eng. Hist. b. 125 (31,758), N.L.I. microfilm pos. 6418), referred to hereafter as 'Letter book'. The secretary's incoming correspondence, along with the greater part of the central and local government records for the period, has been destroyed. Brief accounts of the Hougher outbreak, written before the destruction of these records, may be found in Lecky, *Ire.*, i, 361–7; Froude, *Ire.*, i, 410–16.
3. King to Swift, 16 Feb. 1712 in Harold Williams (ed.), *The correspondence of Jonathan Swift* (Oxford, 1963–5), i, 289.
4. Thomas Wright, *The history of Ireland from the earliest period of the Irish annals to the present time* (London, n.d.), ii, 288. Wright states that this and other Hougher proclamations which he prints are transcribed from 'the private papers of Sir Robert Southwell', then in the possession of Thomas Crofton Croker. It has not been possible to trace these papers.
5. Ibid., i, 286–7. See also *Dublin Intelligence*, 22 Dec. 1711; *Daily Courant*, 21 Dec. 1711. I owe the latter reference to Dr D.W. Hayton.
6. King to Swift, 16 Feb. 1712 in Williams, op. cit., i, 289.
7. Vesey to Joshua Dawson, 22 Jan. 1712 (P.R.O., S.P. 63/367, f.243).
8. 'Calendar of Church miscellaneous papers, 1652–1795' in *P.R.I. rep. D.K. 1951*, p. 76.
9. Joshua Dawson to Vesey, 26 Jan. 1712 (Letter book, f. 15v–16r).
10. All references to government proclamations, unless otherwise stated, are to the incomplete series of printed proclamations in P.R.O.I. Official proclamations also appeared in the *Dublin Gazette*.
11. Vesey to Dawson, 22 Jan. 1712 (P.R.O., S.P. 63/367, f.243v); Dawson to Vesey, 26 Jan. 1712 (Letter book, f. 15v).
12. Dawson to judges of assize, 15 July 1712 (Letter book, f.40r).
13. Dawson to Carter, 15 Dec. 1711 (ibid., f.11v).
14. Dawson to Carter, 26 Jan. 1712 (ibid., f.16r); Dawson to Vesey, 26 Jan. 1712 (ibid.). See also Dawson to John French, 1 Mar. 1712 (ibid., f.22v).
15. Dawson to Carter, 26 Jan. 1712 (ibid., f.16r); Dawson to Vesey, 26 Jan. 1712 (ibid.).
16. Dawson to Sir Ralph Gore, 23 Feb. 1712 (ibid., f.20v).
17. Dawson to Vesey, 26 Jan. 1712 (ibid., ff 15v–16r); same to same, 9 Feb. 1712 (ibid., f.18r).
18. Dawson to John French, 1 Mar. 1712 (ibid., f.22v); Dawson to Colonel Coote, 1 Mar. 1712 (ibid., f.23r). In addition a sergeant, a corporal and twelve men were sent to Belamoe and Dunamon, in response to a request from Colonel Sandford (Dawson to Sandford, 1 Mar. 1712, ibid., f.23r).

19. Instructions to commanding officers, 9 Feb. 1712 (ibid., f.18v).
20. Dawson to Sir Arthur Gore, 9 Feb. 1712 (ibid., f.17v); Dawson to St George, 22 Mar. 1712 (ibid., f.26v) — these were presumably the same arms mentioned to Captain Robert Blakeney, deputy recorder of Galway, on 29 March (ibid., f.27v); Constantine Phipps to Ormond, 12 Feb. 1712 (P.R.O.I. M 2447); and see above, note 18.
21. W.P. Burke, *The Irish priests in the penal times, 1660-1760* (Waterford, 1914, hereafter cited as Burke, *Irish priests*), pp 327, 333, 337, 339, 367, 412-13, 422.
22. Cathaldus Giblin, 'Catalogue of material of Irish interest in the collection *Nunziatura di Fiandra*, Vatican archives' in *Collect. Hib.*, v (1962), pp 14, 18, 25, 28, 30.
23. Burke, *Irish priests*, pp 215-16.
24. Ibid., p. 440.
25. Dawson to Caulfield, 19 Feb. 1712 (Letter book, f.21v).
26. Dawson to Ormsby, 26 Feb. 1712 (ibid.).
27. Burke, *Irish priests*, pp 432, 423, 429, 440.
28. Ibid., pp 195, 398-400.
29. Ibid., p. 447.
30. Dawson to Sir Ralph Gore, 23 Feb. 1712 (Letter book, f.20v); Burke, *Irish priests*, pp 278-9.
31. Burke, *Irish priests*, pp 429, 423.
32. Proclamation, 20 Sept. 1712. For the enforcement of this proclamation see Letter Book, ff 44-50; Burke, *Irish priests*, pp 267-453 *passim*.
33. Dawson to Vesey, 26 Jan. 1712 (Letter book, f.15v); Dawson to Carter, 26 Jan. 1712 (ibid., f.16r).
34. Dawson to Sandford, 18 Feb. 1712 (ibid., f.24r).
35. Dawson to Caulfield, 19 Feb. 1712 (ibid., f.21r).
36. Wright, *History*, cit., i, 290.
37. King to Southwell, 11 Mar. 1712 (N.L.I., MS 2055); *Dublin Intelligence*, 22, 29 Mar., 1 Apr. 1712.
38. *Dublin Intelligence*, 8 Apr., 21 June 1712.
39. Ibid., 29 Mar. 1712.
40. See Southwell to Dawson, 13 Jan. 1713 (P.R.O.I., Calendar of British departmental correspondence, 1683-1714, p. 270).
41. *Dublin Intelligence*, 29 Mar. 1712.
42. Dawson to Lord Mayo, 17 Mar. 1713 (Letter book, f.62r).
43. Dawson to Coote, 20 Dec. 1712 (ibid., f.51v).
44. Dawson to Gore, 9 Feb. 1712 (ibid., f.17v); Dawson to Vesey, 19 Feb. 1712 (ibid., f.20r).
45. Dawson to St George, 19 Feb. 1712 (ibid., f.20v); Dawson to Caulfield, 19 Feb. 1712 (ibid., f.21r).
46. Dawson to St George, 19 Feb. 1712 (ibid., f.20v).
47. 'Calendar of church miscellaneous papers' in *P.R.I. rep. D.K. 1951*, p. 76; Dawson to Sandford, 1 Mar. 1712 (Letter book, f.23r).
48. For some of the evidence relating to the involvement of Catholic landed gentlemen see Froude, *Ire.*, i, 414-15.
49. Dawson to St George, 26 Feb. 1712 (Letter book, f.22r).
50. Dawson to Shaw, 3 May 1712 (ibid., f.31v); Dawson to Morgan, 3 May 1712 (ibid., f.32r).
51. Aquila Smith (ed.), 'Journey to Connaught — April 1709' in *Miscellany of the*

Irish Archaeological Society, i (1846), p. 171. For the attribution to Samuel rather than Thomas Molyneux see J.G. Simms, *William Molyneux of Dublin* (Dublin, 1982), p. 140.

52. Edward Willes to earl of Warwick, c. 1759 (P.R.O.N.I., Mic. 148, pp 16–17).
53. M.A. Hickson, *Selections from old Kerry records, historical and genealogical* (series 2, London, 1874), p. 144.
54. Barton to government, 3 Nov. 1694 (P.R.O.I., Wyche Papers 2/125).
55. Hickson, op. cit., pp 119–22.
56. William Glanvill to Sir Cyril Wyche, 24 Sept. 1700 (P.R.O.I., Wyche papers 1/1/184); William Glanvill senior to Wyche, 4 Feb. 1701 (ibid., 1/1/210).
57. *H.M.C. Polwarth MSS*, v (1961), 152–8.
58. King to Southwell, 11 Mar. 1712 (N.L.I., MS 2055).
59. Dawson to Caulfield, 19 Feb. 1712 (Letter book, f.21r); Dawson to Ormsby, 26 Feb. 1712 (ibid., f.21v).
60. Dawson to judges of assize, 25 Mar. 1712 (ibid., f.27r).
61. Dawson to judges, 31 Mar. 1712 (ibid., f.29r).
62. *Dublin Intelligence*, 8 Apr. 1712.
63. *Dublin Intelligence*, 8 Apr., 21 June 1712.
64. Dawson to officers at Ballinrobe, Hollymount, Tuam and Kilmaine, 27 May 1712 (Letter book, f.35v); Dawson to Miller, 5 July 1712 (ibid., f.38v); Dawson to Bingham, 27 Nov. 1712 (ibid., f.51r).
65. Dawson to Eyre, 13 Jan. 1713 (ibid., f.55v).
66. *Dublin Gazette*, no. 869 (7–10 Feb. 1713).
67. Douglas Hay, 'Property, authority and the criminal law' in Douglas Hay and others (ed.), *Albion's fatal tree* (London, 1975), p. 49.
68. These points are most fully developed in Hay, art. cit. See also E.P. Thompson, *Whigs and hunters: the origins of the Black Act* (London, 1975), pp 258–69. For resistance to the development of more effective agencies of law enforcement, and the reasons for it, see David Philips, ' "A new engine of power and authority": the institutionalisation of law-enforcement in England, 1780–1830' in V.A.C. Gatrell and others (ed.), *Crime and the Law* (London, 1980).
69. Arthur Young, *A Tour in Ireland* (2 vols, London, 1892), ii, 53–6; Edward Wakefield, *Account of Ireland, statistical and political* (2 vols, London, 1812), ii, 773.
70. L.M. Cullen, *The emergence of modern Ireland 1600–1900* (London, 1981), pp 198–201.
71. For the concept of hegemony in this context see E.P. Thompson, 'Patrician society, plebeian culture' in *Journal of Social History*, vii (1974).
72. Vesey to Dawson, 22 Jan. 1712 (P.R.O., S.P. 63/367, f.243r).
73. Burke, *Irish priests*, p. 423; Dawson to Ormsby, 26 Feb. 1712 (Letter book, f. 21v).
74. King to Swift, 16 Feb. 1712 in Harold Williams (ed.), *The correspondence of Jonathan Swift*, cit., i, 289; P.R.O.I., Calendar of British departmental correspondence, 1683–1714, pp 241-2.

The United Irishman as diplomat

Marianne Elliott

In July 1796, six months after his arrival in France, Theobald Wolfe Tone wrote to the French War Ministry: '... I am here in a situation approaching an *official character*. I may say, I represent my country, under the actual circumstances, and ... any attention shown by the French government is to be considered as shown to the nation much more than to me as an individual.'[1] It was a claim to an official appointment by a United Irish Society which scarcely existed. Yet, by 1799, when the Society was reconstructed after the disasters of the 1798 rebellion, the 'diplomatic' representation in France, to which he laid claim, and the negotiations for French military assistance in which he was involved, were singled out as the Society's most important function, with domestic activities pared to a holding process until the French arrived.[2] Historians have tended to treat the United Irishmen in a purely domestic context. In fact the United Irish organisation at home was a fairly chaotic affair and for any widespread popular organisation one needs to look rather to the Defenders.[3] United Irish secret diplomacy abroad, however, is quite another matter, and foreign assistance was considered of greater significance in the independence movement than any domestic effort. Indeed one of the principles on which the post-1795 republican organisation was founded was the futility of rebellion without French help; even before the home movement had got off the ground Tone was delegated to negotiate such assistance and in a recent book I have argued that this is where the Society's real achievement lay.[4] Viewed in the context of France's standing policy towards foreign revolutionaries and the tactics and achievements of the other foreign groups also negotiating for French aid in the 1790s (the Swiss, Belgians, Dutch, Germans, Italians and Poles to mention the most notable) the United Irishmen were remarkably successful and won the lasting support of many top French officials. In view of their constant failure to synchronise internal rebellion with a French invasion and the undignified squabbling into which the negotiations had deteriorated by 1803, this may seem an unlikely claim. But the people of France's sister republics, supporting French armies of 'occupation', might have questioned the nature of the successes won by their own 'patriots' and marvelled at the extremely favourable terms on which the United Irishmen secured the assistance of French arms. To indicate the importance of these achievements the present paper will examine the nature of such overseas activities—and the reason for their prominence in the United Irish programme before 1802—within the context of French policy towards, and the parallel performance of, foreign revolutionaries in general, seeking to establish how—if at all—they altered that policy to Ireland's benefit.

There can be no doubt that in the years before the suppression of the original, non-republican, Society in 1794, the United Irishmen were excessively pro-French; and in December 1792, on the eve of the declaration of war between England and France, the Irish lord lieutenant, the earl of Westmorland, was convinced that they would accept the offer of help recently extended by France to unfree peoples everywhere.[5] The pre-1794 United Irish Society emphatically denied any desire to win liberty through 'interference from abroad', even to the extent of rejecting such offers from French agents sent in 1793 and 1794. The official clamp-down in Ireland in 1794–5, however, these unsolicited offers of French help, and the sense that they were simply asking France to fulfil promises already made, explains the otherwise unrealistic move of making secret diplomatic negotiations in France the basis of a movement which barely existed, and Tone and subsequent delegates were instructed 'to ask of France that which she had already so generously offered us . . .'.[6]

But the confidence of the early agents to France was not based on any strength at home. Indeed such were their fears of social revolution and unnecessary bloodshed[7] that the process of revolutionising Ireland invariably took second place to the quest for French military assistance, and it is important to recognise the haphazard nature of United Irish activity at home after the dissolution of the first Society in 1794 to put in perspective the problems and achievements of its negotiators abroad. What kind of 'credentials' had Tone, their first and most successful negotiator in France, when he sailed from Ireland in June 1795? The answer is rather slim ones. To the French minister in Philadelphia he presented '... the two votes of thanks of the Catholics, [he was Catholic agent 1792–3]... my certificate of admission into the Belfast volunteers, engrossed on vellum, and signed by the chairman and secretaries' and a letter from Archibald Hamilton Rowan, whom the minister had met on an earlier mission by Rowan to France;[8] whilst to Carnot, a leading member of the French Directory, he was to introduce himself as 'an Irishman; ... [who] had been secretary and agent of the Catholics of that country... [and] also in perfect possession of the sentiments of the Dissenters'.[9] In other documents when he speaks of the United Irishmen he is clearly thinking of the Belfast leaders in particular and he extends his 'credentials' also to cover representation of the Defenders. Catholic Committee, United Irishmen, Defenders— could he really speak with authority for them all? Apparently he could, for an effective alliance was cemented between all three in 1795 and, in a full report of United Irish negotiations later presented to Bonaparte, Edward Lewins was to claim that Tone had received his instructions from 'the patriot leaders, Catholic and Presbyterian alike'.[10] Some members of the Catholic Committee who were also United Irishmen, Lewins, John Keogh and Richard McCormick, for example, had continued to meet secretly with leading United men like Thomas Addis Emmet and Thomas Russell after the 1794 suppression. It was this combination which delegated Tone to use his American exile as 'a stepping stone' to Paris, where he was to apply 'for the assistance of France, to enable us to assert our independence'.[11] However, it was in Belfast, to which he travelled in May 1795 to take ship for America, where he found a new, republican United Irish Society in the making. But it was a revival organised from the lower levels upwards, which the original United leaders were only just starting to support and which showed signs of more Defender involvement than is commonly supposed. It was this new system in the north which had resolved to send *him* as their delegate to France, even before he reached Belfast, and his claims to speak for Defender, Catholic and Dissenter alike seem well-founded.[12] Musing in September 1795 on the schemes of the growing colony of United Irishmen or 'seditious convention' in America, Leonard McNally, the Castle's most reliable informant for much of this period, wrote: 'Tone is a keen sensible man, argues with plausibility and cunning and writes with sensitivity and elegance ... He is acquainted with all the private proceedings of the Catholics. No man in Ireland knows so well their resources or the real situation of the country, of course no man so capable to further the scheme of an invasion, I shall not be surprised to hear of his shortly being in Paris.'[13]

Yet the plans adopted in Ulster in May 1795 for a new oath-bound United Irish Society, involving divisions of thirty-six sending delegates to higher divisions on an ascending scale from district, to baronial, to county and finally to provincial level, were only slowly implemented, even in Ulster; and despite efforts at the end of 1796 a proper executive and national society was not established until the following year. Even then the National Committee was composed of Ulster and Leinster executives alone.[14] The Ulster movement was always the most advanced and better organised, with returns of 117,917 in May 1797 against 16,198 for Leinster,[15] and its executive more militant and more enthusiastic for the French 'alliance'. When it was in the ascendant, therefore, there was a remarkable unity of purpose behind the French negotiations. Once a national executive was formed in Dublin, however, as it appears to have been in the early part of 1797, dissension and tensions began to appear in its unwieldy structure and in June resulted in such a violent disagreement between Ulster and Leinster delegates over their French policy that the former began to send their own secret diplomats independently.[16] The United Irish Society then was in the strange position of having a diplomacy without an effective home organisation and was still in the process of completing that organisation when it was shattered by the 1798 rebellion and attendant repression. The retention of many of the civil qualities from its constitutional predecessor, and uncertainty over the respective roles of internal rebellion and foreign invasion in the task of liberation, had been responsible for such organisational difficulties. As a secret combat force it was useless, a fact which the post-rebellion inquest recognised only too well. Only then, with the Society re-organised on a purely military basis and its total dependence on French invasion acknowledged, was the elective structure dismantled and a new trimmed-down command erected in its place. At last the United Irish Society had structured its organisation with a French invasion (always its most immediate object anyway) in mind and the result was a greater sense of urgency and determination in post-1799 missions to secure that end.[17] But the climate for successful secret diplomacy had faded and while the United men were sorting out their home problems, their tried and trusted channels in France had been eroded.

In addition to such ineffectual back-up machinery, early United Irish negotiations in Paris had to contend with entrenched French policies towards foreign revolutionaries, based on many years of frequently disillusioning experiences. The Irish were latecomers to revolutionary diplomacy. French cosmopolitanism was a temporary phenomenon of the Girondin period, 1792–3. It had reached a peak in the so-called propaganda decrees of November–December 1792 when France had offered help to peoples seeking to liberate themselves, but by 1796 had long disappeared. Even at its height few French politicians had been eager to actively export their revolution. Indeed it took the Legislative Assembly fifteen months to accept the request of incorporation from Avignon and the vision of France as the 'mother superior' of a universal republic was largely the creation of a set of international revolutionaries resident in Paris and congregated around the arch-internationalist, the German Anacharsis Cloots, in the *Sociétié des Amis de la Constitution.*[18] The Belgians, Mayençais, Dutch and Swiss were helped in their revolts for strategic rather than idealistic reasons and in each case France soon tired of their divisions. The Belgian patriots returning with the French armies in 1792 spent more time hounding their political opponents than helping France in her campaign against Austria; the Belgian peasantry thought the French had come to avenge true religion against Austrian reforms and the aspect of a Catholic revenge campaign which the venture assumed helped fortify French scepticism of revolutionary sympathies in traditionally Catholic countries. The Irish are 'religious enthusiasts' one informant told the French foreign minister and he cited the example of Belgium as a warning against putting their faith in such peoples.[19]

The Dutch 'patriots' make an interesting study, both in terms of how exiled revolutionaries conducted themselves and of France's response. Like the United Irishmen, their apprehension of the lower orders and fears of spilling blood permitted the Dutch authorities to take the advantage, and they had been in exile since their abortive revolt of 1786–7. In exile their divisions became notorious and make the personal squabbles of the United Irishmen abroad after 1797 seem insignificant in comparison. Differing claims and demands issued from the mutually hostile groupings in Brussels, St Omer and Paris and their squabbles periodically deteriorated into undignified incidents of fisticuffs in the French towns. France lost patience with them, and their efforts to secure French help from motives of material gain, if not idealism, simply elicited Robespierre's sneering comment that if they were so wealthy they could pay for their own revolution. Their next ploy, an attempt to manipulate French political divisions under the Thermidorean régime, almost had fatal consequences when they were carpeted in an awesome audience before the Committee of General Security.[20] Only months earlier, at the height of the foreign plot fear, several foreign patriots, including Cloots, the self-styled 'orator of the human race', had ended their cosmopolitan vision on the guillotine.[21] The Terror had been the most chauvinistic of all the revolutionary régimes, the xenophobia of the Jacobins and Robespierre in particular coming to dominate its attitude towards foreign revolutionaries, and the wise exile fled Paris for its duration.[22]

The pragmatism of the Terror, however, was symptomatic of almost every régime of the period, and from the time of the Girondins France's most consistent policy towards foreign revolution had been one of helping those who helped themselves and whose cause was useful to French war strategy. Thus they helped the Belgians in order to tie down Austrian forces, the Dutch because of the Orangist alliance with England—though Carnot had been so disgusted with the Dutch exiles in 1795 that he would have been quite prepared to negotiate with their opponents instead, if the Orangists could have been weaned away from their English alliance.[23] The Poles had been encouraged to revolt against the partitioning powers by the more internationally-minded Girondins. But Kosciuszko returned from Paris in 1793 to organise the initially successful revolt of the following year, only to be cold-shouldered by Robespierre, who distrusted generals playing at politics (which Kosciuszko, the professional soldier, was doing) and disliked the aristocratic and royalist nature of the Polish revolution. But the main reason for France's failure to follow through initial support for the Polish revolution was strategic, as always: its desire to win the neutrality of Prussia, one of the partitioning powers—which it did in 1794–5—and to retain it thereafter. The thousands of Polish refugees were instead formed into Polish Legions and kept outside France in Italy, Belgium and later the West Indies, where they were used to crush liberty rather than restore it in their own country.[24] The Dutch too, even though assisted by France in their revolution of 1795, fared badly, and the price of French help was a heavy indemnity, the continued presence of a huge French occupation force, the supply of military and naval stores to the French war effort and continued involvement in the European war through a military alliance with France.[25]

No foreign revolutionary movement, therefore, could expect automatic French sympathy, let alone active support. Tone would not have been aware of the finer points of these events when he disembarked at Havre-de-Grace on 1 February 1796 and neither he nor Lewins showed any recognition of the continuing conflict between the Dutch and their French ally when they were sent to the Hague to negotiate a Dutch expedition for Ireland in 1797.[26] Despite their early cosmopolitanism, the United Irishmen were to prove just as isolationist as all the others when it came to competing for the limited supply of armed assistance. Yet Tone's expectations cannot have been high when he was eventually invited to France in January 1796, after the foreign minister had cleared him of suspicions of being an English spy.[27] Rowan had related to him his own experiences in France the year before, when he had narrowly escaped the guillotine under the Terror and was pursued by alarmist *sans-culottes* and Parisian washerwomen as he escaped the turmoil of the reprisals following Robespierre's downfall.[28] Clearly foreigners were no longer welcomed with the same enthusiasm as in the first days of the Revolution and it is little wonder that Tone was impressed to find the rule of law again in operation under the more moderate rule of the Directory.[29] But by now the French were disinclined to accept self-proclaimed foreign spokesmen and the revolutionary movements for which they claimed to speak without careful vetting, until they had shown their commitment in successful rebellion. And yet here was a raw young man of thirty-two, unprepossessing in appearance, speaking 'execrable French' on his own admission, styling himself 'ambassador' of an unformed revolutionary organisation, and, worst of all, proclaiming Ireland's inability to rebel without extensive French assistance, sent under one of her best generals! Such a mission was surely preordained to failure. Moreover, although the five-man Directory which had assumed power in France in December 1795 was then expressing an interest in Ireland as a means of weakening England, it was raking up all the old neo-Jacobite memoirs on Ireland presented under the *ancien régime* and depicting Ireland as priest-ridden and monarchist. But worst of all, it was treating Ireland as perfect terrain for a *chouannerie* in reverse, a way of exporting the kind of banditry England had promoted in Brittany, which Tone was to argue so effectively would simply have turned Ireland into a wasteland and alienated even the staunchest supporters of France.[30]

Against such odds Tone's achievements are remarkable and one has to be totally ignorant of these to claim otherwise, for he was asking France to make an exception in Ireland's case and to lay aside nearly all the principles she had established through hard-earned experience. Here then was a stripling negotiator claiming that a largely peasant populace was ripe for revolution and that most Irish, including the gentry, were anti-English. Well, France had heard that kind of thing before with the Belgians and she already had grave doubts about the revolutionary capabilities of the Irish! Furthermore, Tone was demanding a landing by a large French army, under a famous French general—even before the Irish had shown their hand in a rising—when it had been standing French policy since 1793 to withold the former until the latter had been achieved and when, in 1796, her military reserves were already being concentrated in southern Europe against Austria. There were other problems too for anyone trying to launch a new foreign mission. With French chauvinism at another new height, laws had just been passed expelling foreigners from Paris and every foreigner risked exposure and arrest on the accusation of some zealous Parisian.[31] Conscious isolation from other foreigners, particularly English-speaking ones, was part of Tone's policy from the outset, and only after 1798, when the United Irishmen became part of France's refugee programme, did this practice disintegrate (to the detriment of the United cause).[32] Finally, the Directory was so intensely divided at every level that foreign negotiators risked attaching their cause to a declining party.

It was this last factor which posed the most immediate problem for Tone as he was hived off to the ministry of foreign affairs, notably to a petty official whose Irish background had long singled him out as resident spokesman on English and Irish affairs. This was Nicholas Madgett, one-time priest and native of Kerry, resident in France since the *ancien régime*, and in 1796 charged with the selection and translation of English newspapers. In 1793–4 he had been the central figure of a group of Anglo–Irish residents in Paris, used by France for secret missions to the British Isles. As such he was largely responsible for the exaggerated offers of French help made by secret agents to Ireland in these years, offers on which the United Irish mission to France was based.[33] But Madgett's former influence was fading and Tone quickly sensed that he was attempting to re-create his Irish monopoly and had not the ear of those that mattered. Moreover, his immediate employer, the foreign minister, Charles Delacroix, was a protégé of Reubell, undoubtedly the most talented and hard-headed member of the first Directory, and the director immediately responsible for foreign affairs. But his foreign policy was continent-based, with the acquisition of France's national frontiers his main goal in the war, and he was normally opposed to the kind of overseas naval gamble which fulfilment of Tone's demands would have entailed.[34] Sensing all this, Tone took his case directly to Lazare Carnot, the director in charge of war and undoubtedly one of the most well-known French names in Ireland, because of his victorious conduct of the war in its early days. Remarkably, in view of how badly burnt the Dutch had been in their attempt to manipulate French political divisions, Tone's ploy was entirely successful. At the time he had been anxious about such 'duplicity', and tried to persuade himself that his 'situation' excused it. He nevertheless felt 'awkward' when confronted with it by Madgett, reminding himself for future reference that honesty was always the best policy. But he had sensed correctly that Carnot's party was in the ascendant, he had not concealed his discussions with the ministry of foreign affairs from them, and actually found himself being canvassed by Delacroix as someone who had the ear of the Directory.[35] It would not be the last time Tone was to play upon the political divisions of directorial France. In Carnot Tone had indeed made the correct choice, for Carnot's experience in the suppression of English-sponsored civil war in the west had made the desire to avenge such wrongs on England something of a crusade, and in this he was wholeheartedly supported by France's top general, Lazare Hoche. This sense of crusade against England, a sense almost that England had to be crushed for France to survive, dominated French marine thinking in particular in these years, and was an important factor creating a body of opinion favourable to Ireland's case.[36] But it was of little immediate use if France could not be disabused of its belief in the feasibility of rebellion in England itself and convinced instead that a French landing in Ireland was the easiest way of attaining the desired end. This was all the more important when France seemed to think Ireland another Brittany where England might be aggravated by a French-sponsored *chouannerie*; it took Tone months of negotiating to dissuade them from employing 'this horrible mode of war' in Ireland and he was not enthusiastic about its use in England either.[37]

Considering the passion with which the *chouan* idea was held until as late as June,[38] this was quite an achievement, as was the conversion of the planned naval attack on England into an expedition to Ireland. Instructions for the latter were issued on 19 June and further refined on 19 July. Many of Tone's recommendations had been incorporated, and Hoche was appointed commander. When he arrived in Ireland he was to establish a republican form of government, with an elective convention and an executive composed of the leaders of the Catholic Committee and the United Irishmen. Disruption was to be minimised and existing civil officials unremoved, where possible. Worries persisted about the overwhelming Catholicism and supposed monarchism of the Irish, and whilst Tone had denied any need to make Catholicism the established religion and religious freedom instead was stipulated in the instructions of 19 July, Hoche was still left the option of finding a suitably Catholic and pro-French candidate if the prevailing preference was indeed for monarchy. Hoche had asked whether the country should be retained as a conquest if it appeared that England might regain control.[39] The Directory's answer was that the French should only assume temporary control of government while their troops were in the country—a precaution which the United Irishmen had always allowed for, until fears of French domination began to take over after 1797.[40] On this occasion, however, it does look as if the Directory and Hoche wanted to avoid alienating any significant portion of the Irish population, since their ultimate object was the humiliation and defeat of England by a joint Franco–Irish invasion. For the next six months the western ports buzzed with preparations to get nearly 15,000 troops and 50,000 stand of arms to Ireland—one of the largest naval expeditions to leave French ports before the Egyptian venture of 1798.[41]

But given the predisposition of the French to send an expedition to the British Isles and signs that Hoche hoped also to use Ireland as a stepping-stone for his own ambitions, was Tone's role really as significant as suggested, particularly since there were doubts about him in French minds until as late as May, and they were taking advice independently from two other eminent Irishmen lately arrived in Hamburg, Arthur O'Connor and Lord Edward Fitzgerald? Was Tone instead something of 'a joke' to the Directory as Thomas Flanagan's novel *The Year of the French* suggests, the hopeless romantic who misled the French or the cynical individualist of Tom Dunne's recent study, whose French mission was an outlet for political ambitions unfulfilled in normal constitutional channels?[42] In May 1796 the Directory had indeed sent an agent independently of Tone to check his story in Ireland. But the bare facts distort. The French were no fools when it came to negotiating with foreign 'patriots'; they were naturally suspicious and would only accept their credibility after careful cross-checking. Every other United agent sent to France in this period underwent the same scrutiny;[43] whilst the decision to double-check on Tone took place against revived fears of a foreign plot after the recent discovery of the Babeuf conspiracy in Paris. A number of disgruntled foreigners had been involved, and fears of wider ramifications led to a further clamp-down on foreigners resident in Paris.[44] Furthermore, the agent, Richard O'Shee, was still sent to the leaders in Ireland designated by Tone and on the whole far too much has been made of this incident, particularly since O'Shee never actually completed his mission. Indeed the entire incident is more explicable in terms of internal French divisions, with the Carnot group anxious to substitute their own candidate for one chosen by Delacroix in consultation with Tone, and almost simultaneously Carnot was exempting Tone from the laws against foreigners residing in Paris in the most laudatory terms.[45] Tone's credibility was eventually so well-established by mid-1796 that thereafter his opinion was automatically sought on new arrivals from Ireland, and even after his death association with him became the badge of Irish patriotism in French eyes.[46]

Of more significance is the tenor of O'Shee's instructions, which show France retaining many of the misconceptions about Irish Catholicism and monarchism, and whilst these prejudices are more muted in the July instructions, they are nevertheless still apparent. It is important to understand the strength of such beliefs to see why Tone was so emphatic in his denial of them (as were Lord Edward and Arthur O'Connor also). Exaggeration, perhaps; necessary polemic, certainly; genuine conviction, undoubtedly; and since all the other United Irish negotiators shared his belief in the widespread disaffection of the Catholic populace, Tone can be forgiven for thinking likewise. He was clearly impressed by the Catholic Defenders as a popular revolutionary force, even if he made the same mistake as future historians in considering it a 'peasant' organisation. Tone was violently anti-clerical; he fumed when an ex-friar was proposed for a mission to Ireland, applauded when 'that old priest' in Rome was forced to make terms with the French after 'fleecing all Europe' for 'many a.long century'. But anti-clericalism is not the same as anti-Catholicism; Tone had long been a friend to the Catholics and what he was refuting was not the overwhelming Catholicity of the island, but its priest-ridden nature.[47]

Thus far the United Irishmen at home had little idea of the progress of Tone's negotiations. Indeed it was only with Lewins's arrival in France the following May that he learnt of the formal organisation of a United Irish executive.[48] Until then United Irish diplomacy continued to stem from a few individuals, and such too was the starting point of the June–October 1796 mission of Lord Edward Fitzgerald and Arthur O'Connor to Hamburg, Switzerland and eventually to France. Lord Edward had approached almost the same people responsible for Tone's mission and offered to travel to Hamburg and intercede with France through his old friend, Charles Frédéric Reinhard, French chargé d'affaires there. Reinhard was a German and one of the few cosmopolites of the early 1790s to actually enter French service. But he was a moderate, who had never wanted the Revolution exported to his own country, and was frequently even more suspicious of foreign revolutionaries than the Directory itself. It was through him that the negotiations of every United agent after Tone were channelled, and it was frequently his mistrust, rather than that of Paris, which was carried back to Ireland to aggravate the disputes already gathering by 1797 over the question of French assistance.[49] Reinhard did, however, like O'Connor, clearly a talented diplomat who, despite a poor command of French, gained the respect of every French government right up to the defeat of Napoleon.[50] But by this date, July 1796, the Directory was loath to admit any more foreigners to Paris and was suspicious of Lord Edward's aristocratic connections— notably in the *emigré* world of his wife's relatives taking refuge in neutral Hamburg—and when O'Connor was permitted to meet Hoche in western France Lord Edward was not allowed to accompany him. O'Connor finally met Hoche at Angers about 14 August and his emphasis on the same points as Tone, the need for arms, a French landing before an Irish rebellion, the strength of the north etc., both fortified Tone's position in Paris and caused the preparations for the Irish expedition to be pursued with new vigour thereafter. But the decisions of 19 June and 19 July owed nothing to Lord Edward and O'Connor's influence; Lord Edward assured Reinhard that they recognised Tone's position in Paris and only came to offer more recent information. Tone in turn, whilst left uninformed by the Directory of these negotiators, spoke highly of their patriotism when questioned informally.[51] There was no sense of competition between the two missions.

From mid-1796 until his premature death in September of that year, Hoche was the main hope of the United Irishmen in France. But with the failure of the Bantry Bay expedition which had finally sailed in December 1796, largely through his efforts, Ireland lost its best chance of securing independence at French hands without also incurring the dangers of military government. Hoche was indeed ambitious, but unlike Bonaparte he was an ardent republican and his respect for the rights and liberties of the Rhinelanders in 1797 was a token of what the Irish might have expected under him. Tone was clearly enamoured of the young general, but so too were Lewins and MacNeven, though already influenced by the creeping United disillusionment with France and more recently by Reinhard's cool reception.[52] Military intervention to preserve or restore liberty was one thing, military government quite another, and Hoche in that respect was not another Bonaparte.[53] Certainly Tone, Lewins, and a number of secondary United agents on the continent by the end of 1797, were stunned at his loss and the recognition that their best hope of attaining Irish independence had also died with him lay behind their half-hearted discussions in the months when events at home were fast approaching the crisis of 1798.

Secret diplomacy is often in danger of becoming so secret that it ceases operating from any basis of reality, and the maintenance of contact with home developments is as much a fundamental of secret, as it is of normal, diplomacy. In the secret variety it is necessarily pared to a minimum and with British naval strength making necessary communication by sea hazardous, this side of United Irish diplomacy was much more difficult than that of the continental-based patriots. Even so, the United Irishmen were particularly ineffective in this respect, relying instead on the personal qualities of a handful of negotiators abroad. It is a commentary on the concentration of effort in France that more importance was attached to the flow of information from there than the reverse, and Reinhard expressed surprise that so little contact had been maintained with Ireland.[54] Given the French promises of 1794-5 and 'payment' in the form of a major expedition the following year, few can have foreseen the need to establish some long-term communications network, and for a long time the Paris negotiators remained unaware of the crippling home division and the changing nature of the movement in 1797.

No one had been more alive to his increasing estrangement from Irish affairs than Tone himself and in 1796 he had repeatedly urged the Directory to send agents to Ireland. After the Bantry Bay failure the need seemed all the more imperative, for the French were baffled by the lack of Irish response to the attempt. At Hoche's behest Tone wrote to his friends asking them to send another confidential agent. The result was the mission of Edward Lewins, a former member of the Catholic Committee, fluent in French (he had been a seminary student in France until 1793) but 'scholastic, pedantic and sophisticated' in argument, and lacking the directness and vivaciousness of Tone or O'Connor.[55] The French never took to him as they had to the other two and it is unlikely that he would have taken such a prominent part in the negotiations thereafter without the full support of Tone. Lewins had been instructed by Dublin to contact Tone, who would vouch for his mission, and in the event of a successful invasion of Ireland to remain behind in Paris as Irish ambassador.[56] But Lewins never replaced Tone as United Irish negotiator, even if Tone deferred to his more recent knowledge, and they worked together as a team, most immediately in the Hague, sent there by Hoche to advise on Dutch preparations for another Irish expedition.[57]

But it is a quirk of history that, just as the home Society was graduating from the individualism of early years to recognition of the need for more regular communication with France, the conditions favourable to secret diplomacy abroad were deteriorating. The Irish and English authorities had not known of Tone's presence in France until after the Bantry Bay expedition. But improving British intelligence in 1797 and the necessity of United agents entering France through the neutral ports of northern Germany meant that Whitehall was kept informed of the traffic to and fro, even before Samuel Turner, one of the United agents in Hamburg, turned informer in October 1797.[58] The kind of immunity Tone had enjoyed was gone forever.

Moreover, France had returned to its standing policy towards foreign revolutionaries after the aberration of Bantry Bay and was refusing assistance to the Irish until they had first shown their desire to be free in a rising[59]—and this at a time when the United Irishmen at home were holding back an expanding movement from rebellion until the French had arrived. The upshot was the arrival of younger, more militant leaders on the continent, chafing at the delays in negotiations for French help at a time when they felt Ireland would never again be so ripe for revolution, and questioning the exclusive right of Tone and Lewins to conduct such negotiations. The timing of Lewins's arrival had been unfortunate, not only because of the return of a chastened Directory to a waiting game with the foreign revolutionaries, or the declining fortunes of the pro-Irish party in the months before the *coup d'état* of Fructidor, but because the Batavian Republic, which had temporarily assumed responsibility for sending help to Ireland, had specifically instructed him not to divulge any information about preparations until the expedition was ready to sail.[60] But since the home leaders were using the hope of French invasion to discourage their supporters from independent action until it arrived, the demand for information on the French negotiations had reached a peak at a time when silence had been imposed on their negotiators. Rumours that Lewins was not fulfilling his duties were temporarily calmed by an Ulster delegate sent to check later that summer.[61] But with signs that Ulster's strength was being eroded by General Lake's disarmament of the province, one cannot blame the militant leaders for thinking the French negotiations too leisurely—though in truth there was little else Tone and Lewins could do.

The time had come again to send someone with more recent credentials and in the winter of 1797–8, with the despatch of Arthur O'Connor and the establishment of semi-permanent stations in London and Hamburg to facilitate communication, it looked as if the United Irish mission to France might again achieve the kind of successes won in Tone's heyday.[62] Secret diplomacy like normal diplomacy moves on well-established tracks, with foreign governments preferring ambassadors who know the ropes, and after Tone's initial clearance the French adhered doggedly to him as Ireland's main spokesman. Apart from Tone, O'Connor was the United leader most respected by France, and his arrival with recent information about the situation at home would surely have injected a new urgency into preparations for another Irish expedition. But the new network was entirely destroyed over the next few months with O'Connor's arrest and the arrest or death at the time of the '98 rebellion of many of those most trusted by the French, including Tone. This left Lewins, already distrusted by many of the home leaders, as the only permanent representative in France.[63] Secrecy had gone for good and, with the movement's internal destruction in 1798 and the increasing flow of United men to the continent as refugees rather than ambassadors, so too had its negotiating strength.

United Irish diplomacy after 1797 had been weakened by oscillation between the desire for French help and the fear of it, and above all they were never prepared to barter their national self-determination for political redemption. But the conflict between need and apprehension continued to erode the post-1798 military organisation, and the candid acceptance of their own incapacity, without overwhelming French aid, in the documentation of Robert

Emmet's and Malachy Delaney's mission to France in 1800, must be placed beside their firm demands for all kinds of guarantees and the more remarkable pre-emptive strike of Emmet's rebellion in 1803—all part of their continuing effort to preserve their national soul against the necessary foreigner.[64] By that date the United Irish Society had come almost full circle as a society with a secret diplomacy but without an effective home organisation. But the climate in both countries was very different from that of 1796, and recognising that under Napoleon their options had been reduced to accepting French help with almost certain French domination, most United Irish agents abandoned the mission to France altogether.[65]

As amateur diplomats, however, the United Irishmen had been considerably more successful than as amateur rebels. In their heyday the French negotiations had been the most successfully organised aspect of an otherwise disorganised movement. Without the sense of strength derived from knowledge of their French 'alliance' it is doubtful whether the Society would have amounted to anything at all, for their inherent fears of uncontrolled social revolution would certainly have deterred them from any alliance with the Defenders. Moreover, there was nothing slavish in their approach to France; theirs was a business arrangement, with France securing the defeat of England in return for such help, an alliance with Ireland, and payment in full from confiscated church property for every expedition and arms consignment—no loophole was to be left for future conquest, no heavy war indemnities like those suffered by the Dutch. How such hopes would have worked out in reality we will never know, for with that fundamental communications weakness the necessary co-ordination of the various invasion attempts with internal rebellion always eluded them. However, the arms supplies and naval expeditions sent to Ireland from French shores and, most of all, the favourable terms on which such help was secured, must place the United Irishmen among the more successful of the secret diplomats then in Paris, and the instructions issued to General Hardy, about to take another expedition to Ireland in July 1798, are a token of how far they had come since the days of Carnot's 'chouannising' plans:

> As soon as possible you ought to gather together the leaders of the patriot party and in concert with them organise a provisional government in the area under United Irish control... Above all you must respect the manners, customs and religious practices of the Irish, and in no case must they suffer in their person or their property. Every

officer or soldier who departs from the line of duty ... will be punished
in the most exemplary manner ... the Irish must be treated as brothers,
as citizens persecuted by a ferocious government ... since they are
fighting for the same cause, they must be joined to us by the same links,
the same sentiments ...

... the intention of the Directory being to maintain the independence
of the Irish, you must avoid ... anything which might create the idea
that the French government has anything else in mind than to help
them win back their freedom ...[66]

To treat the United Irishmen, therefore, as noble failures or
hopeless romantics may be good mythology, but it is bad history
and neglects the fundamental truth that they were diplomats before
they were rebels, more at ease in centres of international politics
than the potato-patch of their domestic hinterland.

Notes

The following abbreviations are used throughout this paper:

A.A.E.	Archives des Affaires Étrangères, Paris.
A.A.G.	Archives Administratives de la Guerre, Paris.
A.D.S.M.	Archives Départmentales de la Seine-Maritime, Rouen.
A.H.G.	Archives Historiques de la Guerre, Paris.
A.N.	Archives Nationales, Paris.
Kent C.R.O.	Kent County Record Office, Maidstone.

1. Tone to General Clarke, 21 July 1796 in A.N., A.F. III 186[b] d.858.
2. For details of the reconstruction after 1798 see S.P.O., 620/8/72/2, 620/47/100 and 620/7/74/1–22; P.R.O., Home Office Papers (hereafter cited as H.O.), 100/86/301–2; A.A.E., Corr. Pol. Ang. 592, ff 386–7; T.C.D., MS 869/1/437.
3. M. Elliott, *Partners in revolution: The United Irishmen and France*, (London, 1982), especially pp 49–50; 'The origins and transformation of early Irish republicanism' in *International Review of social history*, xxiii (1978), pp 405–28.
4. M. Elliott, *Partners in revolution*, especially pp xiii–xv, xix–xx, 77–123, 365–6, 371–2.
5. Westmorland to Pitt, 7 Dec. 1792, in S.P.O., Westmorland correspondence, iv, f. 56. For early United Irish response to events in France see *Northern Star*, I, nos 42, 71, 73, 74, 82 and II, nos 10, 21.
6. For Lewins's account of these events (*c.* 1801) see A.N., AF IV 1671 plaq. 1, ff 99–105; also Rowan's account in A.A.E., Corr. Pol. Ang. 589, ff 23–4, 111.
7. See W.J. MacNeven, *Pieces of Irish history* (New York, 1806), pp 197, 204–5, 211, 218–19; Henry Alexander to Pelham, 20 Sept. 1798 in B.L. Add. MS 33106, ff 79–84; *Report from the Committee of Secrecy of the House of Commons of Ireland* (Dublin, 1798), app. xxxi; and *Life of Theobald Wolfe Tone*, ed. William T.W. Tone (Washington, 1826), i, 293; see also M. Elliott, *Partners in revolution*, pp 27–8, 165, 212, 320, 369 for such fears and their attitudes towards the lower orders in general.

8. Tone, *Life*, i, 132.
9. Ibid., ii, 27, 43.
10. See Lewins's memoir of 1801 in A.N., AF IV 1671 plaq. 1, ff 99–105; for the alliance with the Defenders see MacNeven, *Pieces of Irish history*, pp 117–18, 178–9; see also M. Elliott, 'Origins and transformation...', p. 410 for the multi-sided nature of the revolutionary' movement.
11. Tone, *Life*, i, 125–8, and Lewins's account in A.N., AF IV 1671, cit. For the meetings in Dublin see information of Francis Higgins, 6 and 24 June 1795 in Kent C.R.O., U840/0.143/5, 10.
12. For this new organisation see MacNeven, *Pieces of Irish history*, pp 67–8, 76–7; B. Johnston to J. Lees, 8 Aug. 1795 in S.P.O., 620/22/7[b], 28, 41 and information of Thomas Boyle, 1 July 1796, ibid., 620/18/3. Tone was certainly informed of these developments by his Belfast friends—see letter of Robert Simms, 18 Sept. 1795 in Tone, *Life*, i, 128, 284.
13. Information of 'J.W.' [i.e., McNally], 17 Sept. 1795, in S.P.O., 620/10/121/29.
14. For the slow organisation of the new movement see M. Elliott, *Partners in revolution*, pp 72, 108; MacNeven, *Pieces of Irish History*, pp 181–2; *Report from the Committee of Secrecy...* (1798), app. xiv; statement of R. McCormick, c. 1798, in P.R.O.N.I., D. 272/6.
15. Information of Boyle, 12 May 1797, in S.P.O., 620/30/61; also copy of report of the Ulster provincial, 1 Jan. 1797, giving returns of 99,411 for Antrim, Down and Derry in Kent C.R.O., U840/0.152/1.
16. See M. Elliott, *Partners in revolution*, pp 132–3, 151–3; *Report from the Committee of Secrecy...* (1798), app. xiv–xv; and Samuel Turner's account in P.R.O., H.O. 100/70/335–52. See information of Thomas Higgins, 17 Oct. 1797, on Ulster's greater enthusiasm for the French 'alliance' in S.P.O., 620/18/14.
17. See note 2. Two new agents, George Palmer and William Putnam McCabe, were sent to Paris as soon as plans for the new organisation were mounted; for their mission see S.P.O., 620/7/74/1–2, 8, 620/11/130/60; P.R.O., F.O. 33/19/65, 92; and A.A.E., Corr. Pol. Ang. 592, ff 386, 409.
18. For Cloots see A. Soboul, 'Anacharsis Cloots l'Orateur du genre humain' in *Annales historiques de la Révolution française*, 239 (1980), pp 28–58. For the international community in Paris between 1792 and 1794 see A. Mathiez, *La Révolution et les étrangers: cosmopolitanisme et défense nationale* (Paris, 1910), pp 3–58. For French reluctance to accept the role of Europe's revolutionary mentor see A.A.E., Corr. Pol. Ang. 583, ff 210–12, 348–60; 584, ff 19–22, 67–79; Corr. Pol. Suisse 436, f. 278; and A.N., AF III 74 d.301.
19. Anonymous information (Dec. 1792) in A.A.E., Corr. Pol. Ang. 584, ff 408–11. See also S. Tassier, *Histoire de la Belgique sous l'occupation française en 1792 et 1793* (Brussels, 1934), pp 59–60; R. R. Palmer, *The age of democratic revolution* (2 vols, London, 1959, 1964), ii, 69–82.
20. S. Schama, *Patriots and liberators. Revolution in the Netherlands 1780–1813* (London, 1977), particularly pp 144–55.
21. A. Soboul, 'Anacharsis Cloots...', cit., p. 55.
22. See F. A. Aulard, *La Société des Jacobins* (6 vols., Paris, 1889–97), iii, 614–20, iv, 633–5 and A. Mathiez, *La Révolution et les étrangers*, pp 166–7 for Robespierre's opinion.
23. S. Schama, *Patriots and liberators*, pp 195–7.
24. B. Lesnodorski, *Les Jacobins Polonais* (Paris, 1965), pp 315–21. The Polish Legions eventually became receptacles for foreign revolutionaries in general:

see in particular Lewins to the foreign minister, 28 Oct. 1800, in A.A.E., Corr. Pol. Ang. 593, ff 22–3; A.H.G., X^{n}16 doss. 1812 (Jan.) and doss. pers. 2e sér. G.B. 1840 (William Lawless).

25. Treaty of the Hague, May 1795; see S. Schama, *Patriots and liberators*, pp 206–7, 264–9; also communiqué of 6 Aug. 1797 in P.R.O., F.O. 27/50, for growing Dutch discontent at such terms.

26. Tone, *Life*, ii, 410–15, and for Lewins's account of their Dutch negotiations see A.A.E., Corr. Pol. Ang. 593, f. 422.

27. See correspondence of Delacroix and Adet (Oct–Dec. 1795) in A.A.E., Corr. Pol. Ang. 589, ff 23–4, 111–15, clearing Tone of such suspicions.

28. See Rowan's account in *Autobiography of Archibald Hamilton Rowan*, ed. W. H. Drummond (reprint of 1840 edn, Shannon, 1972), pp 186–302; and Tone's account in Tone, *Life*, i, 131–2.

29. Tone, *Life*, ii, 87.

30. For these early negotiations see Tone, *Life* ii, 14–77, 181–204; A.N., AF III 186^b doss. 857–8 and BB^4 103, ff 135–44. For the Directory's Irish *chouan* plans see A.H.G., MR 501, Armée de L'Ouest; A.N., AF IV 1671 plaq. I f. 65; and A. Debidour, *Recueil des actes du Directoire éxécutif* (4 vols, Paris, 1910–17), ii, 176–8.

31. See the orders controlling foreigners residing in Paris (Feb. 1796) in A.N., F7 7107 and also F7 7144.

32. For the United Irishmen as refugees, see M. Elliott, *Partners in revolution*, pp 266–72.

33. For Madgett see A.A.E., Personnel 1er sér. 47, ff 83–9; F. Masson, *Le Département des Affaires Étrangères pendant la Révolution, 1787–1804* (Paris, 1877), pp 354, 366; and R. Hayes, *Biographical Dictionary of Irishmen in France* (Dublin, 1949), p. 105.

34. For Reubell see G. D. Homan, *Jean-François Reubell: French revolutionary, patriot and director, 1747–1807* (The Hague, 1971); S. S. Biro, *The German policy of revolutionary France* (2 vols, Cambridge (Mass.), 1957), i, 378, ii, 491–2, 508; and B. Nabonne, *La diplomatie du Directoire et Bonaparte d'après les papiers inédits de Reubell* (Paris, 1951), pp 42–58. For Tone's suspicions of Madgett and criticism of the unilateralism within the Directory, see his *Life*, ii, 23–4, 38–9, 52, 57, 62, 90–91.

35. Tone, *Life*, ii, 53, 56–7, 62–3.

36. Truguet to Hoche, 21 June 1797, in A.N., AF III 463 doss. 2801, for a good example of French marine thinking on this point. For Carnot and Hoche see M. Reinhard, *Le Grand Carnot* (2 vols, Paris, 1950), ii, 216–20; A Sorel, 'Les vues de Hoche', in *Revue de Paris*, iv (1895), p. 232; and E. Desbrière, *Projets et tentatives de débarquement aux îles britanniques*, (4 vols, Paris, 1900–02), i, 57–69.

37. Tone, *Life*, ii, 80–82, 85. A. Debidour, *Recueil des actes*, iii, 111, n.112 and E. Guillon, *La France et l'Irlande sous le Directoire* (Paris, 1888), p. 193 credit Tone with having transformed directorial plans for Ireland from a *chouannerie* to a full-scale expedition. For spring naval plans against Britain see A.N., AF III 20 doss. 159 f. 142.

38. See M. Elliott, *Partners in revolution*, pp 91–2.

39. Hoche to the Directory, 16 July 1796 in A.N., AF III 186^b doss. 858; and for the July instructions see A. Debidour, *Recueil des actes*, ii, 688–9, iii, 140–44.

40. The issue of a possible French takeover was never far from United Irish thinking, even if muted by confidence in their own strength. But it does begin

to take over after the rise of Bonaparte. See W. J. MacNeven, *Pieces of Irish history*, pp 216–18; United Irish address, June 1797, in S.P.O., 620/31/86; M. Elliott, *Partners in revolution*, pp 243–4, 282–364.

41. For details of the preparations see A.H.G., B[11] 1; A.N., BB[4] 102 and AF III 186[b] doss. 860; N.L.I., MSS 704–6 (French invasion); E. Desbrière, *Projects et tentatives* i, 135–223 and E. H. Stuart Jones, *An invasion that failed* (Oxford, 1950).

42. Thomas Flanagan, *The year of the French* (London, 1979), pp 80–82; though a work of fiction this book is too often taken as fact: Tom Dunne, *Theobald Wolfe Tone, colonial outsider* (Cork, 1982), pp 11, 23, 55.

43. For the appointment of the agent O'Shee see the correspondence of Delacroix and Carnot (May–June 1796) in A.A.E., Corr. Pol. Ang. 589, ff 259–62 and A.N., AF III 57 doss. 224 ff 7–9 and AF III 373 doss. 1853. Lewins, the accredited United Irish agent sent in 1797, was exposed to the same scrutiny: see Simon to Hoche, 17 June 1797, in A.D.S.M., 1 Mi 62/C.157/2097 and correspondence of Reinhard in A.A.E., Corr. Pol. Ham. 111, ff 148–50 and Corr. Pol. Ang. 590, ff 217–333.

44. See S. Schama, *Patriots and liberators*, pp 255, 677 n. 25; R. C. Cobb, *Les armées révolutionnaires* (2 vols, Paris, 1960, 1963), i, 180 n. 124 and R. R. Palmer, *The age of democratic revolution*, ii, 271–2. See Tone's account in *Life*, ii, 110.

45. For Tone's request for exemption from the law against foreigners and Carnot's supportive statement in the margin see A.N., AF III 369 doss. 1799, ff 48–51; for the divisions within the Directory see M. Elliott, *Partners in revolution*, pp 84–5, 88–92. For O'Shee's instructions see A.N., AF III 186[b] doss. 859 and Tone's 'observations sur les instructions delivrées' in A.H.G., B[11] 1.

46. See comments [by Clarke] on Tone in A.N., AF III 186[b] doss. 857; by Talleyrand in A.A.E., Corr. Pol. Ang. 591, ff 174–88; and by General Rivaud in A.H.G., B[5*] 115. Indeed the references to complete faith in Tone after 1796 are legion: A.N., F7 3511, 7293, 7348, 7440; A.A.E., Corr. Pol. Ang. 592, f. 139 and 593, f. 173 being but a few examples.

47. Sullivan's translation of a memoir by Tone in A.A.E., Corr. Pol. Ang. 589, ff 270–71; Tone, *Life*, ii, 144. See also ibid., pp 83–5, but note his sympathy for the ordinary Catholic as distinct from the clergy on pp 51, 185–6, and his admiration for the Defenders on pp 188–90.

48. See Lewins's account in A.N., AF IV 1671 plaq. 1, ff 99–105.

49. For Reinhard see J. Droz, *L'Allemagne et la Révolution française* (Paris, 1949), pp 53–6; for his friction with Lewins see A.A.E., Corr. Pol. Ham. 111. ff 145–50, and with MacNeven, ff 311–29 and 359; see also W. J. MacNeven, *Pieces of Irish history*, p. 190.

50. Reinhard to Delacroix, 7 June 1796, in A.A.E., Corr. Pol. Ang. 589, ff 277–9; and for the esteem in which he was held in Napoleonic France see A.A.G., doss. pers. 2 sér. G.D. 393 (O'Connor); and A.N., AF IV 1674 plaq. 5 doss. 2, f. 543.

51. For the mission see A.N., AF IV 1671 plaq. 1, ff 99–105, AF III 186 doss. 859 (Particularly Hoche's report 29 Aug. 1796), and A.A.E., Corr. Pol. Ang. 588–9; Lord Edward's endorsement of Tone is in Corr. Pol. Ang. 589, f. 249, and Tone, *Life*, ii, 165–6 tells of Hoche's queries about the two emissaries.

52. See Tone, *Life*, ii, 153–5, 407–15, for Hoche's meetings with Lewins and Tone; also A.H.G., B[11] 1 (Hoche's letter of 30 May 1797) and A.D.S.M., 1 Mi 62/157/2094 and 2097 for Hoche's action to help Lewins; for the stunned

reaction by the United Irish leaders to his death see A.A.E., Corr. Pol. Ham. 112, f. 48.

53. For Hoche in the Rhineland see P. Sagnac, *Le Rhin Français pendant la Révolution et l'Empire* (Paris, 1917), chs vi, vii; and for his very different role in the abortive coup of June 1797 from that of Bonaparte two years later, see M. Elliott, *Partners in revolution*, pp 156–9, and A. C. Thibaudeau, *Mémoires sur la Convention et le Directoire*, (2 vols, Paris, 1824), ii, 170–242.

54. Reinhard to Delacroix, 31 Mar. 1797 in A.A.E., Corr. Pol. Ang. 590, ff 211–13; and see M. Elliott, *Partners in revolution*, p. 159 and the inadequate communication in 1797. An interesting account of such difficulties can be found in anonymous information from London (Dec. 1799) in S.P.O., 620/7/74/39.

55. McNally's comments on Lewins (May 1797) in S.P.O., 620/10/121/53; and see Lewins's claims about Hoche and Tone sending for him in A.N., AF IV 1671 plaq. 1, ff 99–105; W. J. MacNeven, *Pieces of Irish history*, p. 109. See also Tone to Reynolds, 24 Feb. 1797 in A.A.E., Corr. Pol. Ang. 589, ff 277–9.

56. Lewins's memoir of 1801 in A.N., AF IV 1671 plaq. 1, ff 99–100; MacNeven's comments (July 1797) in A.A.E., Corr. Pol. Ham. 111, ff 319–23; and for the early stages of his mission see Corr. Pol. Ang. 590, ff 217–333; Corr. Pol. Ham 111, ff 148–50, 222; A.N., AF III 57 doss. 223, AF III 452 doss. 2685 f. 18.

57. For their mission to the Batavian government see Tone, *Life*, ii, 409–17; A.N., AF III 463 doss. 2801, ff 41–6; A.A.E., Corr. Pol. Ang. 593, f. 422 and A.H.G., B⁵41. Only after Tone's death does Lewins assume all his responsibilities (see A.N., F7 7293 and 7459).

58. See Turner's information in P.R.O., H.O. 100/70/335–72, 100/75/5–9; and M. Elliott, *Partners in revolution*, pp 165–240, for improving British intelligence, particularly in Hamburg.

59. See official statement sent to Hoche, 9 June 1797, in A.D.S.M., 1 Mi 62/157/2095.

60. Lewins's memoir of 1801 in A.N., AF IV 1671 plaq. 1, ff 99–105; for the divisions in the home movement see P.R.O., H.O. 100/70/335–52; S.P.O., 620/10/121/55–63; P.R.O.N.I., D. 714/2/1–3; and *Report from the Committee of Secrecy...* (1798), app. xiv, xv.

61. For Teeling's mission see P.R.O., H.O. 100/70/339–52 and A.A.E., Corr. Pol. Ham. 112, f. 48. See also comments on these suspicions of Lewins in *Memoirs of Miles Byrne*, ed. by his widow, (2nd edn, 2 vols, Dublin, 1906), ii, 179.

62. For the purpose of O'Connor's mission see information of Robert Gray in P.R.O., Privy Council, 1/41/A.136 and O'Connor's own account in A.H.G., doss. pers. 2ᵉ sér. G.D. 393. See also *State Trials*, xxvi, 1191–1432 and M. Elliott, *Partners in revolution*, pp 174–86.

63. For the growing distrust of Lewins see P.R.O., H.O. 100/70/335–52.

64. For the mission of Emmet and Delaney in Sept. 1800 see A.A.E., Corr. Pol. Ang. 593, ff 288–9, 594, f. 173; also Bonaparte's comments in A.N., A.F. IV* 204 no. 1182.

65. See for example the letters of T. A. Emmet (1804–5) in P.R.O.N.I., T. 1815/4 and Madden, *United Irishmen* (7 vols, London, 1842–6), 3rd ser., iii, 79–81.

66. Instructions to General Hardy, 30 July 1798, cited in E. Desbrière, *Projets et tentatives*, ii, 134–5.

The 1798 rebellion in its eighteenth-century context*

L. M. Cullen

The purpose of this paper is to relate the rebellion to the perspective of the eighteenth century at large. It does not deal with the immediate social background, part of which has been touched on elsewhere,[1] and other parts of which will be examined at a later date. Along with the Vendée it was the last rural civil war in western Europe north of the Pyrenees, and it is no accident that both events, though widely different in background and purpose, took place in the traumatic decade of the 1790s. As the Defender organisation was widespread, the United Irishmen powerful at least on paper, and both bodies were deeply inter-connected, the contrasts in 1798 are at first sight very puzzling: either why did a rebellion take place at all, or why was it not more general?

Lecky's view, which has dominated the interpretation of the rebellion, was ultimately one of identification with the loyalist cause.[2] It had darkened perceptibly between the writing of his first volume, which appeared in 1878 and the fourth and fifth, which appeared in 1890,[3] coloured by the land war and by radical home rule agitation. His history was now becoming an apology for the fears of the 1880s. He saw loyalist savagery in repressing the rebellion as a response to savagery displayed by the rebels in the first instance, and Cornwallis's dislike of the blood-lust in government circles around him in Dublin was held to be exaggerated. His account of the 1790s is riddled with contradictions and non-sequiturs. The precise place of the Orange Order in the background

* I am indebted to Dr Anthony Malcomson for a number of comments and corrections.

is ambiguous. The magistrates are defended as having exercised a serious and responsible role, while elsewhere he castigates the so-called middlemen from whom they were drawn as reckless and violent, in his anxiety to shield the gentry from a share of responsibility in the blood-lust and violence which disfigured the 1790s. The worst excesses of brutality in putting down the rebellion are attributed not very plausibly to the Welsh and Hessian regiments and to the militia who were largely Catholic in rank and file. Lecky virtually excludes as partisans on either side the writers Edward Hay and Sir Richard Musgrave who were the only contemporaries involved in the post-rebellion polemics to look at the background at any length. However, even Musgrave and Hay were coy on the immediate background to events; anxious to emphasise the innocence of their own sides, they necessarily had to play down the provocation to the other side. Thus Musgrave, who was in the councils of the Orange Order, is remarkably vague on its progress in Dublin and the south, and Hay is not only vague about the United Irishmen in Wexford before the rebellion, but also evasive about the presence of the Orange Order whose role was so provocative that Catholic calm before the rebellion would not appear a plausible argument if Orange attitudes were stressed: he contents himself with saying that the first *public* appearance of the Order in the county was in April 1798. Indeed the myth of good relations preceding the rebellion was first manufactured at the time. The violently loyalist *Faulkner's Dublin Journal* on 7 June 1798 printed a report from Wexford that 'Roman Catholic and Protestant seemed to vie in a desire of forgetting all dissention'.

It is hardly surprising that the assumptions of loyalist and nationalist historians alike tend to make the background incomprehensible. First, in contemporary and later writing evidence of eccentric, socially odd and stupid behavour by rebels, at any rate Catholic ones, has been seized on. This is the Protestant parallel to colourful Catholic accounts such as that of Hunter Gowan entering Gorey with the finger of a Catholic on a sword and using it to stir a bowl of punch. This sort of information has an anthropological character, providing more evidence about the state of mind of the people who retail it than of the other side. Secondly, the numbers have been exaggerated, both by participants who wanted to stress their own contribution and as a reflection of paranoia about the active disloyalty of Catholics.[4] Thirdly, just as the numbers involved were said to be large and the motivations irrational, the rebel leadership was held to have been acquired irrationally by the press-ganging by crowds of prominent Catholics or liberal gentry. Even Charles Dickson assumed that this was the case.[5] Fourthly, the fear of massacre was widespread. This is held to account both for the large numbers and for the terrified press-ganging of the Catholic or liberal gentry as leaders. The fear of exterminating Orangemen was held by Lecky to have been irrational, and he argued that there were scarcely any Orangemen in Co. Wexford.[6] Senior erected this proposition into a still more general principle: 'the Orange bogey aided by United Irish propaganda was most effective where there were no Orangemen.'[7]

Given these four propositions, it is clear that the rebellion has to be regarded as something of an oddity, largely unrelated to the mainstream of political happenings and to the political ethos of eighteenth-century Ireland. The causes of the rebellion under this approach are necessarily vague. The first, and most plausible one is that the rebellion was irrational. The second is that it was caused by frenzied oppression, although as Charles Dickson observed, we then run up against the question as to why it broke out in Wexford and not in counties such as Tipperary where oppression was worse.[8] A third reason is that the land system was responsible. No contemporaries said this, but as modern writing on the subject coincided with the growing interest in the land question in the 1870s the assumption appeared increasingly plausible in the late nineteenth century. Lecky himself had already assumed that the 1641 rebellion in Wexford had a peculiarly agrarian character and he repeated this assumption for 1798.[9] He had however no comprehension of social differentiation among Catholics, and seems to have equated the resentment by the minor gentry which comes out so strongly in Miles Byrne's memoirs with agrarian unrest. Of course the rebellion in Wexford has to be seen in the context of the entire country. Like the Mayo rebellion and the northern rising it cannot be isolated and all instances of disaffection or of overt rebellion have to be seen in the context of the pan-European revolutionary decade of the 1790s. The rebellion is not treated as an integrated phenomenon, whose causes are deep seated, and writers like Senior have never chosen to distinguish clearly between Anglicans and Presbyterians, just as the literature generally has also greatly underestimated the role of Catholics within the United Irishman leadership. What holds together the somewhat similar behaviour by widely differing social and religious groups, and how and why does the eighteenth-century background impel them towards a similar response? It is not really a problem for traditional, Lecky-type historiography, because much of the response is held to be irrational. Moreover, if the responsibility of the landed political establishment is disclaimed as Lecky disclaims it, or if the strains between the capital, Dublin, and the north are ignored, the events can be held to have been deeply rooted in Irish history only in so far as the amorphous and ultimately unhelpful factor of the land system is adduced.

Ireland in the eighteenth century was an immensely complex society, much less stable than the surface calm suggested, characterised by an intricate network of class relations. It was also politically unstable, or more accurately it was socially unstable behind a façade of political institutions which were not only rigid but increasingly so. The political and economic ascendancy of the landed classes was at its peak in the 1750s and 1760s. Relatively, their share of national income had attained its apogee: politically too they had reached their pinnacle in the 1750s, a position apparently secured by the fact that the capable lord lieutenancies of Devonshire and Bedford who sought to maintain the crown's position were followed by a sequence of short-term appointments from 1761 to 1767. However, the seeds of future trouble lay in success itself. If economic growth boosted the revenues of the landed classes, it was also laying the basis of the future wealth of the trading classes and of the middle groups in rural society. Political triumph itself exposed the landed classes; it was essentially the victory of a rich, arrogant and monopolising clique, and bred resentments founded on both political and social considerations among the gentry themselves. Several discontents in fact coalesced. First, the long-standing resentment of northern Presbyterians with the Anglican establishment sharpened in face of the increased ambitions locally and nationally of this establishment. The increased wealth that linen was bringing to Presbyterian rural districts was no small factor in this. Secondly the Catholics became more assertive, encouraged subtly by the celebrated but underrated lord lieutenancy of Chesterfield in 1745 and more positively by Bedford's policy as lord lieutenant of reaching out to the groups beyond the political establishment. Thirdly, merchants became more aware of their rights; the first committee of merchants, a Dublin one, was established in 1761. Fourthly, the political radicalism of Lucas, which in the 1740s was an isolated cause, ceased to be so. Resentment among the gentry at the monopolising role of the grandees was reflected in the emergence of a small but respectable Patriot party in the 1761 general election. Presbyterian, Catholic, merchant and 'new look' patriot all represented variously a challenge to the establishment. They also overlapped. The Committee of Merchants included Dissenter, Quaker and Catholic businessmen in the capital; and its Catholic members were also active in the Catholic Committee. The parliamentary links of the Committee of Merchants were both with the law officers of the crown and with the Patriot members,[10] a pattern which highlights the gulf between them and the grandees.

The political establishment in the 1760s was in the early stages of facing a growing challenge to its hegemony. Committees of merchants appeared in Waterford and Cork as well as Dublin. When the Dublin committee became a Chamber of Commerce in 1783, Belfast established a chamber as well. Presbyterian distinctiveness became more marked in the 1770s and 1780s, and northern businessmen in particular were now consciously seeking to free themselves from establishment Dublin. In Dublin itself the trading and professional classes were growing in size, wealth and pretensions. The number of students in Trinity College drawn from outside the landed and clerical classes increased sharply in the 1780s. No less important, a divide widened within the gentry itself. The divide in the dispute over the Tenantry Act of 1780 lay mainly between the greater landowners, usually with the most advantageous land titles, and lesser landowners for whom tenures for lives renewable were often the basis of their property, and the act sigsificantly decided the issue in favour of the latter.[11] In the 1780s and 1790s there was some transfer of political power from the more prominent landowners to the middle figures of rural society: smaller landowners, gentlemen farmers and middlemen. In Maria Edgeworth's writing, there is a nostalgia for a world which no longer existed. Barrington, a contemporary conspicuously influenced by Maria Edgeworth, expressed this mood more explicitly. He lamented the reduced role of the old gentry, and commented on the rise of pedigree makers to meet the needs of the aspiring.[12] The decline of law and order was subtly related to the decline of the landed classes, and peace and happiness in Ireland for him as for Maria Edgeworth would be found in the reinvigoration of paternalism. *Faulkner's Dublin Journal* on 5 September 1797—and the fact that it was a government journal is itself significant—lamented the rise in the number of esquires and satirically proposed 'a tax on squires':

Is it necessary that every industrious man who retires from business, and every idle fellow that would never take to business, should be a squire? These squires compose so very numerous a body that no part of the kingdom is without them.

As elections came to be contested more frequently, these figures acquired an enhanced political role: as immediate landlords of tenantry they became local power brokers, representing the interests of their patrons, the greater gentry, at local level. Paying low rents to their head landlord, and often social upstarts, they were heartily disliked by these head landlords. This dislike had loomed in the background to the Tenantry Act and Young's views about middlemen were acquired from the conversations he heard around him at aristocratic dinner tables in Ireland in 1776–7. By the 1780s they were frequently being eliminated, though local political necessities modified this policy and account for ambivalence in putting it into practice. Middlemen were frequently Protestants, and the policy posed the dilemma of replacing otherwise loyal Protestant large tenantry with Catholic and more doubtful smaller tenants. They were also frequently magistrates. The low social position of many magistrates was a frequent source of comment among Catholics as well as Protestants. Thomas Russell through his friendship with the Knox family acquired a magistrate's commission in Tyrone in 1791.[13] The fact that, through friendship with a powerful family, a young man in need of cash could receive a commission is itself a comment on the low social level of much of the magistracy. Ironically, though the standing of magistrates was being derided, they were in receipt of new powers in the 1780s and 1790s. In particular the Insurrection Act of 1796 gave them a discretion which worried contemporaries. On law and order issues, magistrates, operating within narrow horizons, were less cognisant of political realities than the grandees. They were poorly equipped in outlook, intellect and experience to deal with social and political tensions. This was conspicuously evident in Armagh. The military officer who had charge of the area, Dalrymple, had a poor view of the magistrates and of the impact of their partial actions on the countryside.[14] In Wexford too the indiscreet actions of individual magistrates played a crucial role in the deteriorating atmosphere before the rebellion. This hybrid class of rising gentlemen farmers and declining younger sons of gentry, exclusively Protestant before 1793 but facing the uncertain and disturbing possibility of losing the acres which they did not farm directly to an occupying and frequently Catholic tenantry, lacked the calm which would enable them to confront a worrying, sectarian and often violent movement of agrarian and political rebellion.

Political institutions, as I have said, became more rigid as the century wore on. The collapse of the undertakers as an institution in Irish political life had an impact which cannot be exaggerated. Before Townshend's watershed viceroyalty, Irish political life was a delicate and shifting balance of three forces: parliament, undertakers and executive. The undertakers shifted between alliance with the executive and with parliament. In the early 1750s the dominant undertaker of the day, Lord Shannon, led the opposition to the executive. This changeability, though motivated by a cynical self-interest, was crucial in ensuring the sensitivity of government to public issues in an unrepresentative parliament dominated by placemen and borough members. The changes killed off tensions, and even after the undertakers had collapsed the sensitivity of the grandees to public opinion remained a function of Irish political life till the end of the 1780s. Superficially the changes may not have seemed great. Parliament not only remained unreformed, but grandee groups still dominated it, and the Boyle interest remained the largest in Irish political life. However, the political consequences were sweeping. After 1772 the constitution had in effect changed, and this became particularly evident after 1782 when the interest of the grandees lay in staving off further revolution. For the first time politicians were intimately identified with administration; parliament was dominated by the executive more effectively than in the past, and one of the consequences was that the distinction between grandees and executive was now obliterated. Lord Shannon's group was now a source of government support, though the fact that government supported the Longfield interest in the aftermath of the Regency crisis is a reminder that the executive was intent on keeping local patronage out of the hands of an entrenched group. Other former undertakers responded differently. The Ponsonbys, a loose federation of politicians from across the country, often linked by marriage and with no real power base at county level, were perforce sensitive to 'public opinion'. The Gore group was even less cohesive. The Clements segment, because of its financial interests, continued to support government; the Gores, after first supporting government, drifted into an opposition stance, and in 1789 the earl of Arran was a member of the Whig Club. Gores and Ponsonbys had no local base; most of them either resided or held seats in counties with few or relatively few Protestants. The Ponsonbys identified with the English Whigs. The Gores, enjoying an easy relationship with the convert gentry in the west even in the 1760s, were free from the hysteria which marked the southern gentry. Indeed one of the key figures in their political alliance had been Anthony Malone whose father had been a convert and who was probably the first politician in the House of Commons to see the need for accommodation with the Catholics. The Boyles on the other hand had a power base in a county with a large number of Protestants. The fact that it was the most borough-rich county in Ireland added to the significance of this, and easily made them—like the Brodricks before them—the obvious leaders of Munster and Irish Protestantism. But there were other gentry with similar views and a significant number of Protestant gentry in south Tipperary, west Waterford and east Limerick, and family and political ties bound many of the gentry of the region together. Even when the Shannon hegemony was breached in the 1790 election, the Cork political world, both new and old interest, was identified with the establishment. It was over-represented in parliament and together with members in adjoining counties provided some forty supporters of government. This helped to account for its prominence in the privy council and in office. But more important than that was the fact that it was the distinctive views of members from the region which gave the administration its views of the Irish situation. Shannon on his return to the privy council in 1793 after his stand on the Regency question was a powerful supporter of the administration. Three of the ministers of the 1780s sat for seats in the region: Beresford and Fitzgibbon, and one of the staunchly Protestant Tolers who had a large political interest in Tipperary. Significantly too, John Toler the solicitor general in the 1790s held a seat in the borough of Gorey, controlled by the strongly Anglican Ram family.

The power of this group was enhanced by two developments in the 1780s. First, Wexford which had been an independent county swung to the side of the administration. George Ogle's acceptance of office in the 1780s is said to have been prompted by his need of cash, but as it did not at first lead to criticism from the Wexford voters, it responded to a need felt by a majority of the voters to identify with a conservative and distinctively Protestant stance. Lord Ely's failure to support the government in the regency crisis fitted in neatly with Ogle's image, and in fact the Ely–Ogle interest had a resounding sucess in the 1790 election. In the 1790 and 1797 general elections both seats in Wexford went to this interest, perhaps the greatest revolution in Irish county politics in the eighteenth century. Next to Cork, Wexford had the largest number of seats of any county in Ireland. A result was that fourteen of the eighteen seats in the county now supported government. If these fourteen are added to over forty basically conservative members in four Munster counties it meant a solid core, whatever the temporary effect of parliamentary alliances, opposed to any change in the *Protestant* constitution. In rough terms this was a third of the parliamentary majority. The second change was a swing in the outlook of northern members of parliament. If the Gores in the west of Ulster and in its Connaught and Leinster fringes are excluded, Ulster was singularly free of powerful political groups (the Downshire and Abercorn interests being both localised, and run by absentee families). The consequence was that its politics were relatively independent of the Dublin political establishment with the exception of the Conolly and Beresford interests. In particular the counties of Antrim, Down and Armagh did not support the government, and Armagh like Wexford had an especially sturdy tradition of parliamentary independence. A striking change, comparable to the shift in Wexford politics, was the change of allegiance by Brownlow junior who abandoned his father's independence and successfully ran as a supporter of government in 1795. And Castlereagh, although he had been elected as an independent in the celebrated 1790 election, justified his switch of allegiance with some confidence in his 1797 election address.[15] The county, despite its turbulent election of 1790, was in fact uncontested in 1797.

Thus progressively over the 1780s and 1790s political independence was breaking down. Even in counties associated with an independent stance, government supporters were not only emerging but a new breed of conservative of disturbingly tender years, like Castlereagh and Brownlow junior, was coming to the fore. One of the consequences was that the administration itself was firmly identified with the Protestant interest for the first time since before Chesterfield's lord lieutenancy. In the 1750s and the 1760s on the other hand, Catholics had seen the lord lieutenant as an ally against a bigoted undertaker interest. In the 1780s and 1790s such a distinction could no longer be made, and administration and parliament were more firmly entrenched in a common conservativeness than in the past. It was to describe this situation and at this time that the phrase 'Protestant ascendancy' was coined, according to Barrington by John Giffard.[16] Drawing strength from the close and novel links with the administration, this group was in some respects a self-confident rather than a fearful group, who could admit of the luxury of a sturdy independence on issues which did not directly imperil its interests. Thus in 1785 some of them supported the radical opposition to the Commercial Propositions, just as in 1789 the earl of Shannon and Lord Ely, though unwavering in their support of the Protestant establishment, found themselves on the same side as the radicals in the Regency dispute. Radicals overestimated the support for their standpoint in such opposition. Thus when the Dublin Chamber of Commerce thanked those who opposed the Commercial Propositions as the '110 faithful and independent representatives of the people'[17] it overstated the real radical element in the opposition.

Munster members not only provided the basic nucleus of government support, but also provided the staunch Protestantism which covered the new fusion of parliamentarians and administration. This image dates back as far as the time of Alan Brodrick, undertaker of his day. Brodrick was regarded as responsible for the downfall of the Co. Cork Jacobite leader, Sir James Cotter, in 1720. The Cotter episode coincided with the infamous introduction of the castration clause into the anti-popery bill in the Irish privy council in 1719. Brodrick was a member of the privy council, and has indeed been regarded as responsible for the clause.[18] The coincidence of the Cotter episode at local level with the castration clause at national level is haunting. Brodrick was identified in a contemporary Irish language poem as an enemy of the Catholics.[19] Henry Boyle, earl of Shannon, was an opponent in 1758 of the registration bill which would have extended legal recognition to the Catholic clergy.[20] Edmund Burke, the son of a Limerick convert and whose mother was a Catholic Nagle from north Co. Cork, must have reflected the local Catholic image of Boyle when he wrote in 1762 to O'Hara that 'you will be no Cortez, Pizarro, Cromwell or Boyle to the natives'.[21] He painted an unflattering picture of the bloodthirsty law-and-order Munster gentry.[22] King, the landlord of Mitchelstown, identified himself with the threat to enforce the penal laws in 1758 when he was provoked by the ill-advised interdiction of Mitchelstown by the Catholic bishop.[23] This was really the beginning of the religious hysteria which swept south Tipperary in the first half of the 1760s. Cork and Tipperary had the largest number of rural Protestants in southern Ireland under arms in the militia array of 1756. As Shannon inhabited a larger world, his concerns were largely parliamentary, but simpler souls like King of Mitchelstown, or Maude, Bagwell and Bagnell in Tipperary were likely to express and work out their fears at local level. What is particularly significant about the whole episode in north Cork and south Tipperary from 1758 to 1766 is the urge to enforce penal legislation which was already largely archaic: the laws against unregistered clergymen, schoolmasters and the carrying of arms. While the effort to enforce the penal laws was intermittent and symbolic—but more evident than elsewhere in Ireland—it did convey one message loud and clear: a firm opposition to further concessions to Catholics, and was a logical expression of support at local level for what Shannon had expressed in parliament. A long line of tragic episodes involving Catholics in conflict with Protestants as victims of authority was celebrated in Munster verse. The verses were transcribed in manuscript across Munster and over a long period of time. The O'Leary–Morris rivalry in the early 1770s, background to the event in the celebrated *Caoineadh Airt Uí Laoire*,[24] is one such episode, indeed one of the last of these anachronistic rivalries. One of the protagonists was Abraham Morris, high sheriff for Co. Cork, whose son was in all probability the Shannon member for the county in the 1790 parliament.

The fear of the undoing of the settlement, of French alliance and of massacre, was frequently resurrected and expressed in the Cork region and its fringes. It was in Co. Cork that Arthur Young was told that Catholic 'labourers' passed on to their sons the title to estates around them,[25] and this belief was made prominent in the mid-eighties by Bishop Woodward and by Fitzgibbon's defence of the establishment, largely over county Cork issues incidentally. In the early 1790s Westmorland dutifully reported the circulation of a list of the confiscated estates and the fears of massacre to London.[26] He must have received them from the Munster politicians who surrounded him and who crowded the establishment dinner tables of Dublin. Daniel Toler who had been high sheriff in Tipperary in 1766 in 1787 referred explicitly to the notorious Nicholas Sheehy execution in the Commons,[27] and in 1792, according to Tone, the Tolers were compelling tenants in Lower Ormond to sign a paper against the Catholic claims.[28] Most of the violently expressed oratory against Catholics came from the south, if we except Ogle and Maxwell both of whom had Wexford properties. The views of some Munster members were extravagant. Sir Boyle Roche from Fermoy must be instanced. So too must be Sir Richard Musgrave, who regarded Catholics when they were quiet as even more sinister than when they were actively disloyal.

The extent to which Munster politicians were out of touch with the Irish scene was an abiding weakness. Landowners in the north, poorly represented in the ministry (apart from the clear-sighted Castlereagh), could always distinguish between Presbyterian and

Catholic, but Munster politicians viewed northern troubles in a simpler light. Lord Shannon in June 1798 observed of the Co. Antrim rising that 'this too is a popish business'.[29] Plots, assassinations, massacres were a continuing fear of Munster Protestants. The credulity is evident in Shannon's letters.[30] Likewise John Beresford in Waterford was reporting that they were daily threatened with massacre, and the view from Lord Longueville, governor of Cork, was scarcely different.[31] It was particularly unfortunate that one of this rabid group, a Mitchelstown King—Lord Kingsborough—with his staunchly Orange North Cork militia arrived in Wexford in April 1798. To his antiquated political outlook he added a characteristic arrogance, made somewhat more colourful by a rustic and outmoded behaviour where women were concerned. Shannon, writing on 17 May, reported:

> Great complaints from Wexford on the bad conduct of Lord Kingsborough forcing into women's rooms in the night etc.[32]

The Irish parliament was not in fact a particularly liberal body: the measures of Catholic relief in 1778 and 1782 and in 1792 and 1793 were imposed by the British government. Their acceptance, and the votes in the Commons, do not point to liberalism. The general opposition in the Irish Commons was around 100 members. The rejection of the Catholic petition in 1792 in the Commons by 205 to 27[33] is a measure of the real support for Catholic relief. Of course, some of the remainder held the view that they supported civil rights as opposed to political rights for the Catholics. But this itself was to overlook the fact that given the revolutionary temper of the times as well as growing Catholic self-confidence liberality on purely civil matters did not meet the mood of the hour. In the last analysis the Irish gentry at heart were solidly conservative on the most crucial issue of the decade, and the long succession of addresses from grand juries and freeholders in 1792 against the franchise for Catholics made it clear that the ugly issue of Protestant ascendancy was now at the centre of Irish politics.

Just as Protestant ascendancy in name and content was now being sharply defined so also was a more demanding attitude among the Catholics. Irish Catholics, landed and upper class, were no more monolithic than the Protestant gentry. In fact, there were three streams in Irish Catholicism in the eighteenth century. First, there were the truculent Catholics of Munster, the mirror image of unyielding Munster Protestantism. Munster Catholics had lost their land to a greater degree than the Catholics of the other southern provinces in the upheavals of the seventeenth century. They had less to lose than the Catholics of the other provinces, and contrary to what Lecky says Jacobitism was a live issue among them at least into the 1750s. Inflamed though the imagination of Munster Protestants was, their fears were not altogether imaginary. If talk, not deeds, was sufficient justification, then they had some reason. As late as 1748 a Clare poet, Sean ÓhUainín, was indicted by the Clare grand jury.[34] The 1761 election in Tipperary, where Catholics, stronger than elsewhere in Munster, were in a position as owners in fee or holders of beneficial leases to influence Protestant voters to favour a candidate identified with the Catholic cause, was a confrontation of the issues. The second stream among propertied Catholics was the gentry of Galway and Mayo, the 'cream and flower' of the Irish Catholic gentry as Tone described them.[35] They kept their lands in part by their caution in the 1690s and aimed to keep them by conservatism in the eighteenth century. They had no leanings towards Jacobitism, and a complicated *modus vivendi* was worked out with local Protestant society. Radical sentiments made little progress among them in the 1790s. The third group comprised the small Catholic landowners of north Wexford, and of a compact region in north Mayo and along the borders of neighbouring Sligo, Roscommon and Leitrim. In these regions the land settlement had greatly reduced the interest of the surviving Catholic landed families and one branch of the McDermott family was even scattered in the seventeenth century as far afield as Co. Louth. It was from this group that the Catholic Committee drew its real strength from the 1750s to 1790s. It provided the radicalism in the Catholic Committee in 1792 and 1793, and a number of sons of Catholic landed families appeared in the membership of the first Dublin Society of United Irishmen. In the early stages the Catholic Committee depended heavily on Charles O'Conor who displayed more toughness and resentment than he is normally credited with, and on the two Anthony McDermotts, the largest Catholic merchants of their day in Dublin. Significantly, in 1791 the budding revolutionary Thomas Russell chose to enter into correspondence with O'Conor.[36] Wexford members gradually came to prominence after the early days and were the hardliners in the Catholic Convention of 1792. In Dublin the role of the McDermotts passed to Edward Byrne whose daughter married a nephew of Denis MacCarthy of Bordeaux. This linked him to the two MacCarthy branches in Tipperary who were among the rich Catholics whose success was resented in the early 1760s.

Byrne was also associated through the MacCarthys with the Wexford interest, especially through the links between the Bordeaux MacCarthys and the Paris Suttons. The Suttons in both Dublin and Wexford were active in the Catholic politics of the early 1790s, and indeed numerous Dublin links played a vital role in the politicisation and radicalisation of upper and middle class Catholics in north Wexford and across the border in south Wicklow.

Irish county politics closely reflected the complexity of the social structure. Tenants were expected to vote in accordance with the wishes of their immediate landlord, and Catholic middlemen or gentry could play a role in politics as in Tipperary in 1761 even though Catholics did not have the franchise. In Tipperary in 1761 the large landowners moved to the right while the intervening layers of landholders espoused the Catholic cause, thus producing a result in which an overt 'Catholic' candidate pipped an evangelical Protestant. In the 1790 and 1797 elections in Wexford a conflict arose similar to that in Tipperary in 1761, though in a contrary direction. The county's grandees were to a disproportionate extent liberal, but a shift to the right by the middle interest below them produced a sharp swing to the right in 1790 which was accentuated in 1797. The bitterness in Wexford of the Independent interest was all the greater because the election results represented a reversal of the traditional stance of the county. The Wexford election of 1790 was only paralleled in its vigour by the Down and Antrim elections of the same year.

It is ironic that Wexford is frequently represented as having been in a calm state on the eve of 1798. In fact, it was an intensely politicised county, and few people, among the non-voters no less than the voters, can have had a dispassionate or uncommitted view on the great issues of the day. In 1792 no less than 20,000 signatures were collected in Wexford to a petition on Catholic loyalty,[37] and Edward Hay collected 22,251 signatories in 1795 to an address to Fitzwilliam.[38] These seem to stand as unique and unprecedented acts of canvassing in Irish public life up to that date. The key to Wexford politics in the 1790s lies with Viscount Valentia or Lord Mountnorris (Arthur Annesley). His father was the celebrated bigamist earl of Anglesey whose second marriage had been validated by the British parliament, and whose third marriage to Juliana Donovan, daughter of a landowner near the Anglesey seat of Camolin, was validated by the Irish parliament. Religious tensions already revolved about the claims of the two ladies at Camolin; the second countess represented the third countess, Countess Juliana, to be supported by a papist interest. Juliana Donovan does not seem to have been a Catholic, but after her husband's death she later married Matthew Talbot, head of the most distinguished of the numerous small Catholic gentry in the north of the county. Her three daughters by her union with Anglesey were married respectively to Sir Frederick Flood, Robert Phaire and John Toole (the latter intimately connected with the Sutton interest). In 1789 a daughter of Mountnorris married John Maxwell-Barry who contested the Wexford election in the Independent interest in 1797. It was Phaire who, as Thomas Cloney's landlord, prevailed on him to campaign for Maxwell-Barry in 1797, and indeed Cloney for a young man was remarkably deep into the county's politics in 1797. So violent was the election that it caused rather interesting stresses and strains in some of the Catholic families such as the Hays and Kyans who were in consequence deeply divided before 1798. The Annesley family had usually been absentee, and hence played little part in Wexford politics, but, through residence by the widowed wife of the last earl and his own residence, Mountnorris had a profound impact on Wexford politics. His own politics and the alliances of his late mother brought together a novel Protestant and Catholic interest. His political interest was supplemented by that of the Grogan/Colclough/Harvey axis. In fact, Mountnorris may have received more support from the Catholics than from the Grogans or other liberal gentry in the north of the county. Cornelius Grogan had actually toyed with giving his support to Ely,[39] and while Maxwell-Barry's independent credentials in 1797 were impeccable, he had anti-Catholic sentiments to live down. The pattern of voting divisions at magistrates' meetings suggests that the Grogan interest did not always see eye to eye with Mountnorris's more furious opposition to Ely. Other influential gentry such as Carew and Alcock supported the Independent line, and a number of small Protestant gentry were also sympathetic. The weight of broad acres and large rentrolls was on the side of the Independent stand. Only Ely, Ogle, the Rams and the Stopfords (Lord Courtown), of the county's more prominent landowners, represented the ascendancy line. The Ram estate was relatively small, and Courtown's interest in the county was also limited.[40] The Tottenhams of course were prominent, but they had little property in the county and were mere creatures of Ely.

More than Catholic relief, law and order had become the issue by 1795. The Orange Order is a symptom of this. It was not in itself novel. Volunteer groups modelled on the pattern of the groups which had appeared in the south before 1778 were founded in North Armagh in the late 1780s. Lord Shannon's Hanover association in Co. Cork in 1791 represented a similar purpose.[41] The grand jury in Kildare suggested a group in 1795;[42] Carhampton formed one in Dublin.[43] Barrington noted that the first Orange association ever formed had been in Dublin and had been invigorated by 1795.[44] The most interesting thing about the Orange Order in the mid-1790s is not its rise in Armagh, but the alacrity with which it spread in the south and how its national organisation became Dublin-based and Dublin-controlled in early 1798. In moving south, it ascended the social ladder and acquired a social prestige it would otherwise have lacked. Founded in Anglican districts in Armagh, it was essentially southern in its early ethos and appeal. The rapidity of the spread of the Orange Order in Trinity College is striking. Contrary to what Blacker's account might suggest[45] there were few students from Armagh in the college: Cork and Tipperary were traditionally the best represented counties. Its appeal to Armagh's grandees was more immediate than has usually been represented, and whatever Lord Gosford's good public image on law and order, he was as early as May 1796 making representations to the Castle for the mitigation of a capital sentence on an Orangeman, on the grounds that carrying out the sentence would lead to disturbances.[46] The representation was made, it should be pointed out, in the immediate aftermath of an assize stage-managed with the best intentions by the grand jury and the attorney general to prove impartial justice.

Arbitrary though the powers under the Insurrection Act were, their exercise provided grounds for appeal to the assizes, even if the indemnity clause of the act, and the general indemnity acts, of which the first was in 1796, protected officers and magistrates against the consequences of their actions. In fact, long before 1798, irregularities such as house burning and lashing were resorted to, and too readily. How numerous were the instances is not the issue; the real point is the doubtful legality of what began in the north in the second half of 1796. All this was accepted without difficulty by the establishment, and by Shannon.[47] Shannon's view by April 1798 was that 'if those who have now authority to search think they have done their duty by examining houses, they may as well have done nothing. Examples should be made to compel them to make discoveries where arms and pikes are hid'.[48] A disturbing feature of this rough justice was the sexual contempt which accompanied indiscriminate punishment.[49]

The really crucial issue was of course the Insurrection Act of 1796 which not only gave sweeping powers to magistrates, but made it possible for an unrepresentative quorum of magistrates to proclaim a large district or even an entire county. Judge Fletcher, who was a barrister in the 1790s, addressing the grand jury of Wexford in 1814, described the act as 'a complete suspension of the English constitution—of English law—of the trial by jury'.[50] Barrington who knew his Wexford (his wife was a Grogan), observed that 'by these men the peasantry were goaded into a belief that justice was banished.'[51] Crucial too were the arrests made on perjured evidence, which conjured up the spectacle of 1766 in Tipperary. These cases were heard at the Wicklow assizes in March 1798. The accused were acquitted. Two are known from the pages of Miles Byrne, but in all ninety had been returned for trial.[52] Curran and the liberal barristers had a field day, the assizes having the same damaging impact on local opinion as the Orr trial in Co. Antrim in September 1797. In the aftermath of the 1797 election the divide among the gentry in north Wexford in 1797 and 1798 hinged not so much on law and order *per se* as on the question of proclaiming districts under the Insurrection Act. In fact, the magistrates had been keen on measures against rebels within the civil law. A meeting of thirty-one magistrates at Enniscorthy on 16 October 1797, including Mountnorris and a number of the liberals, passed a unanimous resolution congratulating various parties on having lodged in jail sundry persons who had administered or taken unlawful oaths.[53] Division only emerged when it was proposed to take advantage of the Insurrection Act to proclaim districts. At a meeting on 20 November Mountnorris and seven magistrates were in a minority in a meeting of twenty-seven magistrates which requested sixteen northern parishes to be proclaimed. It was in response to this defeat that Mountnorris organised a series of chapel meetings at which memorials were signed, thanking him and the seven other magistrates for their stand and asking him both to assure the lord lieutenant of Catholic loyalty and to undo the magistrates' case.[54] In all memorials were signed in fifteen parishes, apparently bearing the signatures of the parishioners. On 6 April eighteen magistrates were present at a meeting which requested the barony of Gorey to be proclaimed. On 25 April at a meeting at which thirty-one magistrates were present, only twenty-eight signed the memorial requesting the entire country to be proclaimed, and two of these seemed to have signed only on the condition that their own parishes were excluded from the proclamation.[55] Indeed in the interval between the two meetings of 6 and 25 April Mountnorris organised another round of addresses. Some 8,025 signatures were attached to petitions from fourteen Catholic parish unions.[56] The meeting was thus a momentous one. It was a defeat for Mountnorris, and indeed, as some of the moderate magistrates approved the memorial, it showed that fears were now quite general. However, it had the effect of adding to the political divide in the county, and it seems likely that some of the signatories may have lent their names with misgiving. Even at the meeting of 23 May at which twenty-two magistrates called for free quarters if arms were not surrendered in fourteen days, the decision taken may have been at variance with the private opinions of some of the magistrates.[57] Undoubtedly some of them were now in an impossible position, torn between their dislike of the Insurrection Act and the excessive zeal of some of their colleagues on the one hand and the mounting evidence of conspiracy spreading rapidly in the country on the other.

One of the things that makes the Wexford rebellion background intriguing is that the county had so far been free from the house raids by rebels for arms so evident in the neighbouring counties. Why this was the case is not quite clear, although Miles Byrne makes a point of referring to the fact that the United Irishmen had actively avoided such raids.[58] Perhaps the county's intense politicisation offered an alternative outlet, or its Defenders were more indigenous in their philosophy than those of the neighbouring counties of Carlow and Wicklow which had been infiltrated by arms-raiding sectarian Defenders from further north. But at any rate for whatever reasons Wexford had remained outwardly calm, and proclaiming came late. But precisely because it came up in the circumstances in which it did it left the magistracy divided on the issue to a degree which had no parallel in any other county. Some of the magistrates were already over-zealous, even if they had not yet exceeded the bounds of legality. Thus Parson Owens, according to Barrington, was 'a violent, indeed an outrageous royalist... not over popular in *quiet* times'.[59] Disturbingly, the outlook of some of the loyalists was distinctly messianic. The Ballyellis yeoman cavalry, for instance, lamented in 1797 that in addition to the other ills of society 'idleness and drunkenness very generally prevail, to the utter destruction of civil society.'[60] It gives added significance to Gordon's description of the defenders of order as the 'armed saints'.

Space does not admit of going into the issue at any length, but it does seem that there was an exponential growth of fear on both sides in the week or two immediately preceding the outbreak of rebellion on 26 May. Rebel recruitment which had been spreading far afield was now made more successful by fear, while some magistrates, although by no means all, were resorting to illegal acts. In fact, even a moderate magistrate like Turner burned some houses.[61] In the week before the rebellion all the active magistrates above the Slaney and some south of it were activated by panic, either in searching for arms often with questionable methods, or in administering the oath of allegiance and issuing protections wholesale in an effort to restore calm. No one in the north and east of Wexford was now in a calm state. The unfortunate meeting of 23 May in which a rather small number of magistrates intimated a request for free quarters if arms were not surrendered within fourteen days produced results which the moderates cannot have intended. If administered in a hostile fashion, by alarmed magistrates, the subsequent surrender of arms proved the extent of conspiracy; if arms were not surrendered it proved that they were withholding them and in Musgrave-style the conspiracy was even more deadly. People and magistrates panicked, but arguably the magistrates panicked first and the more. In such circumstances it proved possible for determined United Irishmen to manipulate events as at Kilcormick on 26 May and for Wexford to join north Leinster three days late in open rebellion.

We can now come back to the considerations set out at the outset of this paper. The counties where rebels took the field in numbers, Antrim, Down and Wexford, had been intensely politicised. Down and Antrim with their sturdy Presbyterianism had produced a strong backing for reform in 1790, and Wexford was even more politicised, reproducing moreover an embittered context in 1797 in contrast to emerging caution or closing of the ranks in other counties. Even the north of Connacht was moderately politicised, and a McDermott was an unsuccessful candidate in the Roscommon election in 1797. As the situation worsened, pointing to what would be civil war, caution was emerging among the United Irishmen. In the north, evidence of emerging caution in Antrim and Down, prompted by fear of the turmoil spreading out from Armagh, preceded rather than followed vigorous law enforcement in both counties. Only over-vigorous law enforcement slowed this process. Perhaps William Ponsonby had put his finger on the problem when he told Shannon, with Kilkenny in mind, in June 1798 that 'the only quiet barony that he knows is that of Iverk, and the reason is there is not a soldier in it'.[62] Wexford was unique in producing intense politicisation in 1797. In other counties some magistrates had opposed proclaiming of the county, but only in Wexford was this opposition part of a political stance, and it carried into 1798 the political sentiments of the preceding year's election, and public opinion was canvassed on the score by Mountnorris at many of the chapels in the northern parishes. Hence much of the north and east of the county was already aflame politically when superimposed on this were both the Wicklow assizes and the law and order issues of April 1798.

Thus Wexford was highly politicised and in an increasingly volatile situation on the eve of the rebellion. Many of its upper classes, some Protestant gentry and a number of its Catholic gentry and middlemen were implicated in conspiracy. John Hay for instance had a long association with Edward Roche, a large farmer in a parish where Hay held land, and an admitted United Irishman. Cloney was deeply involved in the politics of 1797, and has been assumed to be in a detached state of mind because historians have been remiss in reading beyond the first few pages of his memoirs in which he paints an idyllic picture of life in the vicinity of the Castleboro estate of Robert Shapland Carew, a political enemy of Lord Ely. Barrington's accounts of dinners in South Wexford in April leave little doubt of support for rebellion; the diners on one occasion significantly included both John Hay and the Sheares brothers.[63]

While the context in which they arose is exceptional, the fears in Wexford were in no way irrational, and it is easy to understand why they were so widespread. Some very disturbing elements of communal panic had already been emerging in the spring in Wexford and south Wicklow: whole villages slept out of doors on nights of panic for fear of massacre, in itself an odd form of behaviour which led Protestant neighbours to fear that the Catholics had evil intentions and were preparing to massacre Protestants. As far as these happenings are concerned, it is hard to apportion responsibility, because the United Irishmen were themselves in many respects an unlovely bunch, reckless, irresponsible, doctrinaire and usually out of touch with the realities of Irish rural life. But it can be said without fear of contradiction that it was establishment Protestants who popularised the fear of massacre, and made talk of massacre part of the every-day currency of fear in Ireland in the 1790s. As for irrationality, it seems likely that far from the rebels having a monopoly of this quality it was the gentry and magistrates who first became hysterical. In emphasising law and order at any cost they justified much of what United Irishmen propaganda was saying, and compelled many to lay aside the caution which might have deterred action as Ireland seemed to head for civil war. Caution had been growing rapidly in the years before 1798. It was already a feature of the north, but in Wexford it had suddenly started growing in the liberal gentry ranks too in response to the depth of polarisation which was emerging in the weeks before 26 May. Ultimately the rebellion of 1798 was due to the fact that the Irish gentry as a class were deeply flawed, or at any rate the Munster gentry were deeply flawed. And it was the country's tragedy that the administration was in large measure in the hands of men who came from Munster or were privy to the fears of Munster Protestants. Beresford, Fitzgibbon and Foster triumphed in the recall of Fitzwilliam in 1795, but ultimately what really prevailed was the law-and-order, papist-fearing, and hanging element in the gentry. In putting the emphasis on the role of the government in fomenting rebellion deliberately, a view which comes out in Lecky and more positively in Dickson, the irrationalities and fears of the Irish gentry are greatly underestimated, and the painful relationship of the 1790s and of the attitudes of the day to preceding history is left out of the reckoning.

Notes

1. L.M. Cullen, *The emergence of modern Ireland 1600–1900* (London, 1983), pp 210–33.
2. Lecky, *Ire.*, iv, 329.
3. Volume I originally appeared in 1878 as the second volume of Lecky's *History of England*, vols IV and V in 1890 as the seventh and eighth volumes of the same work. The separate Irish edition appeared in 1892.
4. C. Dickson, *The Wexford rising in 1798: its causes and its course* (Tralee [1955]), pp 32–4; *The Life of Michael Dwyer with some account of his companions* (Dublin, 1944), pp 82–4.
5. Dickson, *Wexford rising*, p. 188.
6. Lecky, *Ire.*, iv, 346, 351, 381, 452–3.
7. H. Senior, *Orangeism in Ireland and Great Britain* (London, 1966), p. 101.
8. Dickson, *Wexford rising*, p. 41.
9. Lecky, *Ire.*, i, 45, 93, 99; iv, 345.
10. L.M. Cullen, *Princes and Pirates* (Dublin, 1983), p. 43.
11. M. R. O'Connell, *Irish politics and social conflict in the age of the American revolution* (Philadelphia, 1965), pp 258–98; L. M. Cullen, review of O'Connell in *I.H.S.*, xv (1967), p. 489; D. Dickson, 'Middlemen' in T. Bartlett and D. W. Hayton (ed.), *Penal era and golden age* (Belfast, 1979), p. 174.
12. J. Barrington, *Personal sketches of his own times*, ii (London, 1827), 61–2, 437; iii (London, 1832), 306.

13. S. N. Mac Giolla Easbaig, *Tomás Ruiséil* (Dublin, 1957), p. 54.
14. P.R.O.N.I., Pelham papers, T. 755/2, 9 Aug. 1794.
15. *Faulkner's Dublin Journal*, 22 July 1797.
16. Barrington, op. cit., i, 243. See W. J. McNeven, *Pieces of Irish history* (New York, 1807), p. 21. On early usage of the term see also D. A. Chart (ed.), *The Drennan letters* (Belfast, 1931), pp 91–2; R. B. McDowell, 'Proceedings of the Dublin Society of United Irishmen' in *Anal. Hib.*, xvii (1949), p. 33.
17. L. M. Cullen, *Princes and Pirates* (Dublin, 1983), p. 51.
18. M. Craig, *Dublin 1660–1860: a social and architectural history* (Dublin, 1952), p. 100.
19. Maynooth College, Gaelic MS 3F6, f.39i. See P. Ó Fiannachta, *Lámhscríbhinní Gaeilge Choláiste Phádraig Má Nuad*, fasc. iii (Maynooth, 1966), p. 25.
20. E. Hewitt, ed. *Lord Shannon's letters to his son* (Belfast, 1982), p. lxx.
21. R. S. Hoffman, *Edmund Burke, New York agent* (Philadelphia, 1956), p. 284.
22. Ibid.
23. J. Brady, *Catholics and Catholicism in the eighteenth-century press* (Maynooth, 1965), pp 94–5.
24. S. Ó Tuama, *Caoineadh Airt Uí Laoghaire* (Dublin, 1963), pp 14–16.
25. A. Young, *A Tour in Ireland 1776–1779*, ed. A.W. Hutton (London, 1892), i, 300.
26. P.R.O.N.I., T. 3319/16, 3 Nov. 1792.
27. *Parl. reg. Ire.*, 1787, p. 342. John Toler, then third sergeant, also seemed to hint at the episode very explicitly in the same year (ibid., p. 241).
28. *Life of Theobald Wolfe Tone*, ed. W. T. Wolfe Tone (Washington, 1826), i, 206. See also Brady, op. cit., pp 284–5.
29. Hewitt, op. cit., p. 113.
30. See Hewitt, op. cit., *passim*.
31. T. Pakenham, *The year of liberty* (London, 1969), p. 36.
32. Hewitt, op. cit., p. 96. On his conduct towards women, see also *Eighteenth century Irish official papers in Great Britain*, i (Belfast, 1973), p. 187.
33. Hewitt, op. cit., p. 29.
34. R.I.A., MS 24 B 11.
35. *Life of Wolfe Tone*, i, 193.
36. Mac Giolla Easbaig, op. cit., pp 45–6.
37. T. J. Powell, 'The background to the Wexford rebellion 1790–98' M.A. thesis, N.U.I., 1970, p. 48.
38. E. Hay, *History of the insurrection of the county of Wexford* (Dublin, 1803), p. 34.
39. The account of Powell (op. cit., p. 161) is not quite complete. For the full story see McPeake papers (P.R.O.N.I., T. 3048/C/18): John Colclough, Tintern, to Caesar Colclough, 17 Sept. 1797.
40. G. O. Sayles, 'Contemporary sketches of the members of the Irish parliament in 1782' in *R.I.A. Proc.*, sect. C, Ivi, p. 277.
41. Hewitt, op. cit., p. 28 n.
42. P.R.O.N.I., Pelham transcripts, T. 755/2, 19 Aug. 1795.
43. Ibid., 5, 25 Oct. 1795.
44. Barrington, op. cit., i, 244–9.
45. Colonel Blacker's account of the battle of the Diamond (P.R.O.N.I., T. 2595/6).
46. S.P.O., 620/23/115, 19 May 1796. This is particularly obvious in the light of the government concern, displayed by Isaac Corry and by Arthur Wolfe in letters in the same carton, to manage the assizes impartially, and shows that

their concerns meant little to one of the county's magnates.

47. Hewitt, op. cit., pp 59, 60, 80, 93.
48. Ibid., p. 78.
49. Ibid., p. 97.
50. *Charge of the Hon. Justice Fletcher to the grand jury of the Co. of Wexford at the summer assizes of 1814* (2nd ed., Belfast, 1814), p. 3. I am indebted to Dr Anthony Malcomson for bringing this address to my attention. Delivered to the Wexford grand jury, it is intended as a retrospective commentary on the administration of justice in Wexford.
51. Barrington, op. cit., i, 307.
52. *Finn's Leinster Journal*, 24–28 Mar. 1798.
53. *Faulkner's Dublin Journal*, 9 Nov. 1797.
54. R. Musgrave, *Memoirs of the different rebellions in Ireland* (3rd ed., Dublin, 1802), ii, 322–4.
55. Powell, op. cit., p. 185. One of the magistrates who signed, Alcock, was one of the two magistrates who had held out for their own parish not to be proclaimed. The other, one of the Poundens, also signed.
56. *Faulkner's Dublin Journal*, 3 May 1798. A further two parishes also drew up addresses, though the number of signatories is not given (ibid., 12 May 1798).
57. Hay, op. cit., p. 74.
58. *Memoirs of Miles Byrne*, ed. S. Gwynn (Dublin, 1907), i, 8.
59. Barrington, op. cit., iii, 279.
60. *Faulkner's Dublin Journal*, 4 July 1797.
61. Hay, op. cit., p. 179.
62. Hewitt, op. cit., p. 127.
63. Barrington, op. cit., i, 267–72. Without there being any direct evidence, it seems likely that the Wexford gentry United Irishmen backed the moderate faction in the United Irishmen directory who favoured deferment of rebellion until the French had landed. This would also help to explain the curiously indecisive and contradictory behaviour of some Wexford leaders like Bagenal Harvey.

Indiscipline and disaffection in the armed forces in Ireland in the 1790s*

Thomas Bartlett

General Ralph Abercromby's devastating verdict on the armed forces serving in Ireland in the 1790s that they were 'formidable to everyone but the enemy', has in general been endorsed by subsequent historians;[1] and the troops serving in Ireland in that period, whether regular army, Irish militia or yeomanry, or British fencibles, have become a byword for indiscipline and disaffection. However, these charges have never been investigated in detail, much less substantiated, and a great deal concerning the twin problems of indiscipline and disaffection has remained obscure.

I

In considering the causes of the alleged indiscipline of the troops in the 1790s our starting point must be the outbreak of war in 1793 and the concurrent upsurge of violence in many parts of Ireland which led to an unprecedented expansion in the Irish army. In the period from 1793 to 1798 the number of troops in Ireland rose from around 14,000 to well over 80,000. This latter figure includes some 35,000 yeomanry and if they are deducted this leaves a front-line defence force, on paper at any rate, of about 45,000. This 'paper' or 'ideal' figure requires further modification and when deductions are made for incomplete regiments, the large number of sick troops, and administrative personnel, we are left with an effective force of about 35,000. In contrast to 1793, regular troops formed a small proportion (perhaps 15 per cent) of this force; the bulk (perhaps 60

* An extended paper on this topic covering the period 1793 to 1815 and with considerably more illustrative detail and fuller critical apparatus is forthcoming in *Past and Present*.

115

per cent) were Irish militia and the balance was made up by English and Scottish fencibles and militia.[2] Lax discipline among the troops in Ireland both in the 1790s and later can largely be traced to the enormous expansion in their numbers. This is not to say that unruly behaviour by troops was a novelty in Ireland in the 1790s: Irish newspapers throughout the eighteenth century contain numerous reports of military wrongdoing usually involving casual violence, rioting or the breaking open of gaols.[3] But the great expansion in the size of the army establishment after 1793 meant that there would be many more incidents of insubordination and unruly behaviour. Besides this obvious yet important point, there is evidence to suggest that the expansion of the Irish armed forces in the 1790s was achieved only by permitting the enlistment of recruits of inferior quality. Admittedly, the standard of recruits had always been low. In Ireland (as elsewhere) it was thought axiomatic that no man in his right senses would willingly submit himself to army discipline (the prevalence of flogging being a major deterrent), and hence recruits tended to be forced into the service through poverty or as an alternative to imprisonment, transportation or worse. Nonetheless, the volume of complaints in the 1790s concerning the quality of recruits prompts the conclusion that there was indeed a significant deterioration even from the usual low standard. As early as March 1794 a memorandum on recruiting declared that 'the worst kind of recruits' was being taken into the army—either 'inexperienced young men' or the 'refuse of mankind'.[4] Such recruits caused the desertion rate to soar. 'Desertion is terrible at present,' complained Edward Cooke, under-secretary in Dublin Castle in June 1794, 'and we know not how to prevent it'. A few months later, the new viceroy, Lord Fitzwilliam, said much the same thing: 'There is no keeping Irish troops in Ireland, they desert so abominably.'[5] Evidence for these assertions is not lacking. Colonel E. P. Trench's regiment when inspected, in May 1794 at Granard, Co. Westmeath, was found to have lost 233 men (out of a total complement of around 1,100) by desertion, and while marching to their port of embarkation they may have lost more.[6] Trench's regiment was by no means unique.[7] Soaring desertion rates—surely an index to the quality of recruits—coupled with a huge demand for troops for both the West Indian and continental theatres led inevitably to a further lowering of standards and an even greater dependence on the 'refuse of mankind' as possible recruits, with negative effects on the level of discipline, and perhaps of 'disaffection'.

Yet, it could be argued that army leaders had long been accustomed to handling large numbers of raw recruits, among whom 'the refuse of mankind', medical rejects and alleged subversives, were well represented, and that in time, as Westmorland put it 'the magic of his majesty's uniform' would work its usual alchemy on even the dullest material.[8] This 'magic' depended ultimately on the officers' and N.C.O.s' diligence, energy and expertise, but in these respects my impression is that the negligence and laxity long associated with the army in Ireland[9] became even more prevalent in the 1790s. Some officers were, of course, outstanding: Sir John Moore's diary of his tour of duty in the Cork area in the late 1790s shows what an energetic and capable officer could accomplish: and the military papers of Colonel Robert Leslie who was stationed in Co. Tyrone at the same time show him to have been an equally dedicated officer.[10] But Leslie and Moore and a few others like them were in a decided minority, remarkable precisely because of their energy and expertise. The general run of officers appears to have been of indifferent quality, on occasion cheating their men or the army, leaving them to their own devices for long periods or (if the complaints of Generals Lake and Carhampton were well founded) simply not showing up to perform their duties.[11] In 1794 the 79th Regiment stationed in Belfast mutinied (much to the delight of the local radicals) over a rumour that the entire regiment had been sold to the East India Company by its 'absentee colonel'.[12] And Colonel Trench's regiment, which, as we have seen, lost nearly one quarter of its strength through desertion, had fourteen officers absent without leave or who had never joined the regiment.[13]

Irish militia officers, in particular, received a great deal of criticism. Some, but not all, of this criticism can be attributed to the professional contempt with which the regular officer regarded his militia colleague. Relations between the two were poor, and there were frequent wrangles over rank and precedence.[14] On the other hand, given the fact that political and family considerations, not military experience or expertise, determined the disposal of commissions, it was preordained that the officer class from a military point of view would be undistinguished. Lord Abercorn, for example, saw the Tyrone militia quite simply as a vehicle for patronage and he had himself appointed colonel of the regiment (though he resided in England) and he managed to get many of his friends into it as officers.[15] Not surprisingly, there were soon complaints that the officers of the Tyrone militia preferred 'walking the streets of Strabane and lounging in the mess room' to doing their duty with the regiment.[16] Moreover, given the fact that the militia officers were Protestant, and the privates Catholic (Craufurd declared that a Catholic was rarely promoted even to the rank of corporal) the gap between officers and men must have been even wider than in British regiments.[17] Nor was religion treated as a matter of private conscience: the Tyrone officers tried to prevent their men from attending Mass on Sundays, an action that led to disturbances, and there were several other instances of this type.[18] Altogether, it is difficult to see how anyone ever expected Irish militia officers, with all their limitations, to discipline some 20,000 raw recruits into an effective force for the defence of Ireland.

And yet, in the final analysis, not all the blame for the indiscipline in the Irish militia can be laid at the door of the officers. Officers, in general, whether regular or militia, kept a loose rein on their unruly troops (and were allowed to do so by their political masters), on occasion even encouraging them to engage in lawless behaviour. For example, as early as March 1793, General Richard Whyte encouraged his troops, his 'charming boys' as he called them, to go on the rampage through Belfast attacking the homes and business premises of known radicals and beating anyone who got in their way. 'There are no lives lost' reported Whyte, 'but many marks of the sharp edge of their sabres.' On a wider scale, in his pacification of Connacht, Lord Carhampton sent scores of suspects to the fleet without even the pretence of a trial and there were numerous houseburnings and floggings—all quite illegal—during arms searches in Ulster and elsewhere.[19] Illegality and indiscipline were closely linked, for it was a short step from illegal action connived at or sponsored by the government to the freelance type. And the licence seemingly extended to the troops as a body appeared to cover individual acts of casual violence. The rape by two officers of Mr Uniacke's maid while she was in custody as a material witness to her employer's murder (only one of a number of such incidents) almost certainly prompted Abercromby's 'General Orders' of February 1798.[20]

'It cannot be denied that some things have been done which are to be regretted,' conceded Thomas Pelham, Camden's chief secretary, 'but at the same time I believe that no army ever behaved better under similar circumstances and I venture to say no army was ever placed in exactly the same situation'.[21] Castlereagh, Cornwallis's chief secretary, also attributed the indiscipline of the troops to the 'irregular service in which . . . [they] . . . have necessarily been engaged'.[22] Even Abercromby, perhaps the army's severest critic, admitted that some of its indiscipline stemmed from its situation in Ireland: 'the dispersed state of the troops is really ruinous to the service. The best regiments in Europe could not long stand such usage.'[23] Traditionally, troops in Ireland had been widely scattered throughout the countryside and there were relatively few concentrations outside of Dublin. To a large extent, the police nature of the military service in Ireland, where troops were frequently called to the aid of the civil power, made some dispersal not just inevitable but also convenient. Yet it was also recognised that the dispersal of the troops was bad for discipline. Dress regulations, parade drill and arms exercise were impossible to keep up, and officers grew bored and negligent or stayed in Dublin.[24] These peacetime problems were greatly exacerbated by the huge expansion of the army in Ireland during the 1790s and by the nature of the counter-insurgency role that it was called upon to adopt. To combat widespread rural unrest, which at times amounted to localised insurrections, a further dispersal of the troops, including militia, was implemented, though, as before, the troops were in theory only to be employed at the request of the local magistrates. By the time of Abercromby's appointment as commander-in-chief in late 1797, however, the role of the army had clearly changed. From acting in aid of the civil authorities the troops had in many districts begun to act in their stead. As early as January 1795 it was recognised that outrage and terrorism had increased so much that in certain areas, as Fitzwilliam put it, 'the soldiery is the only magistracy in real authority';[25] and in 1797 the troops were ordered to act as they saw fit, without waiting for authorisation from local magistrates. There can be no doubt that this removal of the modest restraint of having to seek the permission of the civil power before acting led the army, in Abercromby's words, further into 'irregularities and disgrace'.[26] No doubt the daily crimes with which the army had to deal also had an influence on its conduct. In a single letter of November 1797 Pelham described how a constable had been murdered, his body dismembered and his limbs scattered about a hillside as a warning; how a magistrate had been assassinated; and how a farmer, his wife, their maid-servant and all his pigs and dogs had been killed—'the bowels of the farmer [had been] torn out and a label [put] on his belly threatening all informers'.[27] Freed from legal restraint and dealing with crimes such as these, the army became increasingly a series of vengeful posses traversing the countryside.

The proximate causes of the breakdown in army discipline can, then, be attributed to the dispersal of the forces and the blurring of the vital distinction between civil and military authority. But more important in the long run was the evident confusion of purpose that afflicted military leaders as to the proper role of the army in Ireland. General Abercromby, for example, saw the army's primary function as the defence of Ireland against foreign invaders; hence his dismay at finding the troops so widely dispersed that they could not be assembled rapidly should the enemy effect a landing. His remedy for local unrest and outrage was in general to leave its suppression to the local force, the yeomanry. Yet Camden and his 'cabinet', that is to say his friends and his advisers, were by no means satisfied with this. As far as they were concerned the threat of invasion was secondary to the grim reality of a nationwide conspiracy of urban and rural rebels steadily pursuing their ends by intimidation, widespread tendering of oaths, and murder. Camden's civilian advisers advocated that terror be fought with counter-terror, and their views prevailed among the army staff. As General Knox put it, 'I look upon Ulster [and presumably by extension much of Ireland] to be a La Vendée and [believe] that it will not be brought into subjection but by the same means adopted by the republicans in power—namely, spreading devastation through the most disaffected parts'.[28] Consciously or not, the methods of the French in crushing *chouannerie* were adopted in Ireland. When Camden's advisers clamoured for 'extirpation' of the rebels and the British home secretary, the duke of Portland, recalled the measures used to crush the rebellion of 1745 in Scotland, the response of the military could not afford to be fainthearted. 'If you have an opportunity of attacking the villains,' General Lake instructed General Loftus on 24 May 1798, 'take no prisoners.'[29] The relentless political pressure for a policy of counter-terror which the military command embraced (or yielded to) was largely responsible for the indiscipline in the army. Given the combustible elements among the new Irish recruits and the poor calibre of their officers, to allow or encourage the military to act outside the law was to set in train a process of disintegration that culminated at the notorious 'Races of Castlebar'.

II

But if the troops in Ireland were generally undisciplined, were they also, as observers frequently claimed, disaffected as well? Military disaffection can be usefully separated into 'active' and 'passive' disaffection.[30] The former constitutes a massive threat to military cohesion and effectiveness. In extremities it manifests itself in shooting or conspiring to shoot one's officers, or in going over to the side of the enemy, or both. 'Passive' disaffection, on the other hand, while undoubtedly a threat to military discipline, is not subversive in motivation; it is sometimes indistinguishable from the usual grumbling of soldiers and stems from indiscipline as much as anything else. 'Passive' disaffection (or indiscipline) can, however, through mismanagement by the authorities, become 'active'. What begins as a protest over conditions within the military establishment can become an attempt to subvert it; hence the necessity for constant vigilance by the authorities.

It is clear that when viewed with this distinction in mind active disaffection among the armed forces in Ireland, particularly among the Irish militia, was much exaggerated. There is, for example, no recorded instance of troops shooting their officers, though there were many reports of various militiamen conspiring to do so; but these allegations were never wholly substantiated.[31] Moreover, when faced with rebel insurgents (French troops were another matter), the Irish troops, militia and yeomanry, acquitted themselves well. Ferocity, not disaffection, was the main criticism directed at them. Most remarkably, those regiments which were supposedly the most disaffected were the ones that distinguished themselves in battle. The Westmeath militia, only a month before some of its privates were accused of plotting to murder their officers, fought well at New Ross; the Monaghan militia, four of whose members had been executed for disaffection in 1797, fought bravely a year later at the battle of Antrim; the King's Co. militia, reputedly much disaffected, fought well at Enniscorthy; and the Meath militia and the Royal Irish Dragoons, both regiments under suspicion (indeed, the Dragoons were soon afterwards broken up for insubordination and disaffection) fought heroically at New Ross, the Meath militia losing fifteen men and the Dragoons twenty-six out of the ninety official casualties.[32] In fact, to the exertions of the Irish troops during the rebellion was its failure principally due.

Nor does the conduct of the militia at Castlebar provide evidence of their disaffection. Cooke claimed that the Kilkenny and Longford militias ran away from the French because they were Catholics and 'were many, if not most, of them sworn United Irishmen'. In retrospect the defeat at Castlebar proved to be a turning point in the deployment of the Irish militia for they were never really trusted by Dublin Castle thereafter.[33] But there is no need to choose disaffection as the explanation for the defeat and flight of Lake's force.

It is true that the Irish army outnumbered the French by over two to one (1700 to 800), but Lake's forces were mostly 'half-soldiers' who were probably half-trained as well. With a force thus composed it was most unwise of Lake to risk a pitched battle against French veterans. It is also true that a number of militiamen who fled the field of battle in panic subsequently joined the French. Lake reported a figure (admittedly incomplete) of 278 men missing after the battle, of whom 158 were from the Longford Militia, 44 from the Kilkenny Militia, and 33 from the Galway Volunteers.[34] A small proportion of these men (probably not more than 60) appear to have joined the French; some of them later claimed that they had joined Humbert under duress, and certainly some deserted from the French before the defeat at Ballinamuck. But the remainder—the large majority—seem simply to have fled in panic and taken advantage of their situation to desert.[35] Almost certainly, many more joined one of the bands of robbers abounding at that time than joined Humbert. Among the Irish militia, indiscipline merging with lawlessness rather than active disaffection was predominant in 1798.

Frequently, allegations of disaffection within the militia seem to have been prompted more by an overheated imagination (fuelled by the spectacle of so many uniformed Catholics with firearms) than by reliable evidence. Often there was an inability to distinguish between the traditional grumbling of soldiers and military disaffection, and when disaffection was apparently uncovered it can usually be classed as passive rather than active and can be attributed more to deep discontent than to anything else. Nevertheless, even when the hysterical, the mischievous and the routine allegations are seen for what they really were, and when so-called disaffection is more properly labelled as discontent and traced to pervasive indiscipline and a climate of insubordination, there remains a substantial body of evidence relating to active disaffection within the militia and the yeomanry and one or two regular regiments. Although this evidence requires careful handling, it cannot be ignored or explained away casually.

III

There can be no doubt that many attempts were made to suborn troops in Ireland during the 1790s and later though for the most part they were desultory rather than systematic. The attempts came from two quarters, the United Irishmen and the Defenders, and of the two the United Irishmen were by far the less important. The Society of United Irishmen confined its activities, at least for the first few years of its existence, to increasing its membership and to spreading its message of union between Catholics and Dissenters and parliamentary reform by publicity and propaganda. In common with other radical societies in England and Scotland at the time, the United Irishmen, taking their cue from Paine's remarks on the military in *The Rights of Man*,[36] made an appeal to the soldiers for support. Late in 1792 they issued a handbill addressed to them: 'Soldiers, friends, citizens and brothers! The moment is at last arrived when we may call you so. ... Liberty has destroyed distinction and we who are and will be free are happy in teaching you how to anticipate the hour when you shall be restored to the common Rights of Man...'. Abandoning high-flown rhetoric for more practical concerns, the author of the handbill then listed the soldiers' grievances that would be remedied when their rights were restored: oppressive officers, corporal punishment, poor pay, services abroad, and living in a gloomy barrack, 'the very symbol of a Bastille'.[37]

Once war broke out in February 1793, however, such appeals to the troops to make common cause with the radicals could be construed as sedition, though initially the authorities in Ireland were reluctant to take matters that far. It is most unlikely that any settled plan for suborning the troops or militia existed among Irish radical groups before 1795; provocative handbills were about as far as they were prepared to go and there is no evidence of soldiers being sworn into the United Irishmen. It was not until the middle of 1795, after the society was forced underground, that such a plan emerged. In June 1795 a government spy reported that United Irishmen in the Belfast area had been urged 'to seduce the military by all possible means', and his wording suggested that this was a new policy.[38] A year later, in July 1796, the United Irishmen in Belfast boasted about their hold over the militia 'which they say they are sure of'.[39] This claim was no doubt an exaggeration; as happened frequently with the United Irishmen, it represented the wish rather than the deed. Nonetheless, a great deal of significance attached to the claim, for it indicates that by mid-1796 the United Irishmen had effected an alliance with the Defenders.[40] Quite simply, there was no way that the United Irishmen could have been 'sure of' the militia *unless* they had made such an alliance; it was well known that Defenderism was very strong in the militia. Indeed, it is probable that this consideration played a major role in convincing the United Irish leadership that an alliance with the Defenders, despite its disadvantages, was nevertheless a military necessity. But were the United Irishmen justified in believing that Defenderism could provide them with enough disaffected soldiers to overthrow the state and set up a republic?

The exact nature of Defenderism remains elusive.[41] It is clear however that it was a movement of great complexity blending current grievances over tithes, taxes and rents with a lively folk-memory of confiscation and oppression. It combined sectarianism and millennialism with a fair amount of political realism; and it was avowedly subversive of the established order in church and state. It had a special appeal for soldiers too. At the trial in 1795 of some privates of the South Cork Militia for being sworn Defenders 'it appeared that many were induced to take the oath in consequence of their being able to travel throughout the kingdom with one of the tickets or certificates given to them when sworn, free of expense and in perfect safety, being supplied with liquor and lodged wherever they passed....'[42] Altogether, this mixture of diverse elements made Defenderism a powerful, even revolutionary, force in Ireland in the 1790s and later—all the more potent for defying both easy definition and easy remedy. In a real sense, its strength and its appeal stemmed from its mystery.

Yet the mixture, if powerful, was also unstable, for the various elements that constituted it were highly volatile. No one could predict which single element—the millennial, the sectarian, the economic, or the political—would emerge to define the essential purpose of Defenderism. In allying with the Defenders, the United Irishmen were confident that they could, as the state prisoners later put it, 'melt them down' into the general body of their society and thus define their purpose in terms of the objectives of the United Irishmen.[43] But given the combustible nature of the material with which they were dealing and its distance from their own experience, such confidence could not have been well founded. When the United Irishmen reportedly claimed that they were 'sure of' the militia, apparently because they were sure of the Defenders, they merely revealed their ignorance of the Defenders and they displayed an exaggerated confidence in the degree or quality of the Defenders' penetration of the militia. With respect to military disaffection, the numbers involved, while clearly important, were probably not the crucial factor; more important was the rank of the disaffected and their position within the regiment. It was a major weakness of the Defenders that while they had sworn many privates they had recruited no officers and relatively few sergeants or corporals to their ranks. Moreover, such was the nature of Defenderism that even if many militiamen were sworn Defenders, this cannot be taken as evidence that they were seriously disaffected—that in a crisis or on a given signal they were prepared to shoot their officers or to mutiny or desert in large numbers. The plasticity of Defenderism, the diffuseness of its objectives, the vagueness of some of its oaths and its lack of a consistent national focus—all made such a deduction inadmissible, and, as we have seen, the performance of many 'disaffected' corps during the 1798 rebellion provided clear proof to the contrary. This is not to say that the alliance between the United Irishmen and the Defenders, where it revealed itself in the suborning of troops, and especially militia, constituted no threat to military discipline and effectiveness or ultimately to the security of the island. There was indeed a threat but the fact that it was contained so easily can only be explained by the limited nature of the danger in the first place. The events of 1797, the *annus mirabilis* for mutiny and disaffection, provide an illustration of these points.

The threat posed by military disaffection was at its height in 1797. In April and May of that year occurred the naval mutinies at Spithead and (more serious because more political) at the Nore. Meanwhile in London seditious handbills had been discovered at Chatham barracks and there was open discontent among some of the Guards regiments.[44] In Ireland there was mounting evidence of United Irish-Defender penetration of the garrisons at Blaris, near Belfast, in Dublin itself, and at Bandon, Cork, and Limerick in the south and southwest.[45] Altogether, during the months from April to July an observer might have been forgiven for believing that United Irish conspirators had spun a web of disaffection throughout the armed forces of both England and Ireland and that in alliance with the French and Dutch their plans for an unopposed invasion of Ireland were about to come to fruition. In July 1797 Portland even claimed, with enough truth to make it credible, that 'there was a direct and regular correspondence between the [naval] mutineers and the rebellious corps in the camps of Blaris and Bandon and a constant intercourse between the disaffected or United Irishmen and the French government...'.[46]

As is well known, however, the aggregate threat faded and disappeared as summer gave way to autumn. The naval mutinies were quelled by a judicious mixture of repression and concession, and the grumbling of the troops in England was answered by a boost in pay.[47] In Ireland, disaffection was checked by rough military meas-

ures, either official (the savage punishment of suspects)[48] or un-
official (warnings by individual regiments that they would tolerate
no suborners in their ranks).[49] Dublin Castle, however, on military
and political grounds, did not approve these rough methods, and
Camden dismissed various 'warnings' issued by individual regiments
as 'absurd'.[50] It much preferred the formal means by which discipline and due subordination had traditionally been enforced. Sometimes this meant sending suspected troops abroad. Sometimes again
entire regiments were moved to another less 'disaffected' district
within Ireland and were replaced by English and Scottish fencibles
or militia, though Dublin Castle was embarrassed when on arrival
these regiments issued their own 'warnings'.[51] Attempts were also
made to keep the soldiers from fraternising with civilians. Thus
there was a flurry of orders insisting that troops wear proper dress,
avoid taverns, and remain in barracks after retreat.[52] Above all,
Dublin Castle and the military authorities put their faith in general
courts martial and carefully stage-managed executions (sometimes
pardons were given minutes before sentence was to be carried out).
This combination proved effective, at least in the short term.
During the month of May 1797 general courts martial were con-
vened in Belfast, Dublin, Limerick and Cork to try soldiers for
sedition and fomenting mutiny. These exercises represented an
impressive demonstration of the authorities' resolve to stamp out
military disaffection. In Limerick there were no executions but
those found guilty were sentenced to be flogged and to serve abroad.
In Cork two men from the Wexford militia were executed by a firing
squad; in Dublin the same fate befell two soldiers from the Kildare
militia; and at Blaris camp, about ten miles from Belfast, four men
from the Monaghan militia, Daniel Gillan, Owen McCanna,
William McCanna and Peter McCarron, were shot for sedition.[53]

A consideration of the details of this last affair reveals much
about the level and nature of disaffection among the troops and
demonstrates the appropriateness of the formal response of the authorities to it. Blaris camp contained over 4,000 troops (regulars,
Irish militia, and English and Scottish fencibles). The soldiers constituted both a strategic reserve in the event of a French invasion
and also a force large enough to overawe the north generally and
the nearby town of Belfast in particular.[54] The sowing of disaffection
within this camp would have had the most serious consequences
for the security of Ireland. In fact, during 1796 a conspiracy to sow
disaffection had been uncovered at Blaris but it had been dealt with
easily and leniently, the allegedly disaffected regiments being posted
elsewhere.[55]

In the spring of 1797, however, evidence came to light of a fresh conspiracy involving the newly-arrived Monaghan militia. On this occasion the government's response, probably under the influence of the alarming events at Spithead and elsewhere, was not so restrained. In April the government informer Edward Newall reported that there were many Defenders in the Monaghan militia.[56] His information led to an investigation, and some seventy soldiers of the regiment subsequently confessed to being sworn Defenders.[57] The four eventually selected for court martial were held to be the ringleaders and they were convicted on the evidence of their fellow militiamen. McCarron, Gillan and the two McCannas had been the prime movers in the business and it was they who had made contact with certain Belfast United Irishmen. They had organised a separate and secret officer structure made up of privates within each company. Corporal John Reel testified concerning a conversation with Peter McCarron:

> I then asked him what the purpose of officers was? He told me in the first place to bring news from the townspeople to the men as soon as news came to the townspeople; and secondly when war broke out they were to be officers over the country and the townspeople and that soldiers would all be made officers as they knew discipline well. I then agreed to everything that was said . . . .

There was also some talk that the soldiers would be rewarded with estates when the 'war' was over. The four militiamen were executed in a carefully managed exercise in official terror. It began with a military procession, in which the condemned men were prominent, from Belfast to Blaris camp, where the executions took place before the assembled troops. Afterwards, the soldiers marched in ordinary time past the bodies, which left 'the strongest symptoms of impression on all the spectators'.[58] A few days after this 'awful spectacle' (as the London *Times* called it) the Monaghan Militia wrecked the offices of the *Northern Star* to demonstrate that their disaffection had been exorcised.[59]

It seems clear from this affair that even in regiments that had a notorious reputation for it genuine disaffection did not run very deep, the number of troops sworn being clearly no guide to its seriousness. At Bandon in Co. Cork 145 troops confessed to being Defenders, but as at Blaris this incident was easily tamed by traditional means and the affair blew over. Furthermore, the seditious soldiers of the Monaghan militia were privates (with an occasional corporal), and they were forced to create their own leadership structure because their officers and (crucially) their N.C.O.s stayed out of the conspiracy. This was a major weakness, one that revealed itself in other regiments. Nor was this defect offset by close contact with or leadership from civilian radicals. Such leadership was in any case unlikely, given the different life-experiences of the soldiers and the civilians. The contact between Belfast and Blaris, which had initially seemed so alarming to Dublin Castle, in the end amounted to little more on the part of the civilians than wining and dining the soldiers and offering them flattery and encouragement. Most Belfast radicals were prudent enough not to go further. As Newall remarked contemptuously, they were 'wealthy, wiley and avaricious..., too tenacious of life and property to move themselves, whatever they may effect by means of others.'[60] The calculated terror of the executions at Blaris was as much directed at them as at the troops, and it had the desired effect; by the end of 1797 joint civilian and military sedition—the very aspect of the alliance between Defenders and United Irishmen which a year earlier had promised to deliver to the United Irishmen a domestic substitute army for French troops—was at an end.[61]

Defenderism continued to claim adherents within the armed forces, especially the militia, in the years up to and after 1798, and there were several courts martial set up to try disaffected troops, but Defenderism appeared now as a threat to military discipline rather than as a danger to the state. Contact between Defenders in the army and civilian radicals seems to have been minimal; indeed, as a result of the military executions of 1797 soldiers appear to have been deeply suspicious of such contact. When the Sheares brothers, on the eve of the rebellion, sought to mobilise disaffected troops in the King's Co. Militia to seize strategic points in and around Dublin, they were forced to rely on Captain J. W. Armstrong of that body to do the job on their behalf, a mistake that was to cost them their lives.[62] Shorn of its radical contacts, Defenderism within the armed forces once again expressed itself in a raw indiscipline which included desertion, insubordination and routine sectarian brawling, none of which can really be described as active disaffection. Such misconduct was especially common in the general climate of lawlessness that prevailed throughout Ireland following the suppression of the rebellion, and those regiments which had long been notorious for Defenderism (such as the Meath, Westmeath, King's Co., Louth and Kildare Militias) and some which had recently acquired a reputation for it (the 5th Dragoons for instance) were especially prominent in it. Above all, Defenderism within the armed forces and especially the militia revealed itself in a vigorous anti-

Orange spirit that readily merged into a general anti-Protestantism. In this respect, Defenderism was no doubt rediscovering its old roots, though at one point in the 1790s it had seemed as if, in the interests of unity, the Defenders had pushed anti-Protestantism into the background. At the court martial of two privates of the Kildare Militia in 1797 it was testified that the defendants had agreed 'that it did not signify what religion they were to be of, and that the first that was to cast up to another what religion he was of, was to be hung.'[63] But the murderous sectarian warfare of 1797 and after quashed such tolerant notions. When Philip Reily, Michael Leonard, and Edward, John and Philip McGuire, all privates in the Fermanagh Militia, were sworn into the Defenders late in 1799, one of their first thoughts was apparently to murder all the Orangemen in their regiment. They also drank a toast which pithily summed up the varied experience of Defenderism in the 1790s: 'that the skin of an Orangeman might make a *parapluie* to the tree of liberty.'[64]

IV

Military disaffection, in so far as it had constituted a threat to the effectiveness of the armed forces in Ireland, was a thing of the past by 1800, if not before. Defenderism, that erratic engine of disaffection within the army, now frittered away its energies in unruly and undisciplined behaviour, and after 1798 the remnants of the United Irishmen, chiefly out of a concern for secrecy, tended to avoid any contact with the military. Rumours of disaffection in various regiments, however, persisted for many years. In 1803, Emmet's rebellion predictably gave a boost to such allegations and in 1807 Lord Delvin accused the Westmeath Militia of being disaffected. Further research would no doubt produce other examples, but no reliable evidence ever emerged to substantiate these reports.[65] Sometimes one suspects that Dublin Castle found such reports to be more useful than alarming, as in November 1803 when the viceroy, Lord Hardwicke, used the alleged sowing of disaffection among the soldiers as his main argument in favour of a continued suspension of Habeas Corpus.[66] If the reaction of Dublin Castle to reports of disaffection among the militia was rather opportunistic after 1800 this was understandable. For in a real sense the disaffection of the Irish militia, whether actually present or only imagined, was a matter of relative indifference to the authorities. The reason was that the entire strategy for the defence of Ireland in the 1790s which had given such prominence to the militia and had prompted the great debate on their loyalty had now been discarded and replaced by another. Put simply, whereas in the 1790s the Irish militia had been in the vanguard of the Irish defence forces, after 1800 that position was taken by the Irish yeomanry.

After the 1798 rebellion the Irish militia was progressively downgraded; soon it was little more than a recruiting serjeant or crimp for the line regiments. Year after year, militia regiments 'volunteered' to serve outside Ireland, sometimes in Britain, at other times on the continent. In the first quarter of 1799 no fewer than thirteen regiments offered to serve outside the country.[67] In January 1800 Cornwallis offered a bounty of four guineas to each militiaman who would volunteer for regular service in a line regiment, and he proffered the disposal of an ensigncy to every militia colonel who enlisted just forty volunteers.[68] By 1805 a bounty of between ten and twelve guineas, depending on the terms of service, was being offered, and about 3,000 militiamen a year (in some years, many more) were passing into the line regiments.[69] Such massive drafting on an annual basis, comprising roughly one-sixth to one-quarter of the entire force, rendered the Irish militia ineffective from a military standpoint, since the proportion of raw recruits to trained men in the force was always unacceptably high. As the Irish militia's role had changed to one of supplying semi-trained recruits to the line regiments, the Irish yeomanry had stepped forward into the role vacated by the militia.

Although the Irish yeomanry had begun life as a sort of local police force, with the passing of years its numbers and the range of its duties grew significantly. The yeomanry were undoubtedly as undisciplined as the militia: Thomas Lane, the marquis of Downshire's agent, swore that the yeomanry were 'the most undisciplined, outrageous set of men I ever saw—and the officers boast of being more ungovernable than even those they should control. They are above all civil power...'.[70] Certainly they had had their share of disaffection. The St Sepulchre's corps of yeomanry in Dublin was stood down because of alleged disaffection; Dr Edmund, a physician of Naas, Co. Kildare, and a yeomanry officer, was executed for taking part in the rebel attack on the town of Prosperous during the '98 rebellion; Felix Rourke, a deserter from the yeomanry, was executed for his part in Emmet's rebellion in 1803; and in Co. Galway Lieutenant Kirwan of the Annaghdown yeomanry was court-martialled for being involved in the epidemic of cattle houghing which swept through the west of Ireland in the late 1790s.[71] Such instances of indiscipline and such examples of disaffection were disregarded however, for the yeomanry, unlike the militia, was indisputably loyal. By 1800 loyal was synonymous with Protestant. There had been 'Catholic' yeomanry corps during the late 1790s (Lord Fingall commanded one against the rebels at the battle of Tara),[72] but the trend was unmistakably to Protestantise the force. From some corps, all the Catholics were expelled so as to remove any suspicion of disloyalty, and conversely, groups of Orangemen were enlisted *en bloc* into new corps.[73] After 1803 this trend became almost a settled principle of exclusion. As the yeomanry became more Protestant its size increased from an initial establishment of about 30,000 in 1797 to nearly 60,000 by 1805. Over the same period its function also changed; it became more like a fencible force, that is, light troops on permanent duty for the duration of the war and not limited to their own immediate area for service.[74] Moreover, brigade-majors for each county were appointed by Dublin Castle, and through them the whole yeomanry establishment was controlled at the national level, making it a flexible instrument in the event of invasion or rebellion.[75]

The yeomanry were the true heirs of the Volunteers of 1782, though they generally lacked the 'giddiness' to which their predecessors had been prone. They were the armed Protestants of Ireland, self-reliant and self-confident, once again forming a major portion of the garrison of Ireland, and making a political statement at the same time. Castlereagh pointed with pride to the 'great increase of determined and zealous loyalists since the commencement of the yeomanry armament', and he astutely ascribed this increase 'to no cause more decidedly than . . . the influence of that institution itself'.[76] The remodelled, strengthened and purged yeomanry was, in short, the complete answer to the problems posed by the alleged disaffection of the Irish militia. Defenderism might persist in the militia, but it could now safely dissipate its energies in Spain, the West Indies, or elsewhere. No doubt also, the removal every year of so many young men from Ireland through the agency of the militia helped to lower somewhat the level of disturbance and disaffection in the country. As for indiscipline, there were no easy answers; but even here a modest start was made from the greater concentration of troops in large garrisons. In time this would eliminate that dispersal which many had considered ruinous for discipline. The threat posed by military disaffection, however, was at an end.

131

Notes

1. Lecky, *Ire.*, iv, 203–4; J. W. Fortescue, *A history of the British army* (4 vols, London, 1899–1910, hereafter cited as Fortescue, *British army*), iv, pt i, 595–6.
2. W. D. Griffin, 'The forces of the crown in Ireland, 1798' in G. L. Vincitorio (ed.), *Crisis in the 'Great Republic': essays presented to Ross J. S. Hoffman* (New York, 1968), pp 155–80.
3. J. A. Houlding, *Fit for service: the training of the British army, 1717–1795* (Oxford, 1981, hereafter cited as Houlding, *Fit for service*), p. 56.
4. P.R.O., Home Office Papers (hereafter cited as H.O.), 100/47/272–4.
5. Ibid., 100/48/429, 100/56/218–21.
6. Ibid., 100/48/306, 100/48/429.
7. Altogether, 2,411 soldiers, regulars and militia, deserted in Ireland in 1794: K. Ferguson, 'The army in Ireland from the Restoration to the Act of Union' (unpublished Ph.D. thesis, University of Dublin, 1980), p. 142.
8. P.R.O., Pitt papers, 30/8/331/187–90.
9. See Houlding, *Fit for service*, pp 45–57.
10. J. F. Maurice (ed.), *The diary of Sir John Moore* (2 vols, London, 1904, hereafter cited as Moore, *Diary*); Scottish Record Office, G.D. 26/9/527/bundle 1.
11. See Ferguson, 'Irish army', p. 147 n. and Griffin, 'Forces of the crown', pp 177–9.
12. Westmorland to Dundas, 23 June 1794 (P.R.O., H.O., 100/48/427).
13. Ibid., 100/49/18.
14. See Abercorn to Dundas and General Cunningham, Apr. 1794 (P.R.O.N.I., T. 2541/1K/93–5.
15. P.R.O.N.I., Abercorn papers, T. 2541/1B1/5/31.
16. Vallancey to Abercorn, 8 Nov. 1793, ibid., T. 2541/1C1/48.
17. P.R.O., H.O., 100/79/116–30; Moore, *Diary*, i, 274–5.
18. Vallancey to Abercorn, 5 Feb. 1794 (P.R.O.N.I., T 2541/1C1/12.
19. P.R.O., H.O., 100/43/103, 152–4; Lecky, *Ire.*, iii, 419–20.
20. Major-General Johnston to Abercromby, 19 Feb. 1798 (P.R.O., H.O., 100/73/67). Abercromby claimed that this crime proved the 'want of discipline' in the army (Abercromby to Pelham, 21 Feb. 1798, ibid., 100/73/65). The 'General Orders' were issued on 26 February.
21. P.R.O., H.O., 100/70/181–4.
22. C. Ross (ed.), *Correspondence of the first Marquis Cornwallis* (3 vols, London, 1859, hereafter cited as *Cornwallis corr.*), ii, 504–6.
23. James Abercromby, *Lieut.-General Sir Ralph Abercromby: a memoir by his son* (Edinburgh, 1861, hereafter cited as Abercromby, *Memoir*), p. 86.
24. Houlding, *Fit for service*, pp 45–57. See especially the map on p. 54 showing the quarters of the army in Ireland in 1752.
25. P.R.O., H.O., 100/56/218–21.
26. Abercromby, *Memoir*, pp 93, 101–3.
27. P.R.O., H.O., 100/70/181.
28. General Knox to Abercorn, 21 Mar. 1797 (P.R.O.N.I., T. 2541/1B3/610). Lake agreed: 'Nothing but terror would work' (Lecky, *Ire.*, iv, 49–50).
29. P.R.O.N.I., T. 3048/H/3.
30. My thoughts on military disaffection have been stimulated by several conversations with Professor J. W. Shy of the University of Michigan, Ann Arbor.
31. See for example the *Report from the secret committee of the House of*

Commons, with an appendix (Dublin, 1798), appendix xxix.
32. Castlereagh to Wickham, 3 Sept. 1798 (P.R.O., H.O., 100/82/23–4); Major-General Johnston's report on the battle of New Ross, 7 June 1798 (ibid., 100/77/108–10.
35. Cooke to Wickham, 11 Sept. 1798, ibid., 100/78/330–31.
36. Everyman ed., pt ii, p. 220.
37. P.R.O., H.O., 100/34/43–4.
38. Ibid., 100/55/186.
39. Ibid., 100/62/139–40.
40. Possibly even earlier, for on 22 January 1796 Camden told Portland that the Defenders swore not only to be true to one another 'but to unite and correspond with the Society of United Irishmen' (ibid., 100/62/15–20).
41. For more information on this movement see my 'Defenders and Defenderism in 1795' forthcoming in *Irish Historical Studies.*
42. P.R.O., H.O., 100/58/344–50.
43. Marquess of Londonderry (ed.), *Memoirs and correspondence of Viscount Castlereagh* (4 vols, London, 1848, hereafter cited as *Castlereagh corr.*), i, 357–8.
44. National Army Museum, London (hereafter N.A.M.), MS 6807/370/39; P.R.O., H.O., 100/69/299–300. Incendiary handbills were also found at Woolwich (*Times*, 27 May 1797). See also R. Wells, *Insurrection: the British experience, 1795–1803* (Gloucester, 1983), pp 76–81, 104–6.
45. P.R.O., H.O., 100/69/202–5, 275–9.
46. Ibid., 100/70/17–18.
47. Ibid., 100/68/23–5.
48. S.P.O., Rebellion papers, 620/31/71; P.R.O., H.O., 100/70/191–8.
49. 'Proclamation... of the Mid-Lothian Light Dragoons, Headquarters, Dundalk, 18 June 1797' (National Library of Scotland, papers of the earl of Ancram, MS 5750/119).
50. P.R.O., H.O., 100/72/109.
51. Ibid., 100/64/173; 100/69/245.
52. N.A.M., MS 6807/174/105.
53. *Report from the secret committee...*, pp 283–6; Camden to Portland, 18 May 1797 (P.R.O., H.O., 100/69/307–13).
54. P. Stoddard, 'Counter-insurgency and defence in Ireland, 1790–1805' (unpublished D. Phil. thesis, Oxford, 1972), pp 109, 116, 147.
55. P.R.O., H.O., 100/62/139–43; S.P.O., Rebellion papers, 620/25/68; N.A.M., MS 6807/174/157.
56. P.R.O., H.O., 100/69/202–5.
57. Ibid., 100/69/275–9.
58. *Proceedings of a general court martial held at the town of Belfast*, 8 May 1797 (P.R.O., H.O., 100/70/199–211.
59. *Times*, 23 May 1797.
60. P.R.O., H.O., 100/62/137–8.
61. The execution of William Orr for suborning troops in September 1797 no doubt reinforced the impact of the Blaris executions (Lecky, *Ire.*, iv, 103–15).
62. Ibid., iv, 312–16; v, 22–5.
63. *Report from the secret committee...*, appendix xxix, p. 286.
64. S.P.O., Rebellion papers, 620/17/30/88.
65. Ibid., 620/66/138; P.R.O.N.I., T. 2627/5/9/194–6; P.R.O., H.O., 100/136/38–9.

66. P.R.O., H.O., 100/118/176-8.
67. Ibid., 100/83/60, 75, 90, 98, 140-42, 161, 256-8, 264, 318; 100/84/48.
68. Ibid., 100/90/31-2.
69. Ibid., 100/125/221-3, 100/140/220; Wellesley to Hawkesbury, 7 May 1807 in Duke of Wellington (ed.), *Civil correspondence and memoranda of Field Marshal Arthur, duke of Wellington: Ireland, 30 March 1807 to 12 April 1809* (London, 1860, hereafter cited as Wellington, *Supplementary despatches*), v, 28-36.
70. P.R.O.N.I., Downshire papers, D. 607/9/192.
71. P.R.O., H.O., 100/99/99, 100/81/84, 100/117/153-4, 100/89/53.
72. Ibid., 100/76/293.
73. Ibid., 100/107/33-4; Stoddard, 'Counter-insurgency and defence', pp 288-9.
74. P.R.O., H.O., 100/74/369-75, 100/126/136.
75. Ibid., 100/121/301; Wellington, *Supplementary despatches*, v, 34.
76. Wellington, *Supplementary despatches*, v, 279-83.

The Radical Press in the French Revolution

Hugh Gough

The theme of 'radicals, rebels and establishments' is a broad one, applicable to a wide time span and to a wide variety of historical circumstances. There are radicals and rebels of the right as well as of the left, and establishments too can lie on both sides of the political divide. The focus of this study, however, will be on radicalism of the left, and more particularly on its press during the French Revolution, a decade which saw the birth of constitutional political life in France. In the ten years between the fall of the Bastille and Napoleon's *coup d'état* of Brumaire, over two thousand newspaper titles appeared—most of them in Paris, but with a significant number in the provinces too. Many were short-lived, collapsing after their prospectus or the first few numbers, as their editors fell victims to fatigue or financial shortage. Very few indeed survived the decade in the style of the *Moniteur* which, launched in November 1789 by the publishing magnate Panckoucke, later became the official government newspaper of the Napoleonic Empire.[1] Yet a great many of them played an important role in the political life of the decade. 'It is', wrote Brissot in the spring of 1789 in the first prospectus of his *Patriote Français*, 'the one way of educating a large nation, hindered in its faculties, little accustomed to reading, yet seeking to emerge from ignorance and slavery. Without gazettes the revolution in America, in which France played so glorious a role, would never have come about . . . . Gazettes dragged Ireland from the langour and subjection in which the English parliament had held it; gazettes have preserved the small amount of political liberty that remains in England'.[2]

The Parisian right-wing press of the revolution has been well served by two recent studies, but the radical press has been less fortunate. Apart from biographies of its leading personalities, two excellent unpublished theses on the *Patriote Français* and the *Révolutions de Paris*, and books on the *Journal des hommes libres* and a limited number of Parisian titles between 1789 and 1791, no specific study of its activity has yet been made.[3] Yet it is a subject which merits attention, not only because of its influence and its role in developing a major strand of revolutionary ideology, but also because of the direct political role played by so many of its participants. This study can make no claims to be comprehensive. It covers only the first five years of the revolution, between the fall of the Bastille and the end of the Terror. Yet, within the confines of this increasingly radical phase of the revolution. it is an attempt to draw in the broad lines of the development of the radical press during the revolutionary decade and to highlight its strengths and weaknesses.

During May and June 1789 the Estates General, called reluctantly by Louis XVI in the previous autumn to resolve the crown's financial crisis, was first deadlocked and then transformed into a National Assembly claiming full legislative power. During July the fall of the Bastille in Paris, municipal revolts throughout much of urban France and a simultaneous peasant insurrection, completed the destruction of the social and political order of the *ancien régime*. During these same months the government's control of the newspaper press collapsed too. Mirabeau first successfully defied government censorship in the opening days of the Estates General, a trickle of titles followed during the rest of May and throughout June, and this developed into a full flow during July. By the end of 1789 almost two hundred titles had appeared in Paris. During 1790 this figure climbed to over three hundred, and the following year's total was only slightly less. Some were little more than pamphlets, appearing at irregular intervals and concerning themselves with particular issues of contemporary political debate. But the great majority appeared at set intervals—some weekly, others three or four times a week, and a great many of them daily—and offered to their readers a regular news coverage of debates in the National Assembly, and events in Paris, the provinces and abroad.[4] In viewpoint they ranged over the entire political spectrum, for the early years of the revolution were marked by considerable press freedom, and amongst them were a number of radical newspapers of considerable significance. On 5 July 1789 the *Courrier de Versailles à*

Paris made its first modest appearance, a daily paper owned and edited by Antoine-Joseph Gorsas which was to continue until the spring of 1793. Twelve days later it was the turn of the *Révolutions de Paris*, a weekly which was owned and edited by the bookseller, Louis-Marie Prudhomme. Nine days later, on 26 July, Brissot launched his daily *Patriote Français* — at the third attempt — while 13 August saw the first number of Louise Kéralio's *Journal d'État et du Citoyen* which was subsequently to change title to the *Mercure National*. On 12 September Marat published the *Publiciste Parisien*, which within days adopted the more familiar title of *Ami du Peuple*, while on 3 October it was the turn of the *Annales patriotiques et littéraires*, a daily paper established by the bookseller Buisson after a quarrel with Brissot over the ownership of the *Patriote Français* and soon to be dominated by the personality and industry of its major contributor, Jean-Louis Carra. In late November Camille Desmoulins began his weekly *Révolutions de France et de Brabant*, having already turned down an offer to work for Mirabeau on his *Courrier de Provence*, while an obscure publicist, Pierre-Jean Audouin, produced the first number of the *Journal universel* which, from modest beginnings, was to be the longest lasting of all the early radical papers, finally ending in the summer of 1795. In January 1790 the first edition of the *Bouche de Fer* appeared, produced weekly by a semi-masonic political club, the *Cercle Social*, while several months later, on 22 May, Stanislas Fréron—son of Elie Fréron, the well known opponent of Voltaire—launched the daily *Orateur du Peuple*. On 6 September an obscure and penniless pamphleteer, Jacques-Rene Hébert, followed up with the first number of the *Père Duchesne* which, although politically moderate in its early numbers and notably favourable towards Lafayette, was soon to adopt radical views in the early weeks of 1791.

It is important not to view these titles as a monolithic bloc, for like most newspapers of the period—and this generalisation holds true for the right-wing press as much as for the left—they were highly individualistic enterprises, dominated by the personality of their editors. They employed, for example, a great variety of style and if Hébert was an expert in earthy familiarity and coarse humour, Marat and Fréron were more inclined to direct and violent denunciations of political opponents and their alleged plots. Audouin, on the other hand, was heavily factual, Desmoulins was enthusiastic and polemical, while Brissot held an elevated view of the journalist's role, using measured language, carefully researched material and a high pedagogic tone.[5] Neither were they all on good personal terms, for while Marat and Fréron may have been close—using the same printer on occasion and even writing each other's copy when occasion demanded—Brissot disliked Marat (possibly the result of a quarrel in September 1789 over his alterations to an article written by Marat for the *Patriote Français*), while Gorsas loathed him, Hébert initially distrusted him and Robert refused to have him in his house. Desmoulins, on the other hand, was ambivalent about Marat, but close enough to Fréron to co-operate with him briefly on a newspaper in the spring of 1792. His relations with Brissot, on the other hand, steadily deteriorated, for Brissot was a witness at his marriage in 1790, but they quarrelled in the following spring over their respective attitudes towards Mirabeau and Barnave, and again in the following autumn over womens' education, before the war issue widened the rift irreparably.[6]

Even their social background was by no means uniform. Carra, Brissot Marat and Fréron had all, to varying degrees, been involved in the literary underground of the last years of the *ancien régime*, pioneering new pseudo-scientific theories or penning illegal and subversive *libelles*.[7] So too had Audouin—although little is known of his life before 1789—and possibly Prudhomme, who came originally from Lyons, and had settled in Paris during the early 1780s, publishing a good many political brochures before 1789.[8] Yet involvement in this Parisian style Grub Street was by no means uncommon in the literary world of the late eighteenth century where the supply of would-be *philosophes* outpaced the availability of posts and pensions. It provided many writers with a bare living and, if it engendered in them too a certain rancid bitterness towards a social and political establishment which denied them recognition while manifestly promoting conformist mediocrity, it did not lead them all to become radicals when the dam burst in 1789, for many journalists of the centre and right were drawn from their ranks too.[9] Many radical journalists, moveover, came from other walks of life. Gorsas, for example, was the son of a master-shoemaker from Limoges who, through the patronage of the secretary to the local bishop, had been educated in Paris and then, turning down the possibility of a legal career, had established a school in Versailles. His literary interests then drew him towards pamphleteering in 1786, bringing him a brief prison spell, the closure of his school and a move to Paris where he mixed in the political world of the Kornmann circle.[10] Hébert was a straightforward down-and-out from a respectable Alençon family, who had been ruined by a trivial legal case in his youth and moved to Paris where he had spent the 1780s in a variety of menial jobs. He was drawn into journalism through pamphleteering work in 1790.[11] Others, including François Robert, Desmoulins and Loustallot were lawyers—although Desmoulins and Loustallot were probably not particularly successful—while Louise Kéralio herself came from a respectable Breton noble family with established literary interests.[12] The most that can be said about them is that, Kéralio excepted, they came from bourgeois backgrounds—all, except Audouin and Kéralio, from provincial France—and that most had shown some literary or political interests in their pre-revolutionary careers. Yet few of them had enjoyed much success in those careers, and journalism therefore offered the opportunity for money and advancement as well as an outlet for their political views.

Behind these differences of style, personality and background there were a number of unifying factors which distinguished the radical press. The first of these was, naturally enough, an ideology which marked it out as radical not only against the *ancien régime* but also against the reforms of the early revolution between 1789 and 1791.[13] Opposition, for example, to the *marc d'argent* decree which set a high wealth qualification for eligibility as a deputy, or to the division of citizens into actives and passives with the effective disfranchisement of over three million adult males. Political democrats, most radical journalists favoured more extensive direct democracy in the Rousseauist sense, with the use of referenda on major issues and the devolution of power down to municipal, district or section level, much as the Parisian *sansculottes* were to do during Year II.[14] Anticlerical they certainly were, critical of the clergy by the spring of 1790 and favourable to the elements of democracy contained in the civil constitution enacted that summer. They were hopeful too of a more widespread moral reform—'point de liberté sans moeurs privées' claimed Brissot—as the basis for true revolution, and saw as the essential elements of such reform the retention of press freedom for all shades of opinion, and the extension of the elective principle to areas such as juries, army officerships and local government.[15]

Most of these ideas, if very much the preserve of a minority on a national scale, were common enough in Parisian democratic circles. Yet they inevitably led to a progressive disenchantment with the major personalities and institutions of the early revolution, a disenchantment shown as early as August and September 1789 by Loustallot and Marat in their opposition to the attempts of the

Parisian municipality to limit the autonomy of individual districts and to impose police controls on the press.[16] Necker, for many one of the heroes of 1789, came under fire from the early months of 1790 for alleged corruption and collusion with counter-revolution, while Bailly, mayor of Paris, fell from grace in the eyes of Marat and Loustallot in December 1789, with Desmoulins following closely behind and most of the other titles echoing their criticism during the summer and autumn of 1790. Lafayette's reputation lasted longer, but Marat turned on him in May 1790 for his activities as commander of the Paris National Guard, Desmoulins after his unduly prominent role at the *fête de la fédération* in July, and Loustallot in early August. The Nancy massacre later that month brought in the *Mercure universel*, and the *Orateur du Peuple*, while Hébert too had changed his initial allegiance by the end of the year.[17] The king himself came under criticism during 1790 on the size of the civil list and the question of the right to declare war. Robert and Desmoulins suggested the idea of a republic late in 1789, and Robert avocated it more decisively in a pamphlet of late 1790, *le Républicanisme adapté à la France*. Brissot, on the other hand, although a republican by conviction, argued that France was not yet ready to abandon the monarchy, while most of the others, although increasingly distrustful of Louis XVI and of Marie-Antoinette, still regarded the institution itself as the most convenient form for the executive branch of government until the flight to Varennes.[18]

A second common factor which united radical journalists was their political involvement. Brissot, for example, had been active in radical pamphleteering circles prior to the revolution and was a founder member of the anti-slavery group, the *société des amis des noirs*. Elected to the provisional Paris municipality in September 1789, he was an early member of the Jacobin club and, through the reputation that he acquired from the *Patriote Français*, was elected to the Legislative Assembly and Convention. Robert was a member of the Paris Jacobins, president of the Cordeliers club, a leading light among the *sociétés fraternelles* that sprang up in 1790 and 1791 to provide a political education for the poor, president of their *comité central* when it was formed in May 1791, and prominent in the republican agitation that led up to the Champ de Mars in the following July. From this base, and through his friendship with Danton, he was later elected to the National Convention.[19] Desmoulins, who sat with him there, was also a member of both the Cordeliers and Jacobin clubs, as was Hébert—a member of the Paris municipality from December 1792 onwards—and

Loustallot until his premature death in August 1790. Prudhomme too was a member of both clubs, founder of a *société des indigents* in 1790 and entrusted with political missions by the minister of the interior in the Seine-et-Marne and to the *armée du Nord* in September 1792. Marat was both a Jacobin and Cordelier, as well as being a member of the Convention, while Carra was secretary of the powerful Jacobin correspondence committee between July 1791 and April 1792, then active on one of the secret revolutionary committees behind the downfall of Louis XVI in August 1792, and a member of the Convention. Audouin too was in both clubs, secured election to the Convention for the Seine-et-Oise and later sat in the Council of the Five Hundred during the Directory. Radical journalism was therefore, for many, closely linked to political involvement and frequently proved a useful introduction to a political career.

The Cordeliers district and its club recur frequently in these careers and provide a third unifying factor for, situated on the left bank of the Seine, the district itself was noted from an early stage for its political radicalism. When districts were abolished in the spring of 1790 and replaced by some sixty sections, the area became the *section du théâtre français* but, to maintain its former identity, the district assembly was transformed into the Cordeliers club and was always more democratic in tone and clientele than its Jacobin counterpart.[20] It was from here, the historic centre of the Parisian printing trade, that the radical press predominantly operated, and it gained much of its strength from the sense of geographical and political unity that the area offered. Marat settled there in December 1789 to shelter from the first of many prosecutions and when, in the following month, the Paris Châtelet attempted to arrest him, the district authorities obstructed their attempts until he had time to go into hiding, and then cross to England. When he returned in the summer it was to the Cordeliers district again, and in February 1791 the club offered him assistance to keep the *Ami du Peuple* going.[21] The *Révolutions de Paris* was printed in the Cordeliers district too, at first in Prudhomme's premises on the rue Jacob, then later on the rue des Marais after he had bought his own presses in January 1790. The *Orateur du Peuple* was published from the rue Saint-Jacques and the place Dauphine, while Desmoulins moved to the rue Serpente and the rue du Théâtre Français in 1790, lodging in the same house as Danton—who dominated the district's political life—and expressing his feelings in almost lyrical terms in his *Révolutions de France et de Brabant:*

Je ne me promène pas sur son territoire sans un sentiment religieux, en pensant à l'inviolabilité qu'il vient d'assurer aux honnêtes gens; et sur toutes les rues, je ne lis point d'autre inscription que celle d'une rue de Rome, la rue sacrée.[22]

If ideology, political involvement and geography acted as unifying factors for the radical press, so too did adversity and prosecution. After the collapse of press censorship in the summer of 1789 press freedom was guaranteed in the Declaration of the Rights of Man, subject to the provision of future legislation to control possible abuse. That legislation, however, never enjoyed a high priority in the Assembly's debates, and whenever it was discussed it provoked serious rifts, with right-wing deputies favouring restrictive legislation and left-wing deputies opposing any legislation at all, fearing that it would be used to stifle legitimate criticism. When a law was finally passed, at the end of August 1791, it proved ineffective.[23] In the meantime it remained possible for the government or administrative bodies to prosecute individual journalists if their articles were thought to have provoked a breach of the peace, or for individuals to sue for libel. And, until the judicial reorganisation of the autumn of 1790 these cases were heard in Paris before the Châtelet, an *ancien régime* court which was both obsolete and conservative. It was the Châtelet which attempted to arrest Marat in January 1790, and between December 1789 and July 1790 it also imposed a number of heavy fines on radical journalists who chose to stand and fight instead of flee. In December Gorsas, Carra and Prudhomme all carried stories on the public executioner, Charles-Henri Sansom, alleging that his home served as a centre for counter-revolutionary meetings and the distribution of brochures. When prosecuted, Prudhomme and Desmoulins promptly retracted but Gorsas contested the case, lost and was eventually sentenced to a 20 *livre* fine plus the costs of a public retraction.[24] Two months later Desmoulins was fined 10,000 *livres* for allegations of corruption made against a tithe colector and, in June, was compelled to make a public apology for calling the duc de Crillon a 'citoyen douteux et anti-Jacobin' in order to avoid a 100,000 *livre* fine that would have broken him. In the following month he had to retract allegations made against the court itself, to avoid a 10,000 *livre* fine.[25] The radical press was certainly not alone in suffering in this way, but it was the hardest hit, and other cases—including one involving Fréron shortly after he had started up the *Orateur du Peuple*—led to the formation on Loustallot's initiative of a *société des amis de la liberté de la presse* which first met in July 1790 at the

Cordeliers club. Chaired by Danton, it included Desmoulins, Loustallot, Marat and the Swiss financier Clavière among its fifty or so members, and set to work immediately to draw up a 'mathematical' defence of press liberty for submission to the National Assembly. What happened to this we do not know, but the *société* appears to have met spasmodically until at least October before finally disbanding.[26] Perhaps the abolition of the Châtelet in the judicial reforms of the autumn of 1790 did away with the very reason for its existence, and indeed prosecutions appear to have diminished during the latter months of 1790. However Marat and Fréron experienced problems in December, and the Champ de Mars massacre in the following July was to lead to arbitrary arrests and closures which hit the left and right wing press alike.

One final unifying aspect of the radical press, perhaps implicit in what has gone before, was its heavy Parisian concentration. The history of the provincial press during the revolution remains to be written, but it is clear that the majority of new journals that sprang up in so many towns throughout France between the autumn of 1789 and the spring of 1792 were moderately patriotic, and favourable towards the liberal reforms of these early years. There are occasional cases of right-wing or counter-revolutionary papers, but they were all short-lived, and none carried the same influence as their more glittering Parisian counterparts.[27] On the other hand, only a few towns saw a genuinely radical press. In Lyons a *Journal de la société populaire des amis de la constitution* appeared during the first four months of 1791, and a printer named Prudhomme, related to the owner of the *Révolutions de Paris*, launched a *Moniteur de Lyon* in April of the same year, rapidly raising several hackles by his acerbic comment. In Marseilles a future Girondin, Barbaroux, was on the editorial board of the *Observateur marseillais* in the summer of 1790, while in Avignon the pro-French radical party found support from Sabin Tournal's *Courrier d'Avignon* and Paul Capon's *Courrier du Midi*, both editors themselves being active in the conflict over annexation by France. In Strasbourg the *Courrier de Strasbourg*, which began publication in December of 1791, voiced the views of a radical faction within a badly divided club, while elsewhere there were radical newspapers too in Périgueux, Angers, Aurillac and Montpellier. But, taken as a whole, these titles form only a minority of provincial press and it was Paris, placed at the hub of political affairs and at the centre of a national postal distribution network, which had the greatest influence. The *Patriote Français* with possibly 10,000 subscribers as early as the end of 1789, soon established its strongest clientele in Paris, the future federalist areas of Lyons, the Bouches-du-Rhône and the Gironde, the frontier departments of the north-east and the departments of the Bas-Rhin and the Isère.[28] The *Révolutions de Paris*, with a much larger circulation figure in its early months, was strong too in the Paris area, the Gironde and the north-east, but also had a sizeable readership in the Seine-Maritime and the other Norman departments, as well as in the central departments and the Midi.[29] Marat, within months of his first number, had readers from as far apart as Charleville and Marseilles, Vannes and Mountpellier, Tours and Belvès, building up his print run to over 4,000 within a year. By this time too, in the winter of 1790–91, the *Orateur du Peuple* printed some 15,000 copies daily, while the readership for Carra's *Annales patriotiques* was not far behind, strong on the ground in the Midi, the Gironde and the Parisian area.[30] Tiny figures by modern standards, they were nevertheless sizeable totals for the eighteenth century, when illiteracy debarred over half the population from access to the printed word. Moreover, they form only the tip of the iceberg as for every person who subscribed there were probably four or five others who read every copy because of club or group subscriptions, or through the simple practice of circulating copies to friends. Public reading sessions too enabled many of the illiterate to hear what they could not read, and so participate in political debate.

The massacre of the Champ de Mars in July 1791 marked a turning point in the development of the radical press. Some titles closed down, such as the *Révolutions de France et de Brabant* which finished publication on 25 July as Desmoulins, active at the Cordeliers in the agitation leading to the fateful petition, went into hiding. Others, such as the *Père Duchesne*, suspended publication for a short time, while Marat went to the provinces and abandoned his *Ami du Peuple* in late September, despairing of the future until marriage brought a fresh flow of hope and funds in the following spring. Several journalists, along with their printers, were briefly arrested, but procedures were cut short by the amnesty which accompanied the promulgation of the constitution in mid-September.[31] More significant in the long run, however, was the fact that the king's flight to Varennes had brought France's relations with Europe, and the prospect of war, to the forefront of political affairs and it was this issue more than any other which dominated the debates of the newly elected Legislative Assembly when it first met in October 1791 and largely determined the future course of the revolution itself. For the war issue—with its attendant social, economic and political pressures—split radicals into Jacobins and Girondins, leading to the overthrow of the monarchy, the *journée* of 2 June 1793 and the subsequent emergence of the revolutionary government of Year II. The path to the Terror affected the press as a whole, leading to the outlawing of royalist journals in December 1792, and legislation in March and September 1793 which rendered journalists liable to arrest for a wide variety of political offences. It also affected the radical press more specifically, as newspapers reflected political divisions. The *Patriote Français*, increasingly dominated by the enthusiasm of its new editor-in-chief, Girey-Dupré, who rose to prominence as Brissot abandoned much of his control on entering the Legislative Assembly, became a leading Girondin newspaper. So too did Gorsas' *Courrier*, while the *Annales Patriotiques* and the *Révolutions de Paris*, although less openly committed, rapidly moderated many of their radical views and opposed the growth of *sansculotte* influence.[32] Hébert, Marat and Audouin, on the other hand, allied themselves to the less popular cause of radical Jacobin-inism, articulated by the Mountain within the Convention, and were helped by the emergence of some new titles in the winter of 1792–3, including the *Républicain*—launched by a Rennes printer Réné Vatar in November 1792 and later to change title to the *Journal des hommes libres*—and the *Batave*, launched by a group of Dutch exiles in February 1793.[33] Although largely outnumbered in both readership and influence at first, the Jacobin press was thrust into prominence by the *journée* of 2 June 1793 which saw the expulsion from the Convention of the leading Girondin deputies. Most of the leading Girondin papers rapidly disappeared, as Brissot, Gorsas, Carra and others were arrested and executed, while those few that did survive carefully paid lip-service to the new political orthodoxies. In their place the radical Jacobin press rapidly expanded, often with government support. The Committee of Public Safety, for example, secretly established its own daily newspaper in August 1793, the *Feuille de Salut Public*, while the Paris Jacobin club founded the *Journal de la Montagne*, which was soon followed by newspapers established by provincial clubs in Limoges, Douai, Toulouse, Rheims, Marseilles, Nancy, Châlons-sur-Marne and Bordeaux.[34] Army commanders published newspapers for their troops in areas where they were involved in the repression of civil war or of federalism, while in Perpignan the army of the Pyrenees, facing a Spanish invasion threat, had its own newspaper in the spring of 1794 to revive troop morale. Representatives on mission in the provinces followed suit in cities such as Marseilles and Lyons, in an effort to encourage local Jacobin minorities and win over converts, while substantial amounts were paid out by the Committee of Public Safety, the Provincial Executive Council and the Ministry of War in the form of subscriptions to independent radical titles such as the *Père Duchesne,* the *Journal de la Montagne* or the *Journal universel* for distribution throughout the country.[35]

A radical press established or supported by the political establishment was an important innovation of the Terror, but there was also a radical press which remained outside the establishment, and critical of it, for at least some part of the period. The Enragé newspapers, the *Ami du Peuple* and the *Publiciste* established by Leclerc and Roux after the death of Marat in July 1793 in an effort to don the martyr's reputation in order to spur the Convention on to more radical social and economic measures, are an early example of this. The *Père Duchesne* was then spurred by their rivalry into radicalising its own stance in order to retain its influence and audience, campaigning for economic and political change in August and September 1793, then joining the dechristianisation campaign in November. The consequent growth in Hébert's influence was then a factor in the appearance of the *Vieux Cordelier*, launched in Frimaire of Year II by Camille Desmoulins to spearhead the indulgent counter-offensive for a diminution of the terror and a return to liberal democracy. None were successful in their aims, and their editors either ended up dead—Hébert and Desmoulins on the guillotine, Roux committing suicide in prison—or hidden in protective obscurity, like Leclerc in the anonymity of the army. Nevertheless they bear witness to the way in which the press could remain, for at least part of the Terror, an outlet for political criticism and it may well be that further analysis of other titles will reveal a greater degree of unorthodox political radicalism than has so far been suspected.[36]

The collapse of the Terror after Robespierre's arrest and execution in Thermidor of Year II marked an end to the radical phase of the revolution. The radical press survived, though in a markedly more hostile atmosphere, and played an important role in the survival of Jacobinism during the difficult years of the Directory. But that role in itself requires a separate study. What had the radical press achieved, then, by 1794? What was its political impact and what its wider significance for the development of radicalism?

Any answer to these questions requires the press to be viewed in the wider context of the political media and its propaganda, for the years between 1789 and 1794 saw a wide variety of methods used by different groups for the mobilisation of political opinion. Speeches, sermons, public readings, pamphlets, music, song and dance, festivals, games, architecture, town planning, art, sculpture, pottery, playing cards and jewellery—all had a part to play in the celebration of the revolutionary event and the building of the new Jerusalem. Newspapers were just one medium among many, but they were an important one nevertheless, for the written word could carry a more sophisticated message than the spoken voice, visual imagery or music, while regular appearance enabled them to provide a more continuous commentary on news than pamphlets. As Brissot had noted in 1789 in his reference to the American, Irish and British experience, the press was a potentially powerful political weapon and one which governments were naturally anxious to control. Not all newspapers were political and not all journalists saw their role as leaders of opinion. For some it was merely a job that provided much-needed money, while for others it was a business enterprise which, to survive, steered clear of the contentious and controversial. Yet for most, including the radical journalists reviewed in this article, it was a means of making a political statement and of publicising a political cause. The radical press was consequently an ideological press which helped to give life and continuity to democratic ideas in a country which, unlike Britain or the newly-formed United States of America, had no long heritage of constitutional democratic thought and action on which to draw. It provided information and comment to the literate—and through them to the illiterate—and helped to throw down the roots of a radical democratic tradition which was to become an important component of French political culture. It also served in the short term as an apprenticeship for political activists in both Paris and the provinces, providing many with the springboard for later political careers. Camille Desmoulins communicated this new sense of the journalist's role in the second number of his *Révolutions de France et de Brabant* in December 1789:

> Here I am a journalist, and it is a rather fine role. No longer is it a wretched and mercenary profession enslaved by the government. Today in France it is the journalist who holds the tablets, the album of the censor, and who inspects the senate, the consuls and the dictator himself.[37]

His optimism proved premature, as he himself discovered when he attempted to 'inspect' the 'senate, the consuls and the dictator himself' in the dark winter of 1793–4. Yet in the long run the link that had sprung up between political life and journalism was there to stay. The Jacobin press of the Directory was to strengthen that link still further and bequeath it to the nineteenth century.[38]

Notes

1. Suzanne Tucoo-Chala, *Charles-Joseph Panckoucke et la librairie française 1736–1798* (Pau-Paris, 1977), part iv.
2. *Le Patriote français ou Journal libre, impartial et national, par une société de citoyens, le 16 mars 1789*, p. 1.
3. P. Laborie, *Étude sur le Patriote Français,* (Diplôme d'Études Supérieures Toulouse, 1959–60); G. Villacèque, *Les Révolutions de Paris. Journal patriote 1789–1790,* (Diplôme d'Études Supérieures, Toulouse, 1961); Max Fajn, *The Journal des hommes libres de tous les pays 1792–1800,* (The Hague and Paris, 1975); Jack Richard Censer, *Prelude to power. The Parisian radical press 1789–1791* (Baltimore and London, 1976). For the right-wing press, see W.J. Murray, *The right-wing press in the French Revolution 1789–1792,* (Ph.D., Australian National University, 1971) and Jeremy D. Popkin, *The right-wing press in France, 1792–1800,* (Chapel Hill, 1980).
4. C. Bellanger and others (ed.), *Histoire générale de la presse française,* (5 vols, Paris, 1969–1976), i, 405–37; A. Chuquet, 'Les journaux de Paris en 1789' in *Feuilles d'histoire du XVIIe au XXe siècle,* i (1909), pp 219–227.
5. *Patriote Français,* no. 511, (1 Jan. 1791), p. 1; Loustallot followed a similar style in the *Révolutions de Paris,* and see also Desmoulins' comments in the *Révolutions de France et de Brabant,* xiv. p. 263.
6. Laborie, *Étude,* pp 139, 142–7; *Révolutions de France et de Brabant,* ix, pp 426–9; L. Gottschalk, *Marat* (Chicago and London, 1927), p. 104; Louis Guibert, *Un journaliste girondin* (Limoges, n.d.), p. 49; Jules Claretie, *Camille Desmoulins, Lucille Desmoulins, étude sur les dantonistes d'après des documents nouveaux et inédits* (Paris, 1875), pp 85–6.
7. Robert Darnton, *Mesmerism and the end of the Enlightenment in France* (Cambridge (Mass.), 1968), pp 83–125; see also two of Darnton's articles, 'The Grub Street style of revolution: J.-P. Brissot, police spy' in *Jn. Mod. Hist.,* xl (1968), pp 301–27 and 'The high enlightenment and the low life of literature in pre-revolutionary France' in *Past & Present,* li (1971), pp 81–115. For Carra, see Michael Kennedy, 'The development of a political radical, Jean-Louis Carra 1742–1787' in *Proceedings of the third annual meeting of the western society for French history,* (Texas, 1976), pp 142–150; for Fréron, see Raoul Arnaud, *Journaliste, sans-culotte et thermidorien. Le fils de Fréron 1754–1802. d'après des documents inédits* (Paris, 1909).
8. There is no good biography of Prudhomme, but see his own autobiographical sketch in *L. Prudhomme aux patriotes. Le 13 juin 1793, l'an II de la République française* (Paris, n.d.); also L.-G. Michaud, *Biographie universelle,* (2nd ed., 45 vols, Paris, 1854–65) xxxiv, 427–8; Fr. Greppo, 'Un lyonnais imprimeur et journaliste: le journal, les *Révolutions de Paris*' in *Revue lyonnaise,* 5e série, xxix (1900), pp 42–3. For Audouin, see *Dictionnaire de biographie française,* fasc. 20, (Paris, 1947), pp 433–5, and the comments of the former lieutenant-

general of police for Paris in his memoirs preserved in the Bibliothèque Municipale of Orléans (MS 1421): 'Audouin, se disant avocat, faiseur de nouvelles à la main, colporteur de livres défendus; il s'est associé avec Prudhomme, Manuel et autres mauvais auteurs et colporteurs. Il est de tout métier; il sera espion quand on le voudra'.

9. See for example the pre-revolutionary activity of the editor of the counter-revolutionary *Journal général de la cour et de la ville* in Armand Lods, 'Un journaliste de la révolution, le Petit Gautier' in *La Révolution française*, lxiii (1912), pp 506–12.

10. Guibert, *Un journaliste girondin*, pp 1–33; Septime Gorceix, 'Antoine-Joseph Gorsas, journaliste et conventionnel (1752–1793)' in *Information historique* (1953), pp 179–80.

11. L. Jacob, *Hébert, le Père Duchesne, chef des sans-culottes* (Paris, 1960), chs i, ii; F. Braesch, *Le Père Duchesne d'Hébert. Édition critique avec une introduction. Tome 1. Les origines-la Constituante* (Paris, 1938), pp 22–9, 89–90.

12. For Robert and Kéralio, see P.-J. Levot, *Biographie bretonne* (2 vols, Vannes, 1852–7), ii, 4–7; L. Antheunis, *Le conventionnel belge, François Robert (1763–1826), et sa femme Louise de Kéralio (1758–1822)* (Wetteren, 1955); and their marriage contract in Archives Nationales, Minuterie centrale, Étude Gobin, X, 786, which carries interesting detail on their respective family wealth. For what little is known of Loustallot, the best introductions are Marcellin Pellet, *Elysée Loustallot et les Révolutions de Paris (juillet 1789–septembre 1790)* (Paris, 1872) pp 1–4, & *Révolutions de France et de Brabant*, xlv, 253ff.

13. For a detailed analysis, see Censer, *Prelude to Power*, ch. iii, *passim*.

14. *Mercure national*, xlii (26 Nov. 1790), p. 1623; *Patriote français*, ix (6 Aug. 1789), pp 3–4; xvi (14 Aug.) pp 3–4; xxv (24 Aug.), pp 2–3 etc; *Révolutions de Paris*, iii, 108–12; xvii, 2–19; xx, 11–19.

15. Laborie, *Étude*, pp 186–95; *Révolutions de Paris*, xxxi, 6 and xxxviii, 25.

16. Censer, *Prelude to Power*, ch. v. *passim:* for the importance of the districts, see R.B. Rose, 'The Paris districts and direct democracy' in *Bulletin of the John Rylands Library*, lxi (1979), pp 422–43.

17. *Père Duchesne*, no. 3, (6 Jan. 1791); G. Walter, *La révolution française vue par ses journaux* (Paris, 1947), pp 99ff.

18. Censer, *Prelude to power*, pp 66–7; F-A. Aulard, *The French Revolution. A political history 1789–1804* (4 vols, London, 1918), i ch. iv. For Brissot's view, see *Patriote Français* no. 498, (20 Dec. 1790), pp 3–4; Loustallot's disillusionment is traced in Villacèque, *Révolutions de Paris*, pp 155–6, while, for Robert, see Antheunis, *Le conventionnel belge*, pp 16ff.

19. Loc. cit.; for Robert's political involvement over the summer of 1791 see also A. Mathiez, *Le club des Cordeliers pendant la crise de Varennes et le massacre du Champ de Mars* (Paris, 1910). For Brissot, see his *Mémoires (1754–1793), publiés avec étude critique et notes. Par Claude Perrot* (2 vols, Paris, 1911).

20. Mathiez, *Le club des Cordeliers*, pp 1–13; N. Hampson, *Danton* (London, 1978), pp 31–2.

21. Martine Abdallah-Pretceille, *L'Ami du Peuple et ses correspondants* (Mémoire de maîtrise, Université de Paris I, 1975), pp 74–5.

22. *Révolutions de France et de Brabant*, x, 465–6. Fréron rented out a small appartment at no. 1, place du Théâtre Français in August 1790, inheriting with its furniture a plaster bust of Lafayette which, no doubt, was soon disposed of (Archives Nationales, Minuterie centrale, Etude Giard, xviii, 891).

23. Alma Soderjhelm, *Le régime de la presse pendant la révolution française* (2

vols., Helsinki and Paris, 1900–1901, i, ch. iii *passim.*

24. Eugene Hatin, *Histoire politique et littéraire de la presse en France*, (8 vols, Paris, 1859–61), iv, 193–204; *Révolutions de France et de Brabant*, ix, 387–407.
25. Ibid., xxxi, 323–50; Soderjhelm, *Le régime de la presse*, i, 215–17.
26. P. Vaillandet, 'Les débuts de la société des amis de la presse' in *Annales historiques de la révolution française*, vi (1926), pp 83–4; *Journal général de la cour et de la ville*, iv, no. 13 (13 Oct. 1790); *Révolutions de Paris*, lii (3–10 July, 1790), pp 237–9. Fears of a conspiracy against press liberty were not confined to the radical press: the *Chronique de Paris* voiced the fear on 2 July 1790 that there might be '...une ligue redoutable contre la liberté de la presse'.
27. In Arras, Caen and Limoges the *Affiches* of the *ancien régime* opposed most of the reform enacted in 1789–1790; the only other towns to see a right wing press were Lyons, Nîmes, Montauban, Toulouse, Arles, Troyes and Auxerre.
28. Laborie, *Étude*, pp 49–63.
29. Villacèque, *Révolutions de Paris*, pp 28–9, 196–200.
30. Archives Nationales, W292 (204), 3, 19; BB3 162, 'Affaire de Marat, Danton et autres'; Walter, *Marat*, p. 199; J.P. Gallais, *Catastrophe du club infernal et sa dénonciation par l'universel d'Audouin*, (Paris, n.d.), p. 18.
31. Hatin, *Histoire politique et littéraire*, iv, 113ff; Soderjhelm, *Le régime de la presse*, i, 186–8.
32. Michael Kennedy has argued persuasively that Carra attempted to hold an independent line in his 'L'Oracle des Jacobins des departements: Jean-Louis Carra et ses "Annales patriotiques"', in A. Soboul ed., *Actes du colloque Girondins et Montagnards* (Paris, 1980), pp 252–3; Prudhomme made the same claims for himself in *L. Prudhomme aux patriotes*, (Paris, 1793), p. 14. Yet this was not what the leading Jacobins of the time believed for, although the *Patriote Français* and the *Chronique de Paris* were the Girondin journals that they most frequently denounced, both the *Annales patriotiques* and *Révolutions de Paris* occur frequently too: see *Dubois–Crancé, Dialogue entre le Père Duchesne et Carra sur l'état actuel de la République française* (Paris, 1793), and *Le mensonge et la vérité ou l'antidote de la calomnie, nouveau journal par un ami de la liberté et de l'égalité*, no. ii, p. 6.
33. Fajn, *The Journal des hommes libres*, pp 17–25; Robespierre too contributed his own *Lettres à ses commettans* between October 1792 and April 1793.
34. F.-Aulard, 'La presse officieuse sous la terreur' in *Études et leçons sur la revolution francaise*, i (Paris, 1893), 229–34; Archives Nationales, AFII 66 reg. 484, 2–5, 8–11, 33; H. Gough, 'Les Jacobins et la presse: le "Journal de la Montagne" (juin 1793-brumaire an III)' in Soboul, *Girondins et Montagnards*, pp 269–76; P. Caron, 'Les publications officieuses du Ministère de l'intérieur en 1793 et 1794' in *Revue d'histoire moderne et contemporaine*, xiv (1910), pp. 5–43.
35. Marc Martin, *Les origines de la presse militaire en France à la fin de l'ancien régime et sous la révolution, 1770–1799*, (Vincennes, 1975), ch. iv; Archives Nationales, AFII reg. 484, 6, 12, 31 and 66; Aulard, 'La presse officieuse', pp 235–8; Caron, 'Les dépenses secrètes du conseil exécutif provisoire' in *La Révolution française*, lxxiii (1930), pp 234–5.
36. A. Soboul, *Les sans-culottes parisiens en l'an II* (Paris, 1958), pp 91–7.
37. *Révolutions de France et de Brabant*, ii, 46–7.
38. For the recovery of the Jacobin press during the Directory, see Isser Woloch, *Jacobin legacy. The democratic movement under the Directory* (Princeton, 1970).

The social composition of agrarian rebellions in early nineteenth-century Ireland: the case of the Carders and Caravats, 1813–16

James S. Donnelly, Jr

This essay addresses perhaps the thorniest problem connected with the study of pre-famine Irish agrarian rebellions: their social composition. It is such a thorny issue because the historical evidence bearing upon it is imperfect in many ways. These imperfections in the evidence, together with differences in methodological approaches to the problem, have led to a substantial degree of discordance in scholars' interpretations of the issue. The competing interpretations must briefly be set forth. For many years prior to the 1970s, and particularly in nationalist historiography, scholars could perceive little difference between the social bases of rural collective action before the great famine of the late 1840s and the class composition of the famous agrarian upheaval that began at the end of the 1870s under the aegis of the Land League. For both periods the battle lines were seen as essentially the same: in one camp oppressed tenant farmers, with holdings of small or middling size, and in the opposite camp rapacious landlords, meaning by that term chiefly proprietors belonging to the Protestant landed *élite*. In 1973, however, Joseph Lee insisted in a brief but highly influential essay that there was a world of difference between pre-famine agrarian unrest and the land war of the late nineteenth century.[1] Speaking of the earlier period, Lee observed: 'Despite the considerable tensions existing between farmers and landlords, the main struggle over most of the country did not occur between them but rather between labourers and cottiers on one side and farmers on the other'.[2] There was, in short, intense conflict *between* social classes below the landed *élite*, conflict over such issues as potato-garden (or conacre) rents, wages, and food prices.

This interpretation seemed to fit the kind of class structure that had developed in Ireland as a result of economic and demographic trends since 1750. At the top of the structure in 1841 there were approximately 50,000 rich and 100,000 'snug' farmers, the mean size of whose holdings was 80 and 50 acres respectively; together with the 10,000 or so landowners, they cultivated roughly half the land and controlled access to most of the rest. In the middle of the structure were 250,000 family farmers; the mean size of their holdings was about 20 acres, and they usually met their labour needs from within the family. At the bottom—the depressingly broad base of the social pyramid—were 1.3 million poor peasants and labourers. These poor peasants, or cottiers (300,000 with a mean holding of 5 acres), and the labourers (1,000,000 with a mean holding of one acre) both worked for wages and purchased food; in addition, most of the labourers hired conacre plots each year from the larger farmers or the landowners, who were also the chief employers.[3] In a society thus stratified, the potential for at least some class conflict of the type identified by Lee was obviously great.

Lee's interpretation was challenged, however, by Michael Beames in an article appearing in *Past and Present* in 1978.[4] From a detailed examination of twenty-seven agrarian murders in Co. Tipperary during the late 1830s and the 1840s, Beames concluded that class antagonism between labourers or cottiers and farmers was a much less potent source of violent conflict than Lee had maintained.[5] Instead, Beames stressed that disputes over the occupation of land were the leading cause of 'peasant assassinations', and in his recently published book he presents evidence purporting to show that such disputes gave rise to more agrarian crime than any other single factor or motive.[6] The aggrieved parties in these disputes, in his view, belonged especially to the class of small landholders, and their enemies were landlords—usually 'improving' landlords bent on the consolidation of farms—and their agents or servants.[7] These would-be modernisers of Irish agriculture, Beames seems to be saying, were threatening the survival of a distinct and solidary peasant community.

For different reasons David Fitzpatrick also finds fault with Lee's class-conflict thesis.[8] Fitzpatrick has closely studied an extraordinarily violent parish (Cloone) in Co. Leitrim during the 1830s and 1840s; his chief conclusion is that 'conflict *within* social strata was probably still more pervasive than conflict *between* strata'.[9] Speaking generally, he argues that the extreme scarcity of such

resources as land and employment in pre-famine Ireland regularly
pitted farmers against farmers, and labourers against labourers,
either as individuals or more often in rival groups or factions. This
emphasis on conflict *within* social strata is related to Fitzpatrick's
perception of pre-famine social stratification, which he sees as
much less static or rigid than either Lee or Beames—more like 'a
ladder which one could climb up or slip down', rather than 'a
pyramid on which each man felt he had been assigned (perhaps
unfairly) his proper station'.[10] Against Beames's notion of a solidary peasant community enforcing its ethical standards through
Whiteboyism, Fitzpatrick contends that rival factions repeatedly
masqueraded as communities.[11]

Despite Fitzpatrick's healthy iconoclasm, and despite Beames's
unintentional resurrection of something approaching the traditional
view, Lee's revisionist position is still dominant. With the important exception of the tithe war of the early 1830s, Samuel Clark
basically accepted Lee's thesis when treating rural collective action
before the famine in his important book of 1979, *Social origins of
the Irish land war*. Even more supportive of Lee's interpretation is a
carefully researched essay by Paul Roberts in the recently published collection entitled *Irish peasants*. In this essay Roberts argues
that the notorious but hitherto ill-understood feud between the
Caravats and Shanavests in east Munster during the early decades
of the nineteenth century was deeply rooted in class conflict over
access to land, employment, and food. As Roberts portrays this
feud, and his account is generally persuasive for the years 1806–11,
the Caravats were lower-class Whiteboys, comprising within their
ranks agricultural labourers, industrial workers, and smallholders.
The Shanavests, by contrast, though they included some farm
workers bound by economic ties to their employers, were drawn
from the rural middle class of farmers, publicans, and
shopkeepers, with large farmers usually in the ascendant. In response to the violent efforts of the Caravats to impose Whiteboy
'laws', the farmer-led Shanavests frequently formed vigilante organisations to keep the Caravat poor in check; they also established
factions that fought pitched battles with their lower-class enemies
at fairs, patterns, and other large public gatherings. Roberts
strongly suggests that the element of class conflict inherent in the
Caravat–Shanavest rivalry between 1806 and 1811 was recapitu-
lated in faction feuding and agrarian rebellion during the rest of
the early nineteenth century.[12]

All of these interpretations possess merit in varying degrees, but none of them does sufficient justice to the diversity and complexity of rural collective action before the famine. The principal weakness of the work of these scholars may be simply stated: it is that the interplay between economic fluctuations and the social composition of agrarian rebellions has not been adequately appreciated. Neither Beames nor Fitzpatrick shows any sustained concern with this issue. Both have chosen not to make particular agrarian movements or upheavals the focus of analysis, even though these waves of unrest accounted for by far the greater portion of the collective violence and intimidation that took place in early nineteenth-century Ireland. Both are too ready to generalise from limited sets of data: Beames (in his article at least) from the single crime of murder in only one county, and in a period when there was no major wave of unrest, Fitzpatrick largely from events in a single parish, albeit a very violent one. As a result, Fitzpatrick and especially Beames seem oblivious to the fact that a whole string of early nineteenth-century movements were essentially conflicts between the organised poor and substantial farmers or graziers. Into this category fall not only the Caravat-Shanavest rivalry illuminated by Roberts but also the Threshers of 1806–7, the so-called Ribbonmen of 1819–20, and above all the Terry Alts of 1828–31. In addition, every one of the three great upheavals — those of 1813–16, 1821–4, and the early 1830s — displayed considerable class conflict of the same kind.

While Beames and Fitzpatrick attach too little importance to class conflict, Roberts and Lee attach too much. Roberts tends to view the Caravat–Shanavest rivalry of 1806–11, a feud that erupted in a period of agricultural prosperity, as the paradigm of the outbreaks of Whiteboyism that marked the early nineteenth century.[13] Lee, on the other hand, puts forward the agrarian upheavals of 1813–16, 1821–4, and the early 1830s—all three fuelled by agricultural depression—as exemplifying the dominance of class conflict.[14] It is the central contention of this essay, however, that prosperity and depression influenced the social composition of agrarian rebellions in certain profound and differing ways. A drastically simplified version of the argument would run as follows. Movements that arose and thrived in periods of agricultural prosperity, when farm prices were buoyant and land values were rising sharply, were usually dominated by the landless and the land-poor, whose fortunes were adversely affected by the prevailing economic winds. Their participation in rebellion at such times is to be explained by their determination to restrain the inflation of conacre rents and food prices, to boost wages, and to frustrate the land-acquisitive tendencies of large farmers and graziers, tendencies which were especially pronounced during periods of strong economic expansion.[15] On the other hand, those agrarian upheavals that were fuelled by a drastic decline in agricultural prices were generally marked by a progressive widening in the social composition of the rebellious groups. In the context of depression, to be sure, the poor had many reasons to maintain their tradition of activism, but they were now less often preeminent among the agrarian rebels.

The agrarian upheaval of 1813–16 partly reflects the differential impact of prosperity and depression because it contained elements of both. In the midlands, where four counties (Roscommon, Longford, Westmeath and King's Co.) were eventually affected by serious unrest, the earliest disturbances actually took place during the winter of 1812–13, while agricultural prices were at or near the peak of the boom ignited by the Napoleonic wars.[16] The sources agree that the rebels (called Threshers or Carders) were cottiers and labourers exclusively. As one gentleman declared in February 1813, 'I cannot find that any person worth ten pounds is at all associated with these Threshers; at least it is the case in my neighbourhood [around Strokestown], and those with whom I communicate tell me the same'.[17] The chief objects of the Carders' hostility, observed another gentleman, were the farmers, who paid high rents and therefore demanded high prices for their crops.[18] (Mention of crops should not obscure the fact that this was mainly a grazing region.) The dominant issues here, both at the outset and later, were food prices, wages, conacre rents, and the eviction of smallholders—all pointing towards the class character of the conflict.[19] The same kind of class antagonism that animated the Carders in the midlands also galvanised rebels known as Caravats or John Does in the Kilkenny–Queen's Co. border country. This was another area in which the efforts of the poor to gain access to potato ground at affordable rates were often blocked or curtailed by the land-monopolising tendencies of chiefly pastoral farmers. In this region too, unrest began during the winter of 1812–13, well before the depression in agricultural prices commenced.[20] Conacre was not the only grievance here. Disputes over the occupation of land were a source of serious trouble as well. But in so far as we can tell, these again generally pitted the poor against wealthy farmers.[21]

The bloody vendetta against the notorious land grabber John Little is a prime example of such conflict. By 1814 Little had acquired at least four separate farms,[22] one of which he had taken from the gentleman Gorges Hely of Johnstown in the spring of 1812, when the sitting tenants refused to give what Hely considered the fair value of the land.[23] Late in the summer of 1812 there began a relentless series of reprisals against Little and his workers lasting almost two years. In October 1812 Little himself was seriously wounded while travelling to the fair of Cullahill. Subsequently, one of his herdsmen was severely beaten and forced to quit, and in April 1813 Ciarán Campion, a new herdsman hired by Little, was murdered in broad daylight. Hayricks belonging to Little were set on fire and sheep were stolen from his pastures.[24] But above all, his servants continued to suffer. (Little himself was by this time constantly protected by two soldiers.) In May 1814 a large Caravat band systematically visited his workmen (at least twelve in all), savagely beat them, and ordered them to leave or face death.[25]

The catalogue of violence connected with the Little affair was even more extensive than this. For apprehending and helping to prosecute seven persons allegedly involved in the reprisals against Little, the magistrate Robert St George was heavily punished. Under strict orders from the Caravats, almost all of his labourers quit, tradesmen refused their services, and St George was obliged to use soldiers to save his harvest in 1813.[26] Subsequently, two workers who had failed to leave as directed were flogged, a magistrate who had dined with the ostracised St George was badly wounded, St George's gardener was beaten almost to death, and finally, in February 1814, his steward James Sutcliffe was shot through the heart while lying in bed.[27]

Eventually, the authorities were able to secure convictions against some of the men reportedly concerned in this long string of related crimes.[28] One of those apprehended, a cooper's apprentice at Durrow named John Fitzpatrick, gave detailed information implicating his accomplices.[29] Though a police official impugned the accuracy of substantial portions of Fitzpatrick's story, he acknowledged that Fitzpatrick was 'well acquainted with most of the noted disturbers' of the Kilkenny–Queen's Co. border country.[30] It therefore seems reasonable to pay attention to the social status of the individuals identified by Fitzpatrick as his cohorts. Besides the landed gentleman Theophilus Chamberlain, an unusual class renegade and a very special case,[31] Fitzpatrick implicated a nailer, a publican, two small farmers (both said to hold seven acres), and four labourers. One of the two small farmers—John Peters of Grenan near Durrow—was, according to Fitzpatrick, the leader of the party of Caravats who had murdered John Little's herdsman

Ciarán Campion in April 1813.[32] It is not without significance that Little's vicissitudes from 1812 to 1814 spanned the transition from prosperity to depression.

With the onset of the depression in the autumn of 1813, forces were set in motion that considerably broadened the social basis of the agrarian unrest. All sections of Irish agriculture were hammered by the collapse of the wartime boom. Grain prices plummeted first, their fall beginning after the bumper harvest of 1813. Between 1812 and 1816 the average prices of wheat, oats, and barley at Dublin market slumped by 39, 51 and 53 per cent respectively.[33] Then came the turn of livestock producers. From rich graziers to poor cottiers, they also had ample cause for despair starting in 1814. Within two years British military demand for Irish salted beef and pork virtually disappeared. To judge from the contracts awarded to Irish provision merchants by the Victualling Board in London, beef and pork prices were more than halved between 1813 and 1816.[34] Dairy farmers were the last to suffer, and suffered least, but still grievously. Between 1814 and 1816 the price of Irish butter in London dropped from slightly over 130s. per cwt (a record long unsurpassed) to less than 90s., or by about one-third.[35]

The arrival of deep depression certainly did not lessen the participation of labourers and cottiers in agrarian rebellion, nor did it reduce class conflict. Whatever the poor gained from lower food prices tended to be outweighed by the contraction of opportunities for employment; hard-pressed farmers cut costs by dismissing workers or hiring fewer of them and by lowering wages. Furthermore, at the same time that pork prices collapsed (a very serious matter indeed for the pig-raising poor), conacre rents remained sticky even as other land rents gradually turned downward. Thus most of the same grievances that embittered relations between the poor and the rural middle class in times of agricultural prosperity were also pressed again in the very different climate of depression. Class conflict continued to predominate in the affected portions of the midlands, in the Kilkenny–Queen's Co. border country, in most of Limerick, in parts of Waterford, and in the Clare barony of Lower Bunratty.[36] In general, these were regions primarily devoted to pastoral farming, with much higher than average concentrations of underemployed agricultural workers. Yet by no means all of the lower-class Carders and Caravats were rural dwellers. There was a marked tendency for conflict over conacre rents to occur in the vicinity of towns and villages. This tendency reflects the fact that the town-based poor were especially dependent on the availability of potato ground at affordable prices in the surrounding rural area. And because of their physical concentration, the task of organisation was that much easier, particularly if common work tightened other social bonds.[37]

But precisely because the effects of agricultural depression were so far-reaching, they swept into rebel ranks not only labourers and cottiers but also many of those higher on the social scale. The involvement of substantial farmers (middling and large) and their sons was a commonly observed feature of the agrarian unrest in Tipperary and parts of Waterford, while in most of the disturbed districts of Clare Whiteboyism rested on a broad social basis. The situation in Clare is the least complicated. As already noted, sustained class conflict was typical only of one region of Clare—the barony of Lower Bunratty; most of it was devoted to pastoral agriculture, as befitted the best land in the county, and the position of labourers there was especially precarious.[38] With this exception, the most disturbed districts were those in southern and south-western parts of the county. Three baronies in this area (Clonderalaw, Moyarta, and Ibrickan) merited the application of the Peace Preservation Act.[39] Here the social structure was thick with small and middling tenants, regarded as a peasantry by the local landed *élite*. And here agriculture was strongly oriented towards tillage. When serious disturbances erupted in this region in 1815 and 1816, they revolved around classic landlord–tenant issues: arrears of rent, distraint, and evictions.[40] Tenant solidarity in the face of landlord demands was high. It was reflected in the general support which the Whiteboys were said to enjoy and almost certainly in the composition of their bands.[41] As one of the largest proprietors in south–west Clare put it in March 1816, 'This country is so thickly inhabited with the lower order of peasantry and so very few of a higher order that it is extremely difficult to suppress these disturbances'.[42] In fact, even larger farmers commonly associated themselves with Whiteboy operations in south–west Clare.[43] Their presence is one measure of how pervasive in this region was the desire of tenants in general to see rents reduced, evictions stayed, and renegade farmers punished for grabbing land.

In Co. Waterford the patterns of unrest were much more complicated than in Clare. With its conflict between social strata, battles within strata, and landlord–tenant disputes, Waterford provides ammunition for all schools of thought, including the revisionism propounded in this essay. The complexity of things arose from Waterford's variegated economy, topography, and social structure. It should first be noted that at the census of 1841 the ratio of farm workers per 100 farmers in Waterford (464) was the fifth highest of Ireland's thirty-two counties. Those counties with even higher ratios (Dublin, Kildare, Meath and Roscommon) were all closely connected with grazing.[44] Waterford's economy, by contrast, was basically a mixture of dairying and tillage, with some regional specialisation between the two sectors. Great portions of west and north–west Waterford are of course mountainous or hilly, whereas the eastern portion of the county and parts of the south-west are lowlands.[45] Dairying was pursued more extensively in the former areas, on upland or mountain pastures, tillage in the latter regions, though in neither was a rigid monoculture the rule. As one would expect in a county with such a high relative concentration of agricultural workers, large farmers with over thirty acres were quite numerous. In fact, they accounted in 1847 for nearly two-fifths of all holdings of an acre or more, and of course these large farmers controlled a still greater proportion of the arable area.[46] It is therefore not surprising that Waterford experienced widespread class conflict. This included attacks on dairymen and (less often) their masters, i.e., usually large tenants who hired out cows and land to the dairymen, much to the disgust of the poor.[47] It embraced numerous attacks on migrant workers coming from outside Waterford for the harvest, and (again less often) on their employers, typically the larger farmers.[48] And it comprised assaults against other so-called strangers of the labouring or cottier class who tried to settle down, or whose native place, after they had settled down, was remembered in lean times to be elsewhere.[49]

Yet hostility to strangers and dairymen was not nearly so productive of intimidation and violence in Waterford as depression-induced antagonism between landlords and tenants—both a very mixed species. Many such disputes, especially in the mountainous areas of west Waterford, pitted small and sometimes middling landholders, along with labourers, against large farmers, gentry middlemen, or proprietors.[50] But Caravatism in Waterford was by no means restricted to the mountainous regions of the county or to small tenants and labourers. One magistrate in the Kilmacthomas district described as 'very wealthy', 'wealthy', or 'in good circumstances' a whole string of farmers arrested for, or involved in, agrarian crimes early in 1813.[51] A second zealous magistrate near Cappoquin informed Dublin Castle at the end of 1814 that in Waterford the farmers were, as he put it, 'in league with' the Caravats. He flatly contradicted a newspaper report that farmers in the Cappoquin district were setting up armed associations in order to check the Caravats there. On the contrary, he declared, the alliance between farmers and Caravats made it enormously difficult to capture agrarian rebels even after informations had been lodged against them.[52] A third magistrate, when announcing in 1815 the apprehension of several Caravats whom he termed 'respectable farmers', insisted that he had finally got to the bottom of the villainy in the Tallow district. He was now perfectly convinced that farmers there were the instigators of outrages for the express purposes of obtaining land on their own terms and of preventing all persons from bidding except the current occupier, who was to have the ground at his own price.[53] Thus, even in a county where there was at this juncture little violence over the grievance of tithes,[54] an issue which frequently served to unify the poor and much better-off landholders, the participation of substantial farmers in agrarian rebellion was quite considerable.

Lastly, we come to Tipperary, where Whiteboyism, so to speak, was first invented, where it had its beginnings in the early 1760s, and where, during all the great waves of unrest in the early nineteenth century, there was intense agrarian activity. In its social structure Tipperary was not a county of extremes. With respect to the size of their holdings in 1847, its farmers were divided fairly evenly among the standard categories: 1–5 acres, 24 per cent; 5–15 acres, 31 per cent; 15–30 acres, 22 per cent; and over 30 acres, 23 per cent.[55] In addition, the ratio of farm workers per 100 farmers in 1841 perfectly matched the average for Ireland as a whole.[56] These basic facts about social structure help to explain why class conflict, though manifest especially in grazing areas of the county and around its numerous towns,[57] did not dominate the patterns of unrest between 1813 and 1816. Tipperary's agricultural economy was both highly diversified and highly commercialised. Its corn growers, along with its graziers and dairy farmers, marketed a relatively high proportion of what they produced, and though parts of the county (the south and north–west) were poorly endowed by nature, much of its land was among the best in the country.[58] Because of this strong market orientation, the agricultural depression struck Tipperary farmers with special severity.

In contrast to nearly all the other counties that experienced serious unrest between 1813 and 1816, Tipperary was convulsed by conflict over tithes. It is easy enough to explain why this grievance was largely dormant in some of the acutely disturbed counties.

Until after 1824, pasture land in Ireland was virtually exempt from tithes, and outside the Munster counties and a small part of Leinster, potatoes were also generally tithe-free.[59] Thus the slight concern with this issue in the four affected midland counties makes economic sense. But in Waterford and Clare, as well as in Kilkenny and Queen's Co., where tithes were indeed paid on grain and potatoes, confrontation over these clerical taxes from 1813 to 1816 remained quite limited.[60] Just why this issue should now have been so uneven in its geographical incidence is something of a mystery.

The most important point to appreciate about tithe is that of all agrarian grievances in the south of Ireland, it was the one most likely to cut across the lines of social class below the landed *élite*, the one that most often produced cooperation between social strata in times of depression and rebellion. It certainly did so in Tipperary, and chiefly for this reason the involvement of large farmers as agrarian activists was greater than anywhere else. Of the four Munster counties overtaken by serious unrest between 1813 and 1816, Tipperary experienced the most violence, including the highest number of agrarian murders.[61] The Cashel neighbourhood became notorious in this respect, and much of the violence there was concentrated in or near the parish of Clonoulty, described late in 1815 as 'the most lawless district' in all of Tipperary.[62]

Certain events in this parish and its immediate vicinity deserve extended consideration because they brightly illuminate important aspects of the problem under discussion here. On 7 September 1815 an unusual display of collective resistance to imminent government repression occurred at Ballagh: a body of over a hundred men, with the aid of sledges brought from the forges of local smiths, demolished a large house which had served as a medical dispensary but which was now scheduled to become a police barracks. In destroying the building, these rebels sought to prevent 'those vagabond Peelers' from being used to protect the tithe proctors of the district.[63] The exactions of one proctor in particular—William Dwyer, employed by the Rev. Robert Carew Armstrong, rector of Clonoulty—had aroused much bitterness. Dwyer received repeated notices warning him that he must prepare his coffin unless he quit his post. Cried the writer of one such notice, 'As to allow[ing] any infernal vagabond to be making riches by this thide [i.e., tithe] and distroying the country, by Christ I will not [permit it]....'.[64] Dwyer, however, refused to be intimidated. In fact, he personally tore down a denunciatory notice posted on the local Catholic chapel and openly bid defiance to his enemies, declaring that if 'the boys' were to pay him a threatening visit, he would surely make them suffer for it. His audacity stemmed from the fact that he was, 'as the term here is, a man of "great faction" in that part of the country'.[65] From this association with a large faction Dwyer acquired a false sense of security. Three days after the destruction of the Ballagh dispensary, he was shot to death within a few yards of his own door in Clonoulty village.[66]

By the time of these events Clonoulty and parts of adjacent parishes had already earned a reputation for murderous violence. In December 1813 in Ballintemple parish the gentleman George Wayland was wounded, and one of his servant boys killed, by an armed band only a short distance from his hall door. Wayland functioned as lieutenant of the Ballintemple yeomanry corps, a force which hunted down local Whiteboys, and this circumstance probably explains why he was the target of assassination.[67] In July 1814 in Ardmayle parish Captain Richard Long, another gentleman, was murdered, for reasons that remain unclear; two of the murderers were identified as residents of Clonoulty.[68] In the following month Isaac Fawcett, Jr, the son of a landowner living in Clonoulty parish, was waylaid and mortally wounded near Cashel; he had been a marked man, it was said, ever since Christmas day in 1813, when he and his brother had repelled a raid for arms on their father's house, killing at least one of the attackers and wounding others.[69] The deaths of Fawcett and Long, together with yet another murder at about the same time—that of William Meany, a waterguard employed by the Protestant archbishop of Cashel— drove the alarmed local magistrates to request that Middlethird barony be declared subject to the provisions of the Insurrection Act, a plea with which the government complied in September 1814.[70]

But nothing, it seemed, could halt the remorseless train of murders and shootings, which persisted in this district around Cashel over the next twelve months. In January 1815 Edmund Scully, a wealthy grazier and landlord, with eminent Catholic relatives, was shot and seriously wounded at Clonbonane in Clonoulty parish, apparently in reprisal for distraining the property of some of his defaulting tenants.[71] Other victims—all murdered—included three process servers, a tithe proctor, and the high constable of Kilnamanagh barony, adjacent to that of Middlethird.[72] In this last case, early in July 1815, Thomas Leahy, who as high constable was responsible for the collection of county cess and certain other public charges, was stoned to death at the fair of Clonoulty.[73] In none of these numerous instances of murder or shooting were the authorities able to bring any of the offenders to justice prior to 1816.

Limited information was available, however, about participants in a number of these crimes, and it pointed in a somewhat surprising direction. Soon after the murder of Isaac Fawcett, Jr, in August 1814, an anonymous informant reported it as well known in Clonoulty parish that three men named Keough, Leahy and Commin had been concerned in the abortive attack on the Fawcetts in December 1813, when one of the rebels was killed, and that these three persons, among others, had vowed to avenge the loss. Thomas Keough and Leahy were both sons of wealthy farmers, and Commin was himself the holder of a large farm.[74] Other evidence indicated that Keough and Commin were the killers of Captain Long, according to the police magistrate Richard Willcocks, who noted that Keough's father was worth as much as £500 per annum.[75] Taken into custody in November 1814, Thomas Keough was indicted for Long's murder at the spring assizes of the following year. Yet he was not then brought to trial, perhaps because the crown lawyers lacked reliable witnesses. The bail to which he was admitted—a sum of no less than £4,000—eloquently bespoke his social status.[76]

Although the authorities were foiled in the case of this rich farmer's son, they were not on the wrong track in their determined search for the chief offenders in Clonoulty parish. This was resoundingly demonstrated by the extraordinary breakthrough that occurred in the closing months of 1815. The revelations that led to this breakthrough came from Michael Dwyer and his son Malachi, the brother and nephew respectively of the murdered proctor of Clonoulty, William Dwyer. A publican and shopkeeper, Michael Dwyer had waited two months before making disclosures to the authorities, a delay which he plausibly explained by saying that he first wanted to dispose of a piece of land and to collect a considerable sum of money owed to him.[77] The information which he eventually supplied, however, was far-reaching and especially worthy of credit, since it was based largely on the direct involvement of his son Malachi with the rebels.[78] Moving swiftly, the authorities then arrested nine persons—all from the Clonoulty area—implicated by Dwyer in his brother's murder and in the destruction of the Ballagh dispensary. Reporting their apprehension to Dublin Castle, a police official remarked at the beginning of December, 'They are mostly full farmers' sons and are known to be the principal disturbers in that lawless district'.[79] The same observations could probably have been applied to another six men identified by Dwyer and taken into custody a few days later, though one of the six was said to be a smith who had brought his sledge to Ballagh for the demolition.[80] Included in the original group of nine prisoners was Patrick Keough, one of the reputed murderers of Captain Long and almost certainly a relative of that Thomas Keough indicted earlier for the same offence.[81]

That these prisoners generally came from solid farming stock was confirmed when they were put on trial at a special commission in Clonmel in January 1816. Patrick Keough, who had allegedly presided as captain of the band at Ballagh in the previous September, was described as a man 'of respectable connexions' whose family had 'a good property';[82] he was hanged for this crime opposite the ruins of the dispensary.[83] Among the fourteen other prisoners were four bearing the surname of Murphy. They belonged to 'the most powerful faction in that part of the country' and, like Patrick Keough, 'were connected by relationship with many persons of property and weight in the county... , particularly with the family of Scully'.[84]

The usefulness of such connections was now shown to good advantage. After Keough's conviction but before his execution, two unidentified friends of the Murphys—both 'very respectable men'—approached the authorities and asked to know whether and on what terms the fourteen other prisoners might be granted mercy if they pleaded guilty to the multiple capital charges against them.[85] When arraigned, they had entered pleas of innocence, but with the Dwyers ready to repeat the convincing performance given at Keough's trial, the prisoners had reason to fear the worst unless, as part of a bargain, they openly confessed their guilt. In return for their doing so, and for the surrender of arms by their comrades still at large, the government agreed to remit the death sentences formally passed upon them, with the condition that they all be transported beyond the seas for fourteen years.[86] The disclosures in the Clonoulty cases thus revealed that in this part of Tipperary there was a strong overlap in personnel and organisation between faction groups and agrarian bands, and that the leaders in both tended to be drawn from the upper section of the farming community.

Perhaps the Clonoulty neighbourhood was exceptional in the degree to which substantial farmers and their sons participated in this agrarian upheaval, just as it was certainly exceptional in the intensity of its violence. But the *Dublin Evening Post* was very wide of the mark when it told its readers in September 1815 that 'the disturbers of the county of Tipperary were of the lowest order in the community'.[87] Knowledgeable local observers often took a different view, not only because of the clear association of farmers with resistance to tithes, but also because of the growing inability or unwillingness of farmers to pay rents fixed in prosperous times.[88] As one Tipperary gentleman informed Dublin Castle at the end of 1815, 'the general distress of the farmers, proceeding from the great depression of the prices of grain and cattle, is likely to add more strength and importance to the existing confederacies than all their resolutions and oaths'. Referring specifically to leaseholders denied adequate abatements of their 'war rents', this gentleman declared, 'The working farmers find themselves hurled into a state of despair and are believed at present *to be combining to resist the payment of their rents with arms in their hands...*'.[89] The principal outgrowth of this radicalisation of farmers' attitudes was that when landlords distrained the livestock or crops of defaulting tenants, agrarian bands appeared and forcibly rescued the goods. Along with the collective removal of property about to be seized in satisfaction of unpaid rent, this type of Whiteboy activity became almost a mania in 1815 and 1816 in Tipperary and other disturbed southern counties. 'A hint of distraining is enough from the landlord', remarked a magistrate at the end of 1815, when cries of general agricultural insolvency filled the air; 'the stock and grain', he observed, 'are instantly carried off and any number of carts immediately procured to effect it'.[90]

In its social composition, then, the agrarian upheaval of 1813–16 defies analysis in mainly one-dimensional terms. Economic fluctuations were of major importance, but they interacted with the nature of the social structure in particular regions. In the affected midland counties as well as in the Kilkenny–Queen's Co. border country, violence first broke out while prosperity that disadvantaged the poor still reigned, and members of the farming *élite* were among the principal victims. Even after the depression began, these midland grazing areas, as well as pastoral districts in the affected Munster and Leinster counties, continued to be dominated by class conflict, with little broadening in the social composition of the rebellious groups. In these regions, where the social stratification was marked by sharp cleavages between the swollen ranks of the poor and a relatively small body of rich landholders, there was a pronounced tendency for agrarian conflict to express itself chiefly in terms of the polar class interests of these groups. But in large portions of Clare, Waterford and Tipperary the effects of the depression served to give Whiteboyism a broad social basis. In south-west Clare the process of social differentiation below the land-owning *élite* had made only modest headway. Rural communities there, thick as they were with small and middling tenants, were able to achieve a high degree of solidarity against landlord claims to the much diminished peasant surplus. In Waterford, on the other hand, social differentiation among non-landowners was extreme by comparison with Clare, leading to much more extensive class conflict. Yet even in Waterford the issues of rent, distraint, and control over the occupation of land brought numerous large farmers or their sons into rebel ranks. And this phenomenon of large-farmer involvement reached its highest level in Tipperary, where the socially unifying goal of tithe reduction was added to the demands for the restraining of rents and evictions.

Notes

1. Joseph Lee, 'The Ribbonmen' in T.D. Williams (ed.), *Secret societies in Ireland* (Dublin, 1973), pp 26–35.
2. Ibid., p. 28.
3. The figures in this paragraph, derived from data in the 1841 census and intended to indicate rough orders of magnitude, were kindly provided by Dr Cormac Ó Gráda of University College, Dublin, to whom I am greatly indebted for permission to use them here.
4. M.R. Beames, 'Rural conflict in pre-famine Ireland: peasant assassinations in Tipperary, 1837–1847' in *Past & Present*, 81 (Nov. 1978), pp 75–91.
5. Ibid., pp 85, 88.
6. M.R. Beames, *Peasants and power: the Whiteboy movements and their control in pre-famine Ireland* (Brighton and New York, 1983), pp 124–5.
7. Beames, 'Rural conflict', pp 88–9.
8. David Fitzpatrick, 'Class, family, and rural unrest in nineteenth-century Ireland' in P.J. Drudy (ed.), *Irish studies 2: Ireland: land, politics, and people* (Cambridge, 1982), pp 37–75.
9. Ibid., p. 44 (emphasis added).
10. Ibid., p. 53.
11. Ibid., p. 47.
12. P.E.W. Roberts, 'Caravats and Shanavests: Whiteboyism and faction fighting in east Munster, 1802–11' in Samuel Clark and J.S. Donnelly, Jr (ed.), *Irish peasants: violence and political unrest, 1780–1914* (Madison, Wis., and Manchester, 1983), pp 64–101.
13. Ibid., pp 64, 66, 95–8. Roberts concedes, however, that 'the worsening economic condition of the rural middle class after 1813 created a more fertile soil for cooperation across class divisions' (p. 98).
14. Lee does not claim that 'the main waves of Ribbon activity' represented class conflict exclusively, but he views cottiers as having constituted 'the backbone of Ribbon societies' during the major agrarian upheavals of the early nineteenth century ('The Ribbonmen', pp 27–8).
15. Roberts, 'Caravats and Shanavests', pp 81–5.

16. S.P.O., State of the Country Papers, ser. 1 (hereafter cited as S.O.C.P.1), 1813/1535/2; 1813/1538/16; *Dublin Evening Post* (hereafter cited as *D.E.P.*), 30 June 1814.

17. George Devenish to Robert Peel, 6 Feb. 1813 (S.P.O., S.O.C.P.1, 1538/16).

18. S.P.O., S.O.C.P.1, 1813/1535/2.

19. S.P.O., S.O.C.P.1, 1813/1535/1, 3, 11, 20, 30; 1814/1564/38, 42–3, 46, 55; 1815/1720/20, 61; 1816/1767/43; *D.E.P.*, 13 Apr., 12 June 1813, 30 June 1814; *Ennis Chronicle and Clare Advertiser* (hereafter cited as *E.C.C.A.*), 8 June 1814.

20. Threatening notices enclosed in Memorial of the magistrates of Kilkenny and Tipperary to Attorney General William Saurin, 17 Jan. 1813 (S.P.O., S.O.C.P.1, 1531/2).

21. S.P.O., S.O.C.P.1, 1814/1554/9, 15; 1815/1712/20–2, 26–7; 1816/1761/22, 32.

22. S.P.O., S.O.C.P.1, 1814/1560/47.

23. S.P.O., S.O.C.P.1, 1814/1554/34.

24. Ibid.

25. S.P.O., S.O.C.P.1, 1814/1554/14; 1814/1550/47.

26. S.P.O., S.O.C.P.1, 1813/1554/88.

27. S.P.O., S.O.C.P.1, 1813/1531/22; 1814/1560/17, 23; *E.C.C.A.*, 2 Mar. 1814.

28. S.P.O., S.O.C.P.1, 1814/1554/26, 29–30; 1815/1712/18; 1815/1721/117.

29. Information of John Fitzpatrick, 14 Nov. 1815 (S.P.O., S.O.C.P.1, 1712/34).

30. Edward Wilson to Robert Peel, 18 Nov. 1815 (S.P.O., S.O.C.P.1, 1722/80).

31. For Chamberlain, see S.P.O., S.O.C.P.1, 1814/1563/16, 18–19; 1815/1712/34.

32. S.P.O., S.O.C.P.1, 1815/1712/34. For evidence confirming the general accuracy of Fitzpatrick's description of the social status of Caravats in his area, see S.P.O., S.O.C.P.1, 1814/1554/36, 40; 1814/1563/23–4.

33. *D.E.P.*, 15 Apr. 1819.

34. In 1813, a year which livestock producers would long remember for its prosperity, the Victualling Board in London awarded to Irish provision merchants contracts totalling 47,000 tierces of beef at an average price of nearly £11 per tierce and over 56,000 tierces of pork at an average price of nearly £12 4s. By 1816, however, the Victualling Board secured all the salted beef and pork that it needed from Ireland—a mere 13,000 tierces altogether—for as little as £5 5s. per tierce (*Report from the select committee on agriculture, with the minutes of evidence taken before them, and an appendix and index*, app. no. 6, p. 631, H.C. 1833 (612), v, 1).

35. John O'Donovan, *The economic history of livestock in Ireland* (Cork, 1940), p. 153.

36. For Co. Limerick, see S.P.O., S.O.C.P.1, 1814/1556/16, 23, 31; 1815/1717/15, 17; 1816/1770/14, 18; *Limerick Evening Post* (hereafter cited as *L.E.P.*), 20, 23 Apr. 1814, 12, 29 Apr. 1815, 16 May, 4 July 1816; *D.E.P.*, 5 May 1814; *E.C.C.A.*, 12 June 1816. For Lower Bunratty in Clare, see, e.g., S.P.O., S.O.C.P.1, 1813/1534/4, 8; 1813/1540/10; *E.C.C.A.*, 2, 9 Apr. 1814. A survey of contemporary sources between 1813 and 1816 yields for all of Clare a total of thirty-two reports of acts of violence or intimidation which were certainly or probably committed by labourers or cottiers. (The sources include *E.C.C.A.*, *L.E.P.*, and S.O.C.P.1.) As many as eighteen of these reports concern events that took place in Lower Bunratty. The area included within the bounds of this barony was almost all fine limestone land, most of it devoted to pastoral agriculture. This was especially true of the rich meadows and grazing grounds called corcasses along the Fergus and the Shannon. See

Hely Dutton, *Statistical survey of the county of Clare* . . . (Dublin, 1808), pp 11–12.

37. Besides the sources cited for Co. Limerick in note 36, see S.P.O., S.O.C.P.1, 1815/1721/42. See also Roberts, 'Caravats and Shanavests', pp 75–8.

38. See note 36 above.

39. *Copy of a dispatch from his excellency the lord lieutenant of Ireland to Lord Viscount Sidmouth, dated 5th June 1816, viz, a statement of the nature and extent of the disturbances which have recently prevailed in Ireland, and the measures which have been adopted by the government of that country in consequence thereof*, p. 9, H.C. 1816 (479), ix, 567.

40. See, e.g., S.P.O., S.O.C.P.1, 1815/1714/46; 1816/1768/6–7, 10–11, 13; *D.E.P.*, 2 July 1816.

41. S.P.O., S.O.C.P.1, 1816/1768/11.

42. John O. Vandeleur to [?], 2 Mar. 1816 (S.P.O., S.O.C.P.1, 1768/6).

43. S.P.O., S.O.C.P.1, 1815/1714/46–7; 1816/1768/30, 38; *D.E.P.*, 19 Oct. 1815.

44. David Fitzpatrick, 'The disappearance of the Irish agricultural labourer, 1841–1912' in *Irish Economic and Social History*, vii (1980), p. 88.

45. T.W. Freeman, *Ireland: its physical, historical, social, and economic geography* (London and New York, 1950), chap. 14, *passim*.

46. *Returns of agricultural produce in Ireland in the year 1847, pt ii: stock*, pp 12–13, H.C. 1847–8 [1000], lvii, 109.

47. S.P.O., S.O.C.P.1, 1813/1540/24, 32, 34.

48. S.P.O., S.O.C.P.1, 1813/1540/25; 1814/1566/68.

49. S.P.O., S.O.C.P.1, 1813/1540/22–3.

50. S.P.O., S.O.C.P.1, 1813/1540/35, 40, 51; 1814/1559/32; 1814/1566/18, 37, 49, 66; 1815/1719/1, 8, 25–6, 44, 50; *L.E.P.*, 22 Dec. 1813, 10 Aug. 1814, 26 July 1815; *E.C.C.A.*, 10, 20 Aug. 1814.

51. See the letters of H. St George Cole to William Gregory, 7 Jan., 22 Apr., 25 May, 1 June 1813 (S.P.O., S.O.C.P.1, 1540/20, 36, 43–4).

52. Richard English to William Gregory, 10 Dec. 1814 (S.P.O., S.O.C.P.1, 1566/89).

53. Robert W. Gumbleton to Robert Peel, 7 Sept. 1815 (S.P.O., S.O.C.P.1, 1719/56). For other evidence pointing to the involvement of farmers, see S.P.O., S.O.C.P.1, 1814/1566/16, 38; 1815/1719/71; *L.E.P.*, 17 Jan. 1816.

54. The murder of the tithe proctor Daniel Hennessy near Tallow in April 1814 was a singular instance, not repeated elsewhere in Waterford. Hennessy may have been killed less because he was a proctor and more because he was suspected of having given information to the authorities (S.P.O., S.O.C.P.1, 1814/1566/25). For Hennessy's murder and the circumstances surrounding it, see S.P.O., S.O.C.P.1, 1814/1566/24–5, 29, 73; 1815/1719/40, 52. For the occasional references to unrest over tithes in Co. Waterford, see S.P.O., S.O.C.P.1, 1813/1540/39, 50; 1815/1719/62–3.

55. *Returns of agricultural produce in Ireland in the year 1847, pt ii: stock,* pp 12–13.

56. Fitzpatrick, 'Disappearance', p. 88.

57. S.P.O., S.O.C.P.1, 1814/1559/29, 86; 1815/1682/26; 1815/1721/39, 42, 46, 48–9, 54, 56, 62, 66, 74, 77, 82, 102; 1815/1722/62; 1816/1772/4–5, 19; *L.E.P.*, 8 Oct. 1814.

58. Roberts, 'Caravats and Shanavests', pp 75–6; T.W. Freeman, *Pre-famine Ireland: a study in historical geography* (Manchester, 1957), pp 203–17.

59. J.S. Donnelly, Jr, 'The Rightboy movement, 1785–8' in *Studia Hib.*, xvii–xviii (1977–8), pp 149–50; W.A. Maguire (ed.), *Letters of a great Irish landlord: a*

selection from the estate correspondence of the third marquess of Downshire, 1809–45 (Belfast, 1974), pp 91–2.

60. Much unrest over tithes did occur in Co. Limerick during these years, but the struggle was waged primarily, it seems, by cottiers and labourers, and revolved mainly around the tithe of potatoes (S.P.O., S.O.C.P.1, 1813/1533/22; 1814/1556/33; *L.E.P.*, 4 Sept. 1813, 23 Sept. 1815, 29 Apr., 6 June, 25 July 1816; *E.C.C.A.*, 23 Mar. 1816).

61. Reports in S.O.C.P.1 and in contemporary newspapers indicate that nearly thirty agrarian murders were committed in Co. Tipperary between 1813 and 1816.

62. Edward Wilson to William Gregory, 4 Dec. 1815 (S.P.O., S.O.C.P.1, 1722/102).

63. Threatening notice enclosed in Edward Wilson to Robert Peel, 10 Sept. 1815 (S.P.O., S.O.C.P.1, 1722/3). See also *L.E.P.*, 27 Jan. 1816.

64. Threatening notice enclosed in Edward Wilson to Robert Peel, 10 Sept. 1815 (S.P.O., S.O.C.P.1, 1722/3). See also *L.E.P.*, 23 Sept. 1815.

65. *L.E.P.*, 23 Sept. 1815.

66. S.P.O., S.O.C.P.1, 1815/1722/6.

67. *D.E.P.*, 23 Dec. 1813.

68. S.P.O., S.O.C.P.1, 1814/1559/27, 31, 67.

69. S.P.O., S.O.C.P.1, 1814/1559/43–4, 46, 48; *E.C.C.A.*, 31 Aug. 1814.

70. S.P.O., S.O.C.P.1, 1814/1559/40, 52, 56, 64, 66.

71. S.P.O., S.O.C.P.1, 1815/1721/11–12. Edmund Scully's uncle was a well-known Tipperary banker and his cousin german was a prominent Catholic lawyer.

72. S.P.O., S.O.C.P.1, 1814/1559/93, 95, 97; 1815/1721/6, 106–7, 110; 1815/ 1722/17, 19, 93; *L.E.P.*, 31 Dec. 1814; *D.E.P.*, 24 Aug. 1815.

73. Leahy was killed supposedly because he had been too zealous in collecting certain fines (S.P.O., S.O.C.P.1, 1815/1721/110).

74. S.P.O., S.O.C.P.1, 1814/1559/45.

75. S.P.O., S.O.C.P.1, 1814/1559/67.

76. S.P.O., S.O.C.P.1, 1814/1559/70; 1815/1721/32.

77. S.P.O., S.O.C.P.1, 1815/1722/70; *L.E.P.*, 27 Jan. 1816.

78. S.P.O., S.O.C.P.1, 1815/1722/85.

79. Edward Wilson to William Gregory, 1 Dec. 1815 (S.P.O., S.O.C.P.1, 1722/96).

80. S.P.O., S.O.C.P.1, 1815/1722/102.

81. S.P.O., S.O.C.P.1, 1815/1722/96.

82. Charles Burke to William Saurin, 18 Jan. 1816 (S.P.O., S.O.C.P.1, 1771/25).

83. In his last words before his execution, however, Keough declared that he had played no part in the destruction of the dispensary at Ballagh (S.P.O., S.O.C.P.1, 1816/1771/30).

84. Charles Burke to William Saurin, 18 Jan. 1816 (S.P.O., S.O.C.P.1, 1771/25).

85. Ibid.

86. S.P.O., S.O.C.P.1, 1816/1771/28, 30, 39; 1816/1772/43.

87. *D.E.P.*, 30 Sept. 1815.

88. S.P.O., S.O.C.P.1, 1813/1544/30; 1815/1722/55.

89. John Cooke to Robert Peel, 13 Nov. 1815 (S.P.O., S.O.C.P.1, 1722/79). See also S.P.O., S.O.C.P.1, 1815/1712/19.

90. H. St George Cole to Robert Peel, 31 Dec. 1815 (S.P.O., S.O.C.P.1, 1719/71). See also S.P.O., S.O.C.P.1, 1815/1714/3; *L.E.P.*, 4, 11 Feb. 1815, 17 Jan. 1816; *E.C.C.A.*, 8 May 1816.

The radical face of Paul Cardinal Cullen

Patrick J. Corish

I think I am fairly safe in saying that many definitions of 'radical-ism', and even many descriptions of it, emerge from the papers at this conference. However, I suppose it may be described, at least in the most general terms, as an attempt by those excluded from the body politic, or with what they regard as inadequate participation in it, to secure a larger share. This description excludes revolution, for revolution aims at the overthrow of the established order. It also implies that history remembers as radicals only those who failed. Successful radicals cease to be radicals. They become the establish-ment.

The description I have given also suggests that movements which may be described as radical are not inclined to originate with the most depressed sections of society. They rather tend to come from those with some substance, enough to make them feel that their social and political standing is not commensurate with their econ-omic strength. This is certainly true of Ireland in the second half of the nineteenth century. The first half of the century had been filled with the turbulence of an increasingly desperate poor. Their clerical leaders had set their faces against this turbulence. So had Daniel O'Connell. What probably set up a more effective control than either was the improvement and centralisation of the police force, culminating in the Constabulary (Ireland) Act of 1836 (6 William IV, c. 13). The Poor Law of 1838 (1 & 2 Vict., c. 109), by setting up the workhouse, was also an instrument of social control in that it offered the poor an alternative, however bleak, to the stark choice between clinging on to the potato patch and dying of hunger. But it was the

great Famine which effectively changed the dimensions of the problem. Inevitably, it was the poor who had suffered most during these
terrible years, from death by disease or starvation, or by panic-
stricken emigration. At least over most of the country, the Famine
changed significantly the social stratification of Irish society. The
once-important 'cottier' class almost disappeared. Those who survived were now labourers working for a money wage, and the overall proportion of landless labourers had diminished. In consequence,
they were more inclined to 'know their place'. Post-famine Irish
society had a decidedly 'middle-class' profile.

This profile was in some respects preponderantly 'lower middle-
class', made up of the kind of people who in most societies of the
time had some hopes of fuller participation in the body politic. In
other words, they were the classic seed-bed of radicalism. However,
there was one feature which distinguished Irish radicalism from
radicalism elsewhere. Irish radicalism was sectarian. Irish radicals,
by and large, were Catholics. The Irish establishment was Protestant.

This division of political interests along sectarian lines had developed under the stresses of the 1790s. Before this date, there had
been some indications that the sectarian issue might be avoided, even
in a country with a history as unfortunate as Ireland's. The strains
of the revolutionary decade showed how fragile any such hopes
were. Hitherto, Irish patriotism had been a Protestant preserve almost to the exclusion of Catholics. Afterwards, it became a Catholic
preserve almost to the exclusion of Protestants.[1] It is true that a
liberal Protestant minority tried to stem the tide, but they failed.[2] As
far as the Catholic clergy were concerned, any liberalism in their
ranks was extinguished by the Protestant evangelical revival, the
'Second Reformation' as it called itself. This was the most sustained
effort for centuries at anything like a mass-conversion of the Irish
Catholics. It would have been resented in any case, but it was all the
more resented because it showed up deficiencies in the pastoral
mission of the Irish Catholic clergy. The fact that at least some of
these deficiencies were due to a shortage of material resources, and
were now being shown up by Protestant missionaries well funded
by English evangelicals, added considerable poison to the brew.
'Proselytism' and 'souperism' became very unpleasant words.

As for the better-off Catholic laity, the factor that made them
into 'radicals' was undoubtedly the delay in granting what was regarded as the final instalment of Catholic emancipation. What was
achieved only after long agitation in 1829 was in itself a limited gain,

but it was of great symbolic significance for the Catholic middle classes. The delay in granting it was undoubtedly an important factor in ensuring that the political divide in Ireland would come to be based on religious affiliation rather than on class structures. Perhaps even more significant was O'Connell's success in rallying wide support from a hitherto turbulent poor for the right of middle-class Catholics to sit in parliament.

This had been their principal remaining grievance. Closely associated with it was the question of control of the boroughs, where there was much Catholic wealth. It is true that the Act of Union, by drastically reducing Irish borough representation in parliament, had anticipated reforms that came in England only in 1832. What boroughs remained were, however, rich sources of power and patronage, and in them the Protestant element fought a hard defensive action that was lost only with the Irish Municipal Reform Act of 1840 (3 & 4 Vict., c. 108). The symbol of victory was the inauguration of Daniel O'Connell as lord mayor of Dublin on 1 November 1841.

The Irish county franchise had been restricted to £10 freeholders by the Emancipation Act of 1829. The legislation for Ireland in 1832 had been far more restrictive than that for England or Scotland. The franchise continued to be restricted to £10 freeholders, and in the poorer parts of the country the Irish county electorate seemed to be in some danger of disappearing when the Representation of the People (Ireland) Act of 1850 (13 & 14 Vict., c. 69) trebled its numbers (it did reduce the borough electorate by a quarter). In particular, this measure enfranchised considerable numbers of tenant farmers, irrespective of the conditions of their tenancy, and though the secret ballot was not to come for another twenty years it did make possible a certain amount of 'popular' politics, especially where the land-question was an issue, as was made clear in the election of 1852.

The Irish Protestant community nevertheless continued to resist Catholic advancement. An M.P. had to be a man of fairly substantial means, so it is not perhaps altogether surprising that it was only in the 1880 election that Ireland returned a Catholic majority to parliament. The Protestants started off with a very preponderant share in manufacture and industry and in the professions, but in these areas the Catholic share did not increase in proportion to the increase in Catholic wealth. The most striking example is, however, in the public service, for here patronage was yielding to competition, but despite this, and even allowing for differing levels of education, the Protestant share remained disproportionate, surviving even the disappearance of landlordism.[3]

Any man who took up an important ecclesiastical appointment in Ireland in 1850 would have found himself with functions of a nature that have to be described as 'political', to a degree hard to parallel in other western European countries. In some respects they paralleled the position of the 'ethnarch' of Greek Christians under Turkish rule, where the archbishop was responsible for his religious community to the civil rulers. In Ireland, the archbishop would have found the politically vocal section of his community in some sense 'radical'. It was Paul Cullen's achievement that he did not close his mind to the possibility of being in some sense 'radical' himself.

There was no necessity about this development. His predecessor as archbishop of Armagh, William Crolly, had been, if we must use political labels, a 'Whig'. So was Archbishop Daniel Murray of Dublin, but in 1850 he was eighty-two years of age, and when he died in 1852 Cullen moved to the political capital. It is not so easy to pin English political labels on the other giant of the Irish Catholic hierarchy, Archbishop John MacHale of Tuam: it may be that the best starting-point in exploring him is that of the Irish concept of *taoiseach*. He and Cullen had been friendly: indeed MacHale had played an important role in Cullen's nomination as archbishop of Armagh. However, differences soon appeared between them, and by 1860 MacHale had been more or less reduced to the position of 'his Holiness's loyal opposition', and in the pontificate of Pius IX that was no great role.

At this stage it will be helpful to take a look at Paul Cullen's family background. He was born in 1803 of comfortable farming stock at Ballitore, Co. Kildare. The family tradition was that they had been dispossessed of their ancestral lands in south Co. Wexford in the 1650s, and this is quite probably true.[4] What is undeniably true is that the Cullen family of Ballitore existed as part of a wide network of relationships, in-laws and cousins, all of them prosperous farmers. It is quite in keeping with this background that an uncle and namesake of the future cardinal should have been executed in that year of crisis, 1798. It is also very much in keeping that a brother, Thomas, and a brother-in-law, Peter Verdon, should have been among the pioneers of the Irish cattle trade with Liverpool.

Paul Cullen went to Rome as a clerical student in 1820, and remained there until he returned as archbishop of Armagh in 1850. In 1830 he became rector of the Irish college in the city, a position important in itself, but even more important in that as rector he acted as agent of the Irish bishops in their growing business with the papacy. It was especially important in that a number of questions were coming up, particularly in the field of education, where the issues were quite new to the Roman authorities, and in consequence the advice tendered by an informed Irishman like Paul Cullen was particularly valuable. In fact, the Roman decisions on both the National schools and the Queen's Colleges followed Cullen's advice. The National schools, while wrong in principle, could be tolerated in practice because of the benefits they brought, but the Queen's Colleges were wrong in principle and intolerable in practice. On this latter issue he split with Crolly and Murray—indeed he had already split with them shortly before over the Charitable Bequests Act. This breach was not healed. Indeed, the more conservative clergy in Ireland were concerned at the atmosphere in the Irish college in Rome, where, it was said, students could expect no favour unless they offered communions and novenas for O'Connell and Repeal.[5]

When Cullen returned to Ireland as archbishop Crolly was dead, Murray was soon to die, and MacHale was soon to be kept in bounds if never exactly vanquished. Inevitably, Cullen would be involved in the politics of the day. While it is true, as E. R. Norman put it, that 'he had, in fact, no political theories, only religious and ecclesiastical ones',[6] in Ireland this involved him in political issues rather than excluded him from them.

To any Catholic ecclesiastic, the issue of the Established Church inevitably loomed large. Though the fifth article of the Act of Union had laid it down that 'the churches of England and Ireland, as now by law established, be united into one Protestant episcopal church', and that this arrangement 'shall remain in force for ever' and 'shall be deemed and taken to be an essential and fundamental part of the Union',[7] one did not need to be a Catholic archbishop to reflect that here was an area where a parliament might well follow the good constitutional principle of not being necessarily bound by the acts of its predecessor. Especially after 1832, parliament regulated the affairs of the Church of Ireland, not just in financial matters, like parish rates, church cess, or tithes, but even in its diocesan organisation. The 'second Reformation' in Ireland, beginning in the 1820s, had embittered interconfessional relations. It is true that some of the clergy of the Church of Ireland had considerable reservations about this new development, seeing in it a threat to relationships that were at least long established. It is also true that in some places, sometimes at first sight the most unexpected, Belfast for example, where elements of Presbyterian radical liberalism still remained, relationships could still, at least on occasion, be almost described as easy, but the attitude of some church leaders, notably Archbishop Magee of Dublin, was, to put it mildly, unfortunate. Down to the present day, there is no religious ceremony more socially significant in Ireland than the burial of the dead. At the Reformation, the cemeteries had naturally passed to the established church, but Catholics continued to be buried in them, with Catholic rites, as part of that social consensus that had tempered the asperities of the law. Now Catholic priests found themselves excluded from Catholic funerals. In Dublin especially there was a great need for new cemeteries. They were set up under Catholic auspices, and though they were open to people of all creeds, Protestant and Catholic now tended to be separated in death as well as in life.

The established church, then, was making more difficult the defence of a position threatened from several quarters. As for Cullen, while he was not primarily a speculative theologian, he had no theological respect for Protestantism as he knew it. This attitude was reinforced by the fact that the Church of Ireland archbishop of Dublin was now Richard Whately (1831–63). Whately, an Oxford man, had been the leading spirit of the group in the senior common room of Oriel who called themselves the 'Noetics', Whigs in politics, Broad Church in theology, critical of traditional religious orthodoxy. Significantly, the crisis between the two archbishops of Dublin came over two books written by Whately, and approved by the Board of National Education for use in the schools, *Christian Evidences* and *Lessons on the Truth of Christianity*. In Cullen's eyes, some of what Whately had written was simply heretical, and he demanded that approval be withdrawn. He won his point, and Whately resigned from the Board.[8]

If Cullen had no theological sympathy with Protestanism, he had a deep and atavistic antipathy to the Irish church establishment. For him, there was only one church of Ireland, and it was Roman Catholic. His attitude can be seen clearly in his comments in private correspondence, for example during the state visit of the prince of Wales in 1868. He took keen pleasure in the fact that the prince visited a number of Catholic institutions. Cullen had decided to attend the public functions, including the official banquet in Dublin castle, a place he was usually careful to shun, and he took a very keen pleasure in that as a cardinal he was given precedence immediately after the royal family—'the poor parsons think the world is going upside down when they see popery in high places'.[9] The same precedence given him at the reception by the Royal Dublin Society recalled to him that twenty-five years earlier the society had blackballed an application for membership by his predecessor, Archbishop Murray.

So, he eagerly supported the growing demands for disestablishment. The demand was not altogether free from difficulties, for since the mid-1850s the Irish Catholics had sought and received support from the English Liberation Society, radical in politics and non-conformist Protestant in religion. When Gladstone announced his conversion to disestablishment in 1868 the only remaining issue was church endowment. The Liberation Society was opposed to all endowments for any religion. So was Cullen, where radicalism in the Irish sense was mixed with pragmatism. Since the beginning of the century the Irish Catholics had resisted state endowment because they feared state control. As well, Cullen reflected, if the spoils were to be shared the Catholic share might be expected to be disproportionately small. He met some opposition in getting this viewpoint accepted. At home, he was opposed by David Moriarty, the capable bishop of Kerry. There must have been some explaining to do in Rome, where the *Syllabus* of 1864 had explicitly rejected the idea that church and state should be separated, and where the pope and his secretary of state, Cardinal Antonelli, had had to look on since 1860 while the Italian state confiscated church property on a large scale. The discussions between Cullen and the papacy still await detailed examination,[10] but he won his point. It cannot have been altogether easy, for while it may be presumed that Pius IX and Antonelli had no love for Protestant establishments, the establishment in question was far away, while the principles advocated by Cullen were biting sharply much nearer home.

That Cullen's attitude to the separation of church and state was pragmatic rather than dogmatic appears clearly in his stance on the National schools. None of the churches had been happy when these were introduced in 1831. In view of the clergy of all denominations, education was a matter for the church, not the state. If anything, the Protestants were more opposed to 'mixed' education than the Catholics. The Church of Ireland had sufficient resources to contemplate maintaining its own system. The Presbyterians rather tried to bend the National system in a direction they could approve, thereby increasing Catholic fears. Yet the Catholics had no real alternative, because of their numbers and their poverty. Over much of the country the schools rather inevitably became in practice

Catholic and denominational. There is some irony in the reflection that in the National schools the Catholic church authorities, largely at the expense of the government, were presented with an opportunity for school catechesis they could never have provided from their own resources.

When the schools issue came to a head among the Irish Catholic bishops about 1840 Paul Cullen was an influential figure in Rome, and was naturally an influential adviser of the Roman authorities in what was for them a quite new problem. The advice he gave them then he adhered to all his life. The system was theoretically unacceptable, but in practice it could be tolerated because of the benefits it brought. However, it needed careful watching and constant attempts at improvement, and the only really satisfactory system was a fully denominational one. Cullen pressed for this all his life, but he failed to get it. However, he did get what from his point of view were improvements in the system, to such an extent that by his death in 1878 the theoretical disadvantages looked small beside the practical advantages.

I will take up the question of university education later and in another context. Here it might just be noted that he never relaxed his opposition to the Queen's Colleges or to any form of university education that was not fully Catholic. His Catholic university was probably his dearest ambition. It certainly absorbed a great deal of his time and energy, and equally certainly it was his greatest failure.

The extension of the Irish franchise in 1850 had given the vote to a considerable number of tenant farmers. In consequence, the land-question was always thrusting towards first place in the political debate. While Cullen recognised the importance of the land-question for the peace of Ireland, for him it ranked after church disestablishment and education. And on the land-question Cullen was no radical. He had too much respect for the rights of property, though he did envisage the gradual and peaceful creation of something like a peasant proprietorship. Characteristically, his caution on the land-question was not so much due to political ideologies as to ecclesiastical considerations. Because so many of the Catholic priests were themselves of farming stock, it was in this issue above all others that there was real danger they might take what he regarded as an unacceptable role in politics, by taking a public stance on issues where the laity might legitimately differ, or, worst of all, by becoming involved in the physical violence that could still erupt over political matters. Both bishop and priests in Navan were deeply involved in politics, he wrote to his friend and confidant Tobias

Kirby, rector of the Irish college, Rome, on 23 November 1855. This had led to a fight at a fair in which priests were involved: an example, he commented with heavy irony, of the 'unfettered priest' so dear to the 'popular politics' of the *Tablet* and the *Nation*.[11]

Cullen found himself in a situation where in order to keep the Catholic Church in Ireland the 'popular' institution that history had made it he had to adopt policies that were to some degree 'radical'. It is true that his 'radicalism' tended to decline as he got older, but this may be only part of the human condition. While O'Connell remained his political exemplar, he cooled quite a bit on repeal, or, in the form in which it presented itself in the 1870s, Home Rule, again, characteristically, when he contemplated the possibility of a parliament in Dublin that might be more than half Protestant.[12] As might be expected, he had no time at all for revolution. Here his experiences in Rome in 1830 and 1848 certainly affected his judgement. A man who could see Mazzini in Gavan Duffy would certainly have no time for James Stephens or even for Kickham. Here perhaps one can see his principal political weakness—he gave his confidence only to people who thought like he did, and he was completely indifferent to the judgement of others: as John H. Whyte has remarked, he seemed to 'have made a virtue out of being misunderstood'.[13] Temperamentally, he was in many ways unfitted for the hard road of politics or even of church administration. He consulted only a very limited circle of friends. He found it hard to reach decisions, and in consequence he passed through many bouts of nervous prostration, that at least once, in the summer of 1858, seems to have gone over the edge of total collapse. Significantly, the collapse came when he faced the possibility of a complete failure of the Catholic university. His letters to Kirby at this time are very revealing: 'Dr MacHale will have a great triumph, he always opposed Dr Newman's appointment, and now it appears he was right and I was wrong in the whole case... Why do you not write me a line to tell me what to do?'[14]

While it is true that 'he had no political theories, only religious and ecclesiastical ones', he faced the increasing dilemma that in order to counter the Fenian case that constitutional action was futile he had to involve himself in party politics more deeply than he would have wished. Left to himself, he would have preferred to advance the Catholic position in Ireland by more indirect action, by petition, by publicity, above all by having Catholic laymen placed in posts where they could influence government policy. His alliance with Gladstone in the late 1860s was pragmatic, though at times he could sound enthusiastic.[15] Essentially, however, he would support him in so far as he advanced Catholic interests. Again significantly, the parting of the ways came over Gladstone's Irish university bill, when, under pressure from the Catholic bishops, led by Cullen, thirty-five Irish Catholic Liberal M.P.s voted against it, and it was defeated in the Commons by three votes on 12 March 1873.

The fact is that while the Catholic situation in the peculiar circumstances of Ireland constituted a radical interest, the Catholic church in the pontificate of Pius IX was far from being a radical institution. The hopes raised by the religious revival after 1815 had not been sustained, and the church, increasingly directed by the papacy, had withdrawn into a defensive shell, epitomised in the *Syllabus* of 1864, which appeared to seal off Catholics from all the political and intellectual developments of the age. In all this, Paul Cullen was a faithful follower of Pius IX. It was only to be expected that the crisis-issue should be higher education.

Cullen was implacably opposed to the Queen's Colleges. He devoted more time and effort to the increasingly hopeless venture of the Catholic university than he did to any other cause. His appointment of Newman as rector was expansive and imaginative, but the two men found it hard to work together. The faults were on both sides, and Cullen and Newman were temperamentally less incompatible than were Newman and Manning, as was clearly shown in the attempts to provide Catholic university education in England in the late 1860s and early 1870s. This tangle cannot even begin to be unravelled here. For long years the accepted version was that in Purcell's acid biography of Manning,[16] published in 1895. Indeed, the balance was really redressed only in 1962 by Vincent Allan McClelland, and it is an indication of the complexity of the issues that his dispassionate vindication of Manning can at times leave some impression that he has not quite succeeded in being fair to Newman.[17]

Cullen and Newman never lost a mutual respect. By contrast, relations between Newman and Manning were at best suspicious and frequently hostile. In 1867, a time when Catholic intellectuals were being cut down by papal condemnation, Newman's opponents tried to raise the cry of 'heretic', and in this they had the support of Manning, now (since 1865) archbishop of Westminster.[18] It was Cullen who was appealed to by Pius IX as a judge of Newman's orthodoxy, and Cullen vouched for him.[19] Newman might have complained, during his years in Dublin in the 1850s, of being 'worn down' by Cullen (though one may have a suspicion that of the two

Newman was made of the more durable material), but each man retained a deep basic respect for the other. As Newman wrote to a close friend, Charles William Russell, the president of Maynooth, when Cullen died in 1878: 'We were different men, but I always loved him and felt grateful to him—and highly reverenced him for his works' sake'.[20]

The Irish university question had accumulated such a tangled history since the 1840s that it took courage even to attempt a solution. In particular, it seemed almost impossible for Gladstone to satisfy two interests he did not wish to alienate, the English Nonconformists and the Irish Catholics. He decided to consult no interests outside the government, and he described his proposals, tabled on 13 February 1873, as 'a measure solely of the government alone'. There was to be an Irish national university, with the exclusive right to confer degrees. The university was to have no religious tests. Five colleges were named, Trinity College, the Queen's Colleges in Belfast and Cork, Magee College, and the Catholic University. Other colleges might be added later, but the Queen's College, Galway, was suppressed, and candidates might present for a degree without being attached to any college. No college was to receive further endowment under the bill, but the university was to have endowments from which professorships, exhibitions and scholarships might be provided. University professorships were not to be established in the sensitive subjects, theology, moral philosophy and modern history. In these, teaching was to be the exclusive concern of the colleges.[21]

Cullen made it clear that he was not satisfied. In an attempt to win him over, Gladstone asked the lord lieutenant, Earl Spencer, to ask for a meeting. It took place in the Castle on 25 February, and though it was good-tempered and cordial there was no meeting of minds.[22] Cullen contended that the bill continued the principle of 'mixed education', especially in that poor Catholics would be drawn to the well-endowed Queen's Colleges or Trinity rather than to the unendowed Catholic University. Spencer replied that the Irish Church Act of 1869 had ruled out the possibility of new state endowments to denominational institutions. To this Cullen had no reply, but he was clearly anxious about many areas of teaching. It was not enough to restrict teaching in theology, moral philosophy and modern history to the colleges. Apart from the fact that many Catholics might be expected to be attracted to the Queen's Colleges or Trinity, professors of the university might teach other subjects, and most of the professors of the university, he was certain, would be taken from the staff of Trinity. If outside appointments were to be made, there was nothing to prevent Darwin or Huxley being appointed to chairs of geology or zoology. Here one can see a concern which would have been widely shared at the time by most Christian leaders, but it is not so easy to see the basis for the fears Cullen expressed over non-denominational teaching of English literature, though in this area his fears seem to have been real. Spencer asked him if he considered mathematics and ancient history safe. Here one might perhaps detect a note of irony entering the exchanges, and there may be a similar note in Cullen, who when assenting added that things like engineering were safe too. Though the meeting was completely good-humoured—the word is Spencer's—no common ground was established.

The bishops met on 27 and 28 February 1873. Of the twenty-two present only one, Butler of Limerick, supported the bill. A fall of snow had kept MacHale at home. He would certainly not have supported the bill, but he had declared his view that the only constructive thing the bishops could do was to issue a strong declaration on Home Rule (this might well have been an attempt to sidetrack discussion on the university question). In his absence, Cullen had little difficulty in getting the bishops to agree to send a petition to parliament and lobby the Irish M.P.s.

The debate on the second reading began on 3 March, and the bill was assailed from all sides. When the vote was finally taken, at 2 a.m. on the morning of 12 March, the measure was defeated by three votes.

This issue of higher education shows up most clearly the limits of Cullen's cultural and religious radicalism. In brief, he was no John Henry Newman. But his relations with Newman, though never easy, were infinitely better than Newman's relations with many theological conservatives, such as Henry Edward Manning. It has been noted that at a critical time Cullen underwrote Newman's orthodoxy, and Newman remembered this gratefully. On a more political level, the situation in Ireland had inbuilt elements which must be described as radical. Here, in contrast with his predecessors such as Archbishops Murray of Dublin and Crolly of Armagh, Cullen, admittedly cautiously, pursued a programme that had its radical elements. It may be that the core of his admittedly great achievement was to have imposed from above a restructuring of the Catholic Church in Ireland that left it the essentially popular character that had been its historical inheritance, and this at a time when the Catholic church as a whole was in a very conservative mood.

182

It might well be said that in the end he suffered the fate of all successful radicals, in that he ended up in some sense as the new establishment. Another, and possibly more searching way of putting it—if these shorthand words are to be of any service—is that he presided over the emergence of a pluralist society. What Cullen could not have changed, nor indeed would he have wished to change, was the hard fact that in this society the most important pluralist elements were the religious denominations. Neither could he have changed, nor again would he have wished to change, the hard fact that these denominations carried a heavy legacy of history that made an amicable pluralism very difficult indeed. Recent studies have emphasised the Irish and nationalist element in him.[23] An even more recent work, the first attempt at a formal biography long overdue,[24] would deny that there was any such element, and paints him as a narrow bigot, dominated by an exclusive 'ultramontanism'. He came to a country moving peaceably towards pluralism, but reversed all this and put in its place a Catholic 'cultural ascendancy' and 'imperialism'. To put it bluntly, this is an outrageously simplified version of things which is quite unsustainable. Another recent work, after an examination of Cullen that is far from historically exhaustive, dismisses him as a minor political meddler of little religious significance.[25] It would appear that after a reasonably successful rescue from a role as the *bête noire* of Irish nationalism he is now coming under attack from another quarter. But he is much too many-sided a person to be pinned down to a simple formula such as these two books proffer.

Notes

1. The point is succinctly made by Marianne Elliott, *Partners in revolution* (Yale, 1982), pp 238–9.
2. For recent studies, see Ian d'Alton, *Protestant society and politics in Cork 1812-1844* (Cork, 1980); J. R. Hill, 'The politics of privilege: Dublin corporation and the Catholic question, 1792–1823' in *The Maynooth Review*, vii (1982), pp 17–36.
3. For examples, see Emmett Larkin, 'Economic growth, capital investment, and the Roman Catholic church in nineteenth-century Ireland' in *A.H.R.*, lxxii (1967), pp 872–3.
4. What evidence there is is collected by Peadar Mac Suibhne, 'The early Cullen family' in *Reportorium Novum*, ii, 1 (1957–8), pp 185–98.
5. See E. J. O'Reilly to Cullen, 11 December 1844; William Walsh, bishop of Halifax, Nova Scotia, to Cullen, 29 January 1845. Archives of the Irish college, Rome, Cullen papers, nos 998, 1014.
6. Norman, *Cath. ch. & Ire.*, p. 10.
7. See Edmund Curtis and R. B. McDowell (ed.), *Irish historical documents 1172-1922* (London, 1943), pp 208–13.

8. There has recently been a new biography of Whately: D. H. Akenson, *A Protestant in purgatory: Richard Whately, archbishop of Dublin* (Archon Books, Hamden, Connecticut, 1981).
9. Cullen to Kirby, 27 April 1868. Archives of the Irish college, Rome, Kirby papers 1868, no. 142, calendared in P. J. Corish, 'Irish college, Rome: Kirby papers' in *Archiv. Hib.*, xxx (1972), p. 63.
10. In addition to the ecclesiastical material, there is useful information in the despatches of Odo Russell, the British agent in Rome (P.R.O., F.O. 43/101–103B). The more important of these are printed in Noel Blakiston (ed.), *The Roman question* (London, 1962).
11. Archives of the Irish college Rome, Kirby papers (Manly papers, box 2), calendared in P. J. Corish, op. cit., in *Archiv. Hib.*, xxxi (1973), pp 56–7.
12. Cullen to Kirby, 23 November 1873. Ibid., 1873, no. 425, calendared in P. J. Corish, op. cit., in *Archiv. Hib.*, xxx (1972), p. 75.
13. In Corish, *Ir. catholicism*, v, II, 36–8.
14. Cullen to Kirby, 24 July, 5 August 1858. Archives of the Irish college, Rome, Kirby papers (Further Australian papers), calendared in P. J. Corish, op. cit., in *Archiv. Hib.*, xxxi (1973), pp 92–3.
15. For example, in his letter to the aggregate meeting in Dublin and in his letter to the clergy of his diocese, published in *Freeman's Journal*, 3, 16 November 1868.
16. E. S. Purcell, *Life of Cardinal Manning* (London, 1895), ii, 495–505.
17. V. A. McClelland, *Cardinal Manning* (London, 1962), pp 87–128.
18. For details, as recounted in the biographies published shortly after their deaths, see Purcell, op. cit., ii, 304–52 and Wilfrid Ward, *The life of John Henry Newman* (London, 1913), ii, 150–241.
19. Ward, op. cit., ii, 192.
20. Fergal McGrath, *Newman's university, idea and reality* (Dublin, 1951), p. 504.
21. The main provisions of the bill are conveniently summarised in Norman, *Cath. ch. and Ire.*, pp 448–9.
22. Spencer's memorandum of the conversation is in Gladstone's papers, B.L., Add. MSS 44307, ff 161 ff.
23. E.D. Steele, 'Cardinal Cullen and Irish nationality' in *I.H.S.*, xix (1975), pp 239–60; Emmet Larkin, *The making of the Roman Catholic church in Ireland 1850–1860* (Chapel Hill: University of North Carolina Press, 1980).
24. Desmond Bowen, *Paul Cardinal Cullen and the shaping of modern Irish Catholicism* (Dublin, 1983).
25. Desmond Keenan, *The Catholic church in nineteenth-century Ireland: a sociological survey* (Dublin, 1983). See especially p. 252.

How radical was Irish feminism between 1860 and 1920?

Mary Cullen

I

There has been little recent historical study of Irish feminism in the late nineteenth and early twentieth centuries. The studies that have been done have dealt with particular aspects of feminist activity.[1] and there has not as yet been any óverall survey. The aim of this paper is to make a start in that direction by relating what we know of Irish feminist organisation to the context of international feminism, and by considering how one might attempt to determine what was 'radical' and what was not. In the present state of knowledge both objectives can be only partially achieved, but it is hoped that the study will do two things. It may indicate areas where research should be profitable. Also, while it is concluded here that the question in the title is the wrong question, it seems that the attempt to answer it helps to identify some of the right questions to deepen our understanding of Irish feminism.

The first essential is a perspective within which to place Irish feminist activity and against which to test it. This requirement is filled by Richard J. Evans's book, *The Feminists*.[2] It provides a broad comparative survey of feminist movements in Europe and most of the English-speaking world, while making no reference at all to Irish feminism. It also provides an explanatory hypothesis against which the Irish experience can be tested.

Evans first discusses the origins of nineteenth-century feminist movements, and then follows their development in the different countries he considers. Feminist movements he defines as organisations of women 'expressly created in order to fight for the emancipation of the female sex as a whole.'[3] Their origin he sees in an interaction between ideological and socio-economic forces.

The ideological basis he finds in the fusion of Enlightenment rationalism and the religious individualism of Protestantism, which resulted in nineteenth-century Liberalism. The Enlightenment emphasis on the power of human reason to reform society, and also to criticise it and to legitimate criticism, had obvious potential for feminism. Much Enlightenment literature challenged lack of equality in various areas of human life, and a body of it supported the right of women, on the grounds of shared human reason, to equal education, equal access to employment and equal political rights. Evans sees the Protestant emphasis on the responsibility of individuals for their own salvation as also having clear, if latent, potential for feminism.

Liberalism saw the human race as developing and progressing by way of the removal of restrictions on individual development and achievement. Women were an obvious case where development and achievement were stunted by disabilities imposed on individuals on the basis of birth. In the name of *laissez faire* liberal individualism could be called on to support the equality of the sexes in terms of the removal of positive restrictions on one of them.

Indeed the overt restrictions imposed on women amounted to a comprehensive man-made barrier to any possibility of economic, social or political equality between the sexes. While details might vary from country to country the overall pattern of discrimination was amazingly constant, so that Evans can advance a categorisation broadly applicable across all the countries with which he deals.[4] Women were excluded from participating in political life by holding public office, standing for election or voting. Restrictions on the holding of property, and on involvement in business, trade and the professions, barred them from economic independence. Denial of basic rights in civil and criminal law underlay many of the other disabilities and in itself gave men authority over women's lives. A moral double-standard made women the punishable party in cases of illegitimacy, prostitution and adultery. Finally, the objectives and practice of education differed for males and females, so that girls were specifically trained for domestication and subordination.

In spite of this artifically created and self-perpetuating dependency of women on men Evans does not think that the intellectual support that feminism could claim from Liberal ideology is sufficient in itself to explain why feminist protest, not itself a novel phenomenon, should at this period have produced organised Feminist movements. More than intellectual conviction was necessary, he argues, and he finds an answer in economic and social factors.

He identifies change in class structure as the dynamism behind the emergence of Feminist movements.[5] By this he means the development of the middle classes in line with the expansion of trade, industry, administration and the professions. Within a rapidly-changing society the middle classes advanced in number, wealth, power, self-image and ambition. They abandoned earlier aspirations to rise to the ranks of the aristocracy, and redefined their aims and values in terms of an ethic of hard work and achievement, within which the individual was seen to succeed on the basis of personal merit.

This was an ethic whose practice was strictly confined to males. Indeed, as middle-class men increasingly built their self-esteem on their individual achievement in economic, social and political life, middle-class women were even more firmly than before debarred from the possibility of emulating them. The professionalisation of more and more desired occupations, which protected the interests of middle-class men, squeezed women out more completely than before. It correspondingly devalued the few occupations available to middle-class women. These developments, together with the separation of home and workplace, meant that within marriage also middle-class women found the actual and comparative content of their role as housewife seriously diminished. It became increasingly difficult for them to value either a relatively leisured life in the home or a precarious struggle for survival in the workplace in terms of their men's new ethic of work, achievement and success. Evans sees the first organised Feminist movements as their response to this challenge, a demand by middle-class women that the theory and practice of Liberalism be applied to women as well as to men.

Within any particular country Evans identifies the influences that helped or hindered the development of these movements. 'In favour were Protestant religion, Liberal polity, bourgeois society, against were Catholic church, authoritarian constitution, feudalism and aristocracy.'[6] He also identifies a characteristic model or pattern of development followed by feminist movements,[7] a pattern from which particular movements might of course deviate to a lesser or greater extent. The pattern began with what was called 'moderate' feminism, which was concerned with economic, educational and legal rights, and then it developed into 'radical' feminism, concerned first with issues of moral reform of society and then, and more especially, with the franchise. The first essential prerequisite for full participation in society was economic independence. So feminists demanded for married women control over their own property and for single women access to higher education and the professions. In the next stage of moral reform they were particularly involved in the areas of temperance movements and sexual morality, both of which had something to offer both to women as a group and to middle-class interests generally. Evans sees involvement in these moral dimensions as having a radicalising effect on feminist aims and tactics, or, as he seems to mean, politicising them so that they turned to the demand for the vote as the means of access to political power to enforce their other objectives. The vote then rapidly acquired the status of a symbol of feminist demands generally, around which all feminists could rally, and it became for many a basic objective in itself. After that stage was reached Evans sees organised feminism undergoing further vicissitudes, but this paper is concerned with the model only up to that point in its development.

II

What we know of early organised feminism in Ireland seems to fit Evans's model. The membership of the groups involved appears to have been small and to have been drawn largely from Protestant middle-class women working closely with their English counterparts. Irishwomen and Englishwomen shared the same general disabilities under English law. They also shared similar problems in the discriminatory theory and practice of female education, and in exclusion from the professions and political life. Within the United Kingdom they were both located within a Liberal polity which tolerated organised dissent up to a point. In the early stages, when co-operation was closest, they sought redress from the same representative bourgeois parliament at Westminster.

On some issues Irish feminists seem to have shared a joint campaign with Englishwomen, as in that for the married women's property acts and the Social Purity Crusade. On others, as employment, education and the vote, it seems that they may have initially followed an English lead but their campaigns were separate and developed differently. Differences inevitably arose from the colonial relationship between Britain and Ireland, which increasingly faced feminists with diverging outside influences, problems and opportunities. When Home Rule became an imminent possibility, Irish feminists found themselves pressing for suffrage from the United Kingdom parliament and at the same time demanding its inclusion in any new constitutional arrangements in Ireland.

Feminists themselves could differ on tactics and in their extra-feminist loyalties, as well as on the relative priority they gave the latter in relation to their strictly feminist objectives.

Feminist action on the linked issues of the employment and education of middle-class women was under way by the early 1860s at least with the foundation in 1861 of the Queen's Institute for the Training and Employment of Educated Women in Dublin and in 1867 of the Ladies' Institute in Belfast. The inadequacy of the education of the 'educated women' pushed feminist action towards raising the general standard of middle-class female education. The employment motivation merged with the influence of the English movement to give girls as well as boys an education aimed at intellectual development as an aim in itself. Pioneering institutions were the Belfast High School for Girls, later known as Victoria College, founded in 1859, and Alexandra College for the Higher Education of Women founded in Dublin in 1866.[8] This development is seen as a major breakthrough in women's education as it produced the women teachers who could bring girls' secondary education up to the academic level of that of boys and provided a link between secondary and university education.[9]

The next major breakthrough came with the passing of the Intermediate Education Act in 1878 and the Royal University Act in 1879. Neither was in any way intended to contribute to the education of women. Both were *ad hoc* solutions to the British government's problem of finding some indirect method of subsidising male Catholic education in Ireland. The opportunity for women lay in the fact that the solution adopted in each case was to establish a purely examining and award-giving body and did not require compulsory attendance at any specified institutions. In each case the feminists recognised a golden opportunity, and lobbied successfully[10] to have girls and women included in the legislation.

So far all this had been achieved by a small body of Protestant feminists. Meanwhile development in the secondary education of Catholic girls had been in the direction of distinctly middle-class 'respectable' fee-paying convent schools as a response to the demands of Catholic middle-class social aspirations.[11] The education provided in these by the religious orders was aimed at religious formation and preparation for domesticity. Academic and cultural subjects tended to be taught more at the level of accomplishments than as intellectual disciplines. But once the Protestant women had opened the door to new possibilities in female education the convent schools began to avail of the opportunities. As early as 1884 fifteen convent schools entered girls in the intermediate examinations, in spite of the indifference or hostility of many bishops. Catholic provision of education for university degrees followed and the Dominican St Mary's College and High School, Eccles Street, and Loreto College, Stephen's Green, both in Dublin, were established among the leading women's colleges by the early 1890s. The driving force behind these developments was pressure from the Catholic middle class who made it clear that unless they got the educational provision they wanted in Catholic institutions they would seek it in Protestant equivalents.[12]

When the time came for the final settlement of the university question the feminists, now including Protestant and Catholic, had two organisations in the field to fight their case, the Central Association of Irish School Mistresses and the more recent Irish Association of Women Graduates. They both argued for fully co-educational institutions as the only way by which women could share in the higher standards made possible by endowments. Understandably the women's colleges, both Protestant and Catholic, fought to survive as teaching colleges affiliated to the universities and argued the benefits of the collegiate life they could provide. In the event they lost out while the feminist case triumphed. The Irish Universities Act of 1908 set up two institutions, Queen's University, Belfast, and the National University of Ireland, comprising the other two Queen's Colleges and the Catholic University College. Compulsory attendance was imposed, no women's colleges were affiliated to either university, but women were admitted on equal terms with men to the teaching, degrees, honours and offices of both.[13]

Other areas of early Irish feminist activity await investigation, though it seems that there was activity on all the major issues in international feminism identified by Evans. There was an Irish input into the campaign for legislation to protect married women's property. The issue here was the right of married women to control over their own inherited and earned property, and so it affected women from all social classes. Feminists and others often saw it as concerning working-class and lower middle-class women most immediately in its relation to earnings, since the property of wealthy women could be protected by the legal stratagems developed by the courts of equity to allow propertied families to circumvent the common law. Anna Haslam,[14] a Quaker from Youghal living in Dublin, and Isabella Tod, of Presbyterian stock living in Belfast, both of whom seem to have been active in every branch of Irish feminist organisation, were involved in the campaign. Isabella Tod gave evidence before a select committee in 1868 on the advantages of such an act to working-class women in the Belfast area.[15] Petitions in favour of an act were organised in both Dublin and Belfast, and there was a women's committee at work in Dublin.[16] Considerable progress in establishing the principle of spouses' separate property was achieved with the Married Womens' Property Acts of 1870, 1874, 1882 and 1907.

Irish feminists were also involved in the area of moral reform and sexual equality. Again both Anna Haslam and Isabella Tod were active in the Social Purity Crusade led by Josephine Butler. Haslam and her husband, also a feminist, became associated with Josephine Butler in 1869 and worked 'for ten years in this great fight, rousing public opinion by means of meetings, petitions and various forms of active propaganda'[17] until success was finally achieved. The campaign was aimed at repeal of the series of Contagious Diseases Acts, passed during the 1860s, which regulated prostitution in certain designated areas. They provided for compulsory registration of prostitutes as well as making them liable to compulsory medical examination and, if found to be suffering from venereal disease, to compulsory treatment. Two of the designated areas were in Ireland, the Curragh and Cork–Queenstown. For feminists there was a general moral issue in the tacit encouragement given to vice by any state regulation, and a specifically feminist issue in the double standard which did not interfere with the men involved but treated the women as commodities to be periodically cleansed and recycled as 'clean harlots for the army and navy'.[18]

Most areas of early feminist activity in Ireland still await exploration. Even a superficial testing of Evans's model indicates that most of the major issues attracted action. Petitions, public meetings, letters to newspapers and lobbying of politicians all point to organisation. Women's involvement in temperance movements,[19] abolition of slavery campaigns, women's committees within the churches, and philanthrophy of all kinds, all need investigation. A comparative study of the activity of Catholic and Protestant women in these and other areas would add to our understanding of Irish feminism. Then we need a new look at nuns. The founding mothers of the religious orders of sisters were usually women in the heroic mould who themselves broke out of sex-role stereotyping and organised other women to follow suit. Why did they or their successors turn these organisations into formal religious orders, thereby bringing them under the direct control of the male authority-structure of the Catholic Church? What are the implications for the history of Irish feminism of the availability to Catholic women of a career as a nun? Above all, perhaps, we need knowledge of the lives of as many individual women as possible. But we need biographies which do not concentrate simply on women's contribution to male-defined movements and goals. We need to ask how women saw their own lives, with their opportunities, aspirations and limitations, and how they individually tried to reconcile these to their own best advantage in specific historical situations.

III

The early stages of the suffrage movement again seem to fit Evans's model. The first Irish suffrage society appeared some years after the emergence of feminist organisation on economic, educational and moral issues. Again Anna Haslam and Isabella Tod were in at the beginning, and Haslam founded the first independent Irish group, the Dublin Women's Suffrage Society, in 1876.[20] Its membership was predominantly Quaker, including men as well as women, and it worked by the usual methods of petitions, public lectures, letters to newspapers and lobbying of M.P.s. It expanded its range and changed its name to the Irishwomen's Suffrage and Local Government Association. Progress was slow, but in 1896 women became eligible as poor law guardians and in 1898 they won the local government franchise and the right to be district councillors.[21]

In the early years of the twentieth century a new generation of educated women, beneficiaries of the achievement of the earlier feminists and many of them Catholic, arrived on the public scene. These women had been socialised in the cultural and political renaissance of the late nineteenth century. A more assertive, less patient and often nationalist-oriented type of feminist appeared, ready if necessary to use unconstitutional tactics. The Irish Women's Franchise League (I.W.F.L.), founded in 1908 by a group including Hanna Sheehy-Skeffington and Margaret Cousins, was modelled on the militant English society, the Women's Social and Political Union (W.S.P.U.), whose 'spirited frontal attack on their government'[22] the Irishwomen greatly admired. But they were clear that the Irish situation demanded its own strategies and Irish leadership. Suffrage societies proliferated around the country in a growth and expansion achieved by no other Irish feminist movement. During the early stages of expansion the feminists succeeded in maintaining a united position in spite of individual unionist or nationalist sympathies. Their agreed policy was to support measures of female suffrage from whatever quarter they might come. But over the following years the mounting climax in the colonial relationship between Britain and Ireland imposed severe strain on the policy of 'Suffrage first—above all else!' and under it suffragist unity gradually disintegrated.

The immediate political context was the imminence of Home Rule after 1911. The priorities of the I.W.F.L. were to ensure that female suffrage was included in the Home Rule bill and to pressurise Irish M.P.s to support any women's suffrage bill that came before parliament. Many members of the Irish Party were sympathetic but when Redmond decided that their support might be detrimental to the interests of either Home Rule or the party itself they fell in line and voted against. In 1912 their opposition defeated an all party 'conciliation' bill which would have conceded a limited female suffrage. The English W.S.P.U. retaliated by declaring opposition to Home Rule itself. Irish suffragists stepped up the pressure on the Irish Party to have suffrage included in the Home Rule Bill then before parliament. When Redmond remained immovable the feminists responded with a mass meeting of unprecedented size. Suffrage societies, unionist and nationalist, from all parts of the country, gathered in Dublin to demand that suffrage be included in the bill.[23] When this too was ignored the I.W.F.L. stepped up its militancy from organised heckling of political meetings to breaking windows in public buildings which led to a number of its members serving jail sentences. Between 1912 and 1914 thirty-five women were convicted for suffrage offences.[24]

Public reaction tended to see militant tactics as anti-Home Rule, anti-nationalist, or unwomanly behaviour, and sometimes all three. Such attitudes were reinforced by the intervention of the English W.S.P.U., two of whose members threw a hatchet, variously described as 'small', 'blunt' and a 'toy', at the prime minister, Asquith, during his visit to Dublin in July 1912, and later tried to set fire to the Theatre Royal. The I.W.F.L., blamed for the W.S.P.U.'s activities as well as its own, suffered some bad press and some loss of membership.

Pressure on the alliance between unionist and nationalist suffragists was added to during a brief period of euphoria in 1913 when it seemed that the Ulster Unionist Council might commit itself to the inclusion of female suffrage in its plan for a provisional government to be set up if Home Rule became a reality. The English W.S.P.U. promptly established a branch in Belfast[25] which attracted Ulster suffragists whose own societies tended to be small and non-militant.

Meanwhile the I.W.F.L. had little success in extending into Ulster because it was seen as being 'tainted with Nationalism.'[26] When Sir Edward Carson made it clear that votes for women would not be included the W.S.P.U. retaliated with large scale arson against Unionist property.

The outbreak of war in 1914 increased the strain on suffragist unity. A core group remained committed to a 'Suffrage first — above all else!' position, while others decided that for the time being their unionist or nationalist loyalties must take precedence. Suffrage groups whose allegiance was to unionism tended to drop suffrage activity for the duration and turn to war work for the British cause. The gap between them and the suffrage-first position was widened by the pacifist stance of the suffrage newspaper, the *Irish Citizen*. The gap also widened between the suffrage-first position and those nationalist suffragists who believed that England's difficulty was Ireland's opportunity. By now there were women's organisations, the Ulster Unionist Women's Council (1911) and Cumann na mBan (1914), affiliated to the two male armed forces, the Ulster Volunteers and the Irish Volunteers, on either side of the political divide. These attracted many women who also supported women's suffrage.

The Home Rule bill had now become law, with its operation suspended until after the war and with the position of Ulster yet to be decided. John Redmond adopted a policy of support for Britain as being in the best interests of Home Rule. When the Irish Volunteers split, with the majority following Redmond, Cumann na mBan rejected his policy and opted for the revolutionary nationalist side.

The issues between the suffrage-first position and the nation-first position were fought in the pages of the *Irish Citizen*. They centred on how rather than whether suffrage should be achieved. One side argued that national freedom must come before that of a section, and the emancipation of women follow that of the nation. It also argued that in logic nationalists could not ask Britain for the vote. The *Irish Citizen* editorials insisted that feminists could not compromise on or postpone women's rights and deplored the fact that nationalist women accepted a status subordinate to that of men, the position of a 'slave woman' within the movement.[27]

In spite of these differences and the continuing decline of the suffrage movements in numbers and activity, there was a close relationship between the I.W.F.L. and the revlutionary nationalists which now gave the feminists a major victory. James Connolly was a feminist by conviction, and in turn many suffragists found that interaction with socialist ideas pushed their own aims beyond votes for 'ladies' to votes for 'women'. R. M. Fox in 1935 looked back to the days when the I.W.F.L. and the *Irish Citizen.*

> formed a rallying point for all the best and most progressive elements in dublin. In its pages the anti-conscription struggle, and other vital issues, received attention... Madame Markievicz, Connolly, Pearse, MacDonagh and many other pioneers of the Rebellion, used the platform of the Franchise League to express their views.[28]

The 1916 proclamation recognised women as full citizens and this recognition survived to find constitutional expression in 1922. This achievement is seen as jointly that of the pre-1916 suffrage campaign which 'forced the issue into the political vocabulary' of the revolutionary nationalist leadership, and of Cumann na mBan.[29] The latter became increasingly assertive of women's rights to equality during their 'years of strength'[30] between 1916 and 1921 and insisted on fulfilment of the commitment of 1916.

In a compromise between the Liberal and Conservative parties a limited measure of female suffrage, confined to women over thirty, was granted in 1918. While women in the new state of Northern Ireland had to wait until 1928 for full suffrage, this was given in the constitution of the Irish Free State in 1922. But by then the *Irish Citizen* had disappeared and the I.W.F.L. and organised feminism were becoming less visible on the public scene. Hanna Sheehy-Skeffington, who herself personified the tensions imposed on so many women by the conflicting claims of feminism and nationalism, assessed the situation in the final issue of the *Citizen* in 1920. Ireland, she wrote, was now in 'a state of war', and, just as in other European countries during the recent great war,

> the women's movement merged into the national movement, temporarily, at least, and women became patriots rather than feminists, and heroes' wives or widows rather than human beings, so now in Ireland the national struggle overshadows all else.

Feminism could only mark time and wait. But in the meantime there

> can be no woman's paper without a woman's movement, without earnest and serious-minded women readers and thinkers—and these in Ireland have dwindled perceptibly of late, partly owing to the cause above mentioned, and partly because since a measure, however limited, of suffrage has been granted, women are forging out their own destiny in practical fields of endeavour.[31]

Organised Irish feminism had not disappeared by 1922. But it was reduced in numbers, had lost the incalculable contribution of a specifically feminist public voice in its own newspaper, and was overshadowed in the public eye by the problems of the Free State. Above all perhaps, it had lost the unifying but problematic presence of a single concrete issue like the vote. This loss would have forced reassessment and redirection in any case, even if the other factors had not been present. Feminists could rally round an object like the vote without being forced into serious analysis of longer-term aims, or into examination of their possible internal differences with regard to these, including their reasons for wanting the vote itself. With the achievement of suffrage Irish feminism, in line with the experience of feminism in other countries, entered a new phase, and this too awaits historical investigation.

IV

Evans's book proved a useful starting-point for this tentative approach to an overview of Irish feminist organisation in the nineteenth and early twentieth centuries. In the first place it suggested where one might look for evidence of feminist activity. Then the fact that there *was* organised action of some kind on so many of the major issues does two things. It provides a foundation for further research on the Irish scene and it links Irish feminism directly to the international scene, a link which will obviously repay investigation.

It also seems clear that the testing of his analysis of the inflences favouring and inhibiting feminist development against the Irish situation has potential for deepening our knowledge. Three interacting areas here seem immediately promising. One is his location of Protestantism on the side of the angels with Catholicism in the opposing camp. Another is the relationship between feminism and nationalism. The third is that between feminism and socialism.

The contribution of Quaker women—and men—in the early pioneering days is striking. We need to know more about the ways in which their religion facilitated the development or the articulation and assertion of feminist awareness in individual Protestant women. Does the later involvement of Catholic women in the education struggle and the suffrage campaign constitute an exception to Evans's hypothesis or can it be satisfactorily explained within its terms?

Once Protestant women had forced a breach in the barricade surrounding the male educational preserve Catholic women showed little hesitation in following them. The relative speed with which they forced a revolution in convent secondary school education is impressive. In the final analysis it seems that the bishops capitulated because they set a higher priority on retaining control over the education of Catholic women than they did on refusing to compromise on the curriculum. Closer study of the various issues and participants in these developments should add considerably to our knowledge of Irish feminism and of the actual power and powerlessness of women in Irish Catholic society. How much of the pressure for change came from feminist awareness among Catholic women, and how important was the economic potential of the new education? The role of economic incentives, the question of who was influenced by them, as well as the power structure and politics within Catholic families all need examination. If feminist awareness was a factor, what encouraged its articulation at this time? The extent and limitations of the revolution in convent-school education is also relevant. Did the new examination-orientated curriculum in fact foster changing self-awareness, and how did it interact with values passed on in the hidden curriculum? How did the nuns who implemented the changes see the issues and their own position as women in a changing Irish society? What were their aspirations and what options did they see as available to themselves? Did the Catholic women who moved into leadership roles in the education and suffrage campaigns find problems in reconciling their feminism and their religion, and, if so, which had to yield most in the resolution?

Nationalism Evans found to be 'that profoundly ambiguous force'[32] in its relation to feminism, though he argues that the ideology of nationalism should favour female suffrage since it was based on the sovereignty of the people, which implied 'parliamentary sovereignty and the extension of the franchise.'[33] In Ireland the relationship between the two was certainly on the surface ambiguous. One group of nationalists held up the suffrage movement while another granted full suffrage some years before Britain. However, we need examination at a broader level of the contribution nineteenth-century Irish nationalism may have made to the development of feminism and feminist movements by way of a general legitimation of dissent and the provision of a vocabulary and models of constitutional and extra-constitutional pressure for civil and political demands. This might seem particularly relevant for Catholic women as nationalism and Catholicism became more closely linked. However, the fact that Irish nationalists also provided models and legitimation for the most militant English suffragists[34] suggests that the interactions may be more complex. At a more immediate level the interaction between feminism and socialism is intertwined with that between 'non-constitutional' feminists and revolutionary nationalists in the years leading up to 1916. Closer study of these relationships will add to our knowledge of Irish feminism.[35]

Evans's classification of feminist movements into 'moderate' and 'radical' raises problems. He sees feminism as proceeding from 'moderate' economic and educational demands to progressively more 'radical' stages of moral reform and the vote. This interpretation may be more useful in the controversy it raises than in a direct application of his model. He does not make it clear exactly what are the criteria of radicalism on which he bases his model. If the criterion of 'going to the root' of either a patriarchal or class structure of society is used it is not easy to see a straight progress from moderate to radical along the stages indicated by Evans.

As has been seen, feminists faced a formidable array of economic, legal, political and social discriminations which effectively cut women off from the possibility of challenging men's dominance in all the areas of human activity claimed as 'naturally' male. The wide-ranging sweep of these restrictions, both geographically and effectively, can hardly be accepted as an accidental conglomeration of unrelated inequalities. Taken together they add up to an enforcement of conformity to a paradigm or model of male–female relations, a social construction of gender inequality whose very comprehensiveness queries its claim to a base in human 'nature'. The paradigm comprises a sex-based division of labour within a patriarchal value-system. Patriarchal values see men as 'naturally' superior to and more important than women and as naturally in authority over them. A patriarchal society structures itself accordingly. In this analysis the ultimate establishment under challenge by feminists was, and still is, the model in people's minds of what male–female relations are or should be. The model could find expression in legal, educational or political systems, in a church authority structure, a political party or a revolutionary movement. In the context of a patriarchal paradigm it seems difficult to rate suffrage as a more radical demand than, for example, economic independence. Classification along a scale from moderate to radical runs the risk of pushing feminist movements into artificially separate compartments which may obscure the complexity of interaction between ultimate aims and the available options for action.

Currently historians of feminism are reappraising the place of marriage and motherhood in the historical development of feminist thought. The thrust here is towards a holistic approach to the understanding of feminism and feminists in specific historical situa-

tions. For example, it is suggested that the history of English feminism is distorted if it is seen only in terms of efforts to gain access to
the public and political spheres and if the 'immense concern' of
feminists with the 'private and domestic lives' of women is
ignored.[36] In the light of such reappraisal Evans's implication that
acceptance of 'woman's primary role as housewife and mother' was
necessarily conservative and non-radical[37] may be too limited an
analysis to further the exploration of the full range of feminist
thought. Examination of how these differing hypotheses fit the Irish
experience will help us to determine whether the impetus behind
Irish feminism can be adequately explained by the drive of middle-
class women to join in the bourgeois work-achievement ethic.

If degrees of radicalism are determined by the extent to which
feminist movements transcended class boundaries in objectives
and practice Evans's model of progression from moderate to radical again runs into some problems. As it applies to English feminism it has been challenged on the grounds that some of the progress
was in fact in the reverse direction and that the suffrage movement
actually marked the narrowing and moderation of earlier feminist
objectives.[38] An issue 'of direct importance only to some middle-
class women' replaced earlier concern with the 'problems of all
women' as expressed in the campaigns for social purity and for
married women's control of their property.[39] On the other hand,
however, recent research indicates a higher working-class participation in the English suffrage movement than historians, including
Evans himself, had previously suggested.[40] In Ireland the later
suffrage movement showed considerable awareness of and concern
for the problems of working-class women, though it seems there
was little participation by the latter in the campaign for the vote.[41]

The issues raised are complex and need teasing out in each historical and geographical location. The task of assessing degrees of
radicalism is further complicated by the growing consensus that the
situation of women in any specific historical setting can be adequately explained only by an analysis that includes class and ethnic
differences as well as the forms of patriarchy in the particular
society.

Yet another strand in current historical criticism suggests possible
difficulties with all interpretations, including Evans's, which locate
feminist movements within particular historical and political con-
texts. The value of such location is not challenged, but concern is
expressed that, given the inevitable patriarchal socialisation of
today's historians, there is a danger that feminist thinking and

feminist movements may be seen as purely derivative from pre-dominantly male ideas and movements, when this may be an in-adequate or distorted representation of the reality.[42]

The international scene in the writing of the history of feminism is an open and exciting one at present, and one in which more and more historians are joining. The value of a book like Evans's, especially when set in the context of current debate, for opening up an approach to Irish feminist history does not depend on the extent to which his models prove accurate for the Irish situation, but on the pointers it gives and the questions it raises. The extension and deepening of our knowledge of Irish feminists will probably be best served at this stage by trying to find as much information as possible on how they themselves, as individuals and as groups, saw their aspirations, opportunities, problems and limitations, how they related individual and group strategies to these, and how they dif-fered among themselves on analysis and tactics. In other words, we need to aim at understanding as best we can the range of complexi-ties, contradictions and differences that underlay the lives of the women who created Irish feminist movements.

Notes

1. Rosemary Owens, 'Votes for women; Irishwomen's campaign for the vote, 1876–1915' (unpublished M.A. thesis, University College, Dublin, 1977); Rosemary Owens, '"Votes for ladies, votes for women": organised labour and the suffrage movement, 1876–1922', in *Saothar*, 9 (1983), pp 32–47; Rosemary Owens, *Smashing times: a history of the Irish women's suffrage movement,* (Dublin, 1984); Anne O'Connor, 'Influences on girls' secondary education in Ireland, 1860–1910' (unpublished M.A. thesis, University College, Dublin, 1981); Anne O'Connor, 'The revolution in girls' secondary education in Ireland, 1860–1910' in Mary Cullen (ed.), *Thefts of knowledge; women and education in Ireland* (forthcoming); Eibhlín Breathnach, 'Women and higher education in Ireland, 1879–1914' (unpublished M.A. thesis, University College, Dublin, 1981); Eibhlín Breathnach, 'Women and higher education in Ireland, 1879–1914' in *Crane Bag*, iv (1980), pp 47–54; Eibhlín Breathnach, 'Charting new waters; the experience of women in higher education 1873–1912', in Cullen (ed.), *Thefts of knowledge*; Margaret MacCurtain, 'Women, the vote and revolution' in Margaret MacCurtain and Donncha Ó Corráin (ed.), *Women in Irish society* (Dublin, 1978), pp 46–57; Margaret Ward, 'Suffrage first—above all else! an account of the Irish suffrage movement' in *Feminist Review* 10 (1982), pp 21–36; Margaret Ward, *Unmanageable revolutionaries: women and Irish nationalism* (London and Dingle, 1983).
2. *The feminists: women's emancipation movements in Europe, America and Aus-tralasia 1840–1920* (London, 1977).
3. Ibid., p. 13.
4. Ibid., p. 22.

5. Ibid., p. 28.
6. Ibid., p. 238.
7. Ibid., p. 34.
8. Breathnach, 'Women and higher education' (1980), p. 48.
9. O'Connor, 'Revolution in girls' education'.
10. *Englishwoman's Review*, xi (1880), pp 119–20.
11. O'Connor, 'Revolution in girls' education'.
12. Ibid.
13. Breathnach, 'Women and higher education' (1980), pp 52–3.
14. Newspaper cutting, 23 Aug 1914, Historical Library, Religious Society of Friends, Eustace St., Dublin, Cup. B/65.
15. *Special report from the select committee on the married women's property bill*, pp 74–6. H.C. 1867–8 (441), vii, 339.
16. Ibid., p. 76.
17. *Irish Citizen*, 23 Nov. 1915.
18. Evidence of Josephine Butler before the Select committee on the Contagious Diseases Acts, p. 440, H.C. 1878–9 (323), viii, 397.
19. Isabella Tod had 'taken up the temperance question strongly' from early youth, *Englishwoman's Review*, xxviii (1897), p. 60.
20. Owens, 'Votes for women', pp 8–9.
21. Ibid., pp 17–18.
22. Margaret Cousins in J.H. and M.E.Cousins, *We two together* (Madras, 1950), p. 164.
23. *Irish Citizen*, 8 June 1912.
24. Owens, 'Votes for women', p. 126.
25. Ward, 'Suffrage first', pp 30–31.
26. Hanna Sheehy-Skeffington, Reminiscences of an Irish suffragette' in A.D. Sheehy-Skeffington and R.Owens, *Votes for women; Irishwomen's struggle for the vote* (Dublin 1975), p. 16.
27. *Irish Citizen*, 11 Apr., 23 May 1914.
28. R.M.Fox, *Rebel Irishwomen* (Dublin 1935), p. 138.
29. Ward, 'Suffrage first', p. 35.
30. Ward, *Unmanageable revolutionaries*, pp 119–55.
31. *Irish Citizen*, Sept.–Dec. 1920.
32. Evans, *The feminists*, p. 238.
33. Ibid.
34. Ibid., p. 190.
35. This study has already begun with Owens, '"Votes for ladies"'.
36. Barbara Caine, 'Feminism, suffrage and the nineteenth-century English women's movement' in *Women's Studies International Forum*, v (1982), p. 537.
37. Evans, *The feminists*, p. 234.
38. Caine, 'Feminism, suffrage', pp 549–50.
39. Ibid., p. 550.
40. Joan Wallach Scott, 'Women in history: the modern period', survey article in *Past & Present*, 101 (1983), p. 148.
41. Owens, '"Votes for ladies"', p. 44.
42. Elizabeth Sarah, 'Finding a feminist historical framework' in *Women's Studies International Forum*, v (1982), pp 701–9.

'Labour must wait':
Ireland's conservative revolution

Michael Laffan

The Irish revolution of 1916–22 changed the relationship between
Ireland and Britain. It did not change the relationship between one
class of Irishmen and another. Its impact was nationalist and political, not social and economic. The Irish Volunteers, Sinn Féin, the
Dáil cabinet and the I.R.A. were rebels and revolutionaries but they
were not radicals. With few exceptions they had no interest in
digging down to the roots of Irish society. Their aim was to sweep
away the king, Westminster and the Dublin Castle system rather
than to improve the lot of the poor or curb the power of the rich.

They were 'pure' nationalists in the sense that they concerned
themselves with abstractions rather than with material questions,
they followed a tradition which demanded full independence and
postponed any concentration on other issues until this first objective
had been achieved. Some members of Sinn Féin and the I.R.A.
specified fundamental changes in ordinary Irishmen's lives which
would follow the ending of British rule, but their vision was linguis-
tic and cultural rather than social and economic: citizens of the new
Ireland would speak Irish, not English.

More often the Ireland of their dreams was seen in ethereal, even
mystical terms. Extreme nationalists shared a bland, blithe
assumption that all Irish problems would disappear along with the
Act of Union. In Bulmer Hobson's words, if Ireland were to be
reformed in every respect except that she should continue to be
ruled from London, within a generation her position would be as
bad as ever, 'pauperism and ignorance would have grown, industry
would have failed, education would have deteriorated, and the last

state would be worse than the first'.[1] *Irish Freedom*, the I.R.B. newspaper, put the matter even more bluntly: 'internal problems are only of minor importance, and will rectify themselves if we only get rid of British rule'.[2]

Sinn Féin and the I.R.A. were single-minded, concerned above all with maintaining national unity in the struggle against Britain and with avoiding a split in their own ranks. They wished to represent all elements in Irish society. This did not prevent them from disagreeing violently over forms of government, over the king, lords and commons versus the republic in the years before 1916, or over the treaty versus the republic after 1921. But these were disagreements over issues relevant to the basic task facing the movement: the task of securing as much independence from Britain as possible. Social questions were irrelevant.

In general Sinn Féin's economic policies were based more on nationalist than on social or economic principles. Griffith stressed self-reliance, and he urged industrialisation not so much because it might raise Irishmen's standard of living as because 'an agricultural nation is a man with one arm who makes use of an arm belonging to another person, but cannot, of course, be sure of having it always available'.[3]

Sinn Féin's interventions in labour, agrarian and other social problems were not designed primarily to help the underpaid or the landless, but to calm them, and its leaders showed little concern with improving the living standards of the poor before the British departed. Here Sinn Féin followed an established tradition. Its predecessor, the Irish Parliamentary Party, had feared that British remedies for Irish grievances might blunt the demand for home rule.

There was another line of continuity. The leadership of Sinn Féin, like that of the Parliamentary Party before it, was solidly middle-class. Griffith wrote a letter from Reading Jail at the end of 1916 in which he described his fellow-internees, many of whom were to play a prominent role in the Sinn Féin movement in future years. Their occupations were labourer, farmer, builder, insurance agent, shopkeeper, mechanic, civil servant, teacher, clerk, harbour-master, Gaelic League and Volunteer organisers, Gaelic League secretary, bank-manager, musician, fishery proprietor, printer, sweet-manufacturer, lawyer, journalist and editor.[4] The range was impressive, but few of the Irish nationalists in Reading Jail could be categorised as working-class.

The Sinn Féin T.D.s in the first and second Dáils were also

largely urban and middle-class. The professional and commercial groups, which according to the 1926 census comprised only 6 per cent of the population, accounted for 65 per cent of the membership of the first Dáil and 58 per cent of the second.[5] Such a background made it easy, even natural, for Sinn Féin spokesmen to urge patience and restraint on others less fortunately placed than themselves. It reinforced their strategic or tactical aversion to involving themselves in questions which would turn one class against another.

In 1918 and 1920 the Sinn Féin party was dismayed when it was confronted with outbreaks of agrarian unrest, particularly in Galway, Clare and Roscommon. Its leaders feared a new land war which would deflect energies from military and political campaigns, and which might even result in large-scale desertion from the cause by followers more concerned with land than with politics. Their response, often stated with remarkable frankness, was to dampen rather than arouse or even channel this social radicalism, and they stumbled, reluctantly and hesitantly, into efforts to contain it. A Dáil proclamation laid down that 'energies must be directed towards the clearing out—not the occupier of this or that piece of land—but the foreign invader of our Country'.[6] The Dáil cabinet discussed unrest in Roscommon and decided to send two judges to rule on disputes. The local people were to be advised that the Dáil was dealing with the matter, they must abide by the judges' decisions, and they should 'keep quiet meanwhile'.[7]

Sinn Féin and the Dáil government approved or established land courts which adjudicated between rival claimants. These courts did brisk business, and to an extent they succeeded in supplanting the regular legal system. They were a propaganda boon to Sinn Féin which could portray itself as the responsible party of law and order, in contrast to the lawless forces of the crown. Even though many individual Volunteers and members of Sinn Féin ignored the Dáil courts, putting their own immediate economic interests before what they were told was the long-term interest of the nation, these courts did help to contain the agitation which, in general, did no serious damage to the political and military struggle against British rule.

This agrarian unrest was only one of the distractions which threatened Sinn Féin's efforts to focus attention on the 'national' question. The others were the Labour Party and the trade union movement. These were the only groups of any significance, with any degree of discipline or organisation, which were led by representatives of the working class, which wished to transform the structure of Irish society, and which offered a new deal for the Irish poor. They aimed to level up and down, and to alter the balance of property, of wealth and of power between the classes. The Labour Party's 1918 manifesto (for an election which, in the end, it did not contest) included the following aims:

> To win for the workers of Ireland, collectively, the ownership and control of the whole produce of their labour.
>
> To secure the democratic management and control of all industries and services by the whole body of workers, manual and mental, engaged therein....
>
> To abolish all power and privileges, social and political, of institutions or persons, based on property or ancestry, or not granted or confirmed by the freely expressed wish of the Irish people.[8]

Such objectives were not only far more specific than those of Sinn Féin, they were incompatible with the views of most Sinn Féin members.

In the early twentieth century the Irish Labour movement was confronted with a wide range of obstacles, ranging from clerical hostility to small-farmer conservatism. During the crucial years between 1916 and 1922 one of the most significant forces which it encountered was Sinn Féin's determination to absorb, deflect or crush any rivals.

The Labour Party is the oldest in the state, and the only party older than the state, but throughout its first decade it was a delicate and neglected creature, vulnerable, and totally lacking in self-confidence. It was originally an extension of the trade union movement and for long it lived in the unions' shadow. The Irish Trade Union Congress was founded in 1894 but for nearly twenty years it turned its back on politics. This was partly because industrial workers were divided in their loyalties between Protestants in the north, loyal to the connection with Britain, and Catholic nationalists in the south. The Belfast shipyards employed the largest group of male industrial workers in the country, and at the turn of the century half of Irish trade unionists lived in Belfast.[9] Until the spread of Larkin's Transport Workers' Union after 1909 northerners played a predominant role in the movement. Four times between 1905 and 1910 Belfast Labour contested the parliamentary seat of West Belfast, long before the nominal foundation of an Irish Labour party.

Even among Catholic trade unionists there was a widespread feeling that the workers should operate through the Irish Parliamentary Party rather than form their own political organisation. Not until 1912, when the establishment of a home rule parliament in Dublin seemed imminent and the attractions of a Labour group within that parliament seemed irresistible, did Congress decide to form a party. But despite the efforts of William O'Brien nothing was done for years beyond the addition of the words 'and Labour Party' to Congress's title. The new party's organisation was virtually non-existent, and remained so until 1922. Apart from its involvement in local politics it fought only one by-election during its first ten years. Like Sinn Féin between 1910 and 1917, Labour was a party with a programme, with leaders, with national influence, but with no network throughout the country.

This was partly because of those tensions between northern Protestants and southern Catholics which had delayed the party's foundation. Labour's obsession with doing nothing which might further divide northern and southern workers on sectarian lines was comparable to Sinn Féin's obsession with doing nothing which might divide Irish nationalists on class lines. There were significant differences: Sinn Féin succeeded and Labour failed; Sinn Féin was strengthened by its ruthless single-mindedness while Labour was weakened as it vacillated between conflicting policies. The similarity was striking nonetheless.

With the emergence and subsequent predominance of the Transport Workers' Union, and the leadership of the trade union movement by nationalists such as Connolly, Larkin and O'Brien, Labour began to veer towards republicanism in the years before the Easter Rising. Larkin gave a particularly clear example of his nationalist beliefs in his response to the Anglo–Irish treaty. He began his attack on the treaty with the declaration that

> we stand for the Dead. We entered into a compact with them when living. We will not fail them .... We will never in life, under any conditions, betray the Dead.[10]

His sentiments were in the best traditions of necrophilic Irish nationalism.

But in the years before nationalism was radicalised in 1917–18 the republican tendencies within the Irish Labour movement were normally restrained by fears of alienating not only the northern Unionist workers, but also the Catholic majority of the population, most of whom continued to support the Parliamentary Party. In the south many workers disliked Connolly's involvement in 'national' questions. Sean O'Casey represented many when he complained sourly that Connolly's eyes 'saw red no longer, but stared into the sky for a green dawn'.[11]

Connolly certainly did not believe, unlike Sinn Féin, that once independence was achieved all would be well, but he did believe, like them, that no significant progress could be made until after independence. Despite his years in Belfast he grossly underestimated the strength of Protestant workers' adherence to the Union. He failed to appreciate their consciousness of the advances being made by British Labour, of the better wages and conditions enjoyed by British workers, of the Irish Parliamentary Party's social conservatism. His writings and his participation in the 1916 Rising did much to strengthen the links between socialism and nationalism. His beliefs prevented him from coming to terms with Belfast workers' loyalty to Britain.[12]

The 1916 Rising's middle-class nationalist flavour, the destruction of Liberty Hall, and Connolly's own execution, were serious blows to the efforts he had made to bring socialists and republicans together. A reaction set in, and the down-to-earth, efficient men who succeeded him and Larkin resumed the Labour movement's earlier emphasis on less divisive and more purely 'social' issues. Its unity, badly shaken by Connolly, would have been further undermined by a continuing alliance with the apparently-defeated republicans.

The post-rising years saw a dramatic advance by the Transport Workers' Union which had been so badly mauled by the employers in 1913–14. During and after the first World War it spread from the cities and towns to represent farm labourers throughout the country. At the beginning of 1917 the union's membership was 14,500; by mid-1918 it was 43,000, and in 1920 it peaked at 130,000.[13] Its advance paralleled that of Sinn Féin, though at a slightly lower level. In the absence of an effective Labour party the radicalisation of the workers took a dual form; the trade unions acquired members, Sinn Féin acquired voters.

The result of these developments was that during the very years in which Sinn Féin replaced the Parliamentary Party as the dominant force in Irish public life, the Labour movement concentrated on economic rather than on political objectives. Connolly had associated Labour with extreme nationalism, but after his death it lost no time in distancing itself from such a dangerous ally. Its change of policy, or of emphasis, was symbolised by the 'facing both ways' resolution of the Sligo conference of the Trade Union Congress in August 1916; delegates commemorated those who had fallen both in the Great War and in the Easter Rising.

Labour had no sooner retreated from politics and nationalism than the sudden spread of the Sinn Féin party prevented it from claiming any significant share of the credit for transforming public opinion. Sinn Féin and the Volunteers faced no serious competition in their claim to be the sole heirs to the legacy of Easter Week. From 1918 onwards Labour was carried along by Sinn Féin. It was often a willing partner, despite the backward glances it threw over its shoulders at the disapproving Unionist workers in Belfast, but it was always a junior partner, and its position was even more clearly subordinate than it had been during the Rising.

It is significant that the three brief general strikes of the period, which were effective throughout the whole country except north-east Ulster, had all 'national' or political objectives: the prevention of conscription in April 1918, the release of hunger-strikers in April 1920, and the prevention of militarism in April 1922. They all proved the power of organised Labour. The first two were success-ful, and they benefited Sinn Féin.

Other industrial conflicts, especially the seven-month railway strike of 1920, were aimed at British rule in Ireland rather than at unyielding employers. There were many strikes for more pay and for better conditions, but in a time of rising prices such measures, when successful, tended only to keep wages level with inflation. In the light of Labour's earlier passivity, and the disorganisation of agricultural labourers, this was a considerable achievement.[14] Nega-tively the trade unions sought to protect jobs and prevent wage reductions, and as the post-war depression deepened in 1921 this became an increasingly important part of their activities.

Despite some waving of red flags and indulgence in wild rhetoric there was little sign of revolutionary views, let alone of Bolshevism, in the Irish Labour movement. 'Soviets', the seizure and operation by the workers of creameries, bakeries, foundries, mills, mines and other enterprises, were a feature of the period between 1920 and 1922. A Limerick soviet had been established as early as April 1919, although it was a response to a 'national' rather than an industrial grievance: Labour was drawn into a conflict between the British army and the Volunteers. In their response to an I.R.A. attack the British authorities, displaying either clumsiness or bloody-minded-ness, divided the city in two, established one part as a military zone, and instituted a system of passes and controls for people moving from one area to the other. A general strike resulted, and the work-ers set up a committee to run the city's affairs. After twelve days the strike was abandoned and soon afterwards the British removed their restrictions.

During the course of the next few years this example was followed widely and soviets were proclaimed in Arigna, Bruree, Knocklong and many other places. An eel fishers' soviet was established in Castleconnell.[15] Despite their revolutionary titles these occupations were not intended to bring about permanent workers' control, let alone a socialist Ireland. They were a means of fighting for wage increases or, particularly in 1921–2, fighting against reductions, without resorting to strikes and consequent loss of earnings. As soon as the management gave way or an agreement was reached control was restored to the owners. At times the strikers resorted to force: milk was seized at revolver-point to supply the soviet creamery in Carrick-on-Suir. More often the mood was one of good-humoured excitement; 'glimpses of the Red Flag thrilled those glutted with green'.[16]

Responses to the soviets ranged from cooperation to arson attacks and a boycott of their products.[17] The widespread middle-class alarm which they provoked was understandable but unjustified. While the precedent of one soviet often inspired another, there was no national, organised movement, no unifying force, and the soviets had virtually no political content. The Labour Party did not support them and was careful to describe them as 'strikes'.

Labour indulged in occasional dramatic gestures, such as the declaration in its 1918 election manifesto that 'we adopt the principle of the Russian Revolution', or the alignment of the Irish delegates at the Socialist conference in Berne in 1919 with the dictatorship of the proletariat rather than with parliamentary democracy.[18] Such moves did little more than provide their enemies with welcome ammunition. When it was concerned with Irish realities the party showed less daring; its rhetoric might at times be revolutionary, its actions remained democratic.

At the time and subsequently absurd comparisons were made between events in Ireland and in Russia. A far more accurate parallel would be between the situation in Ireland in early 1922 and that in Germany at the end of 1918. In both countries the most left-wing elements of the opposition were faced with a government which, while well-disposed in principle, drifted to the right and accepted help from its former enemies in its efforts to impose order. In both cases the representatives of the working class declared firmly against any seizure of power. The demand for the election of a constituent assembly made by the Congress of Soldiers' and Workers' Councils in Berlin, the so-called 'suicide of the German revolution', was matched by the declaration of the Irish labour and trade union movement, through the *Voice of Labour*, that until the Dáil had debated and voted on the treaty Labour would not inter-

vene because 'the Dáil and not Labour have been entrusted and invested by the Irish people with the authority and responsibility'.[19]
However moderate and democratic it might be, Labour encountered
a widespread fear of socialists and socialism. The 'red scare' thrived
in Ireland as elsewhere. As so often, this mood is best illustrated by
the *Irish Independent:*

> There is one form of socialism which Christianity is opposed to *in toto*.
> We refer to the doctrines of Marx and Engels, which proclaim the com-
> mon ownership of the means of production, an idea not only abhorrent
> to Christianity, but to every natural instinct of mankind. These are the
> doctrines championed by the Russian Soviets and by the late James
> Connolly, doctrines which the 'Socialist Party of Ireland' distribute
> among the illiterate in Dublin from their headquarters in Liberty Hall.[20]

One Parliamentary Party supporter claimed that the organisers of
the Easter Rising were 'the Socialists who were engaged in the great
strike in Dublin, and who carried innocent little children down to
the docks to have them proselytised and sent to England'.[21] The
clergy joined in with attacks on the menace of atheistic socialism.
The left was forced on the defensive. In 1919 an issue of the *Watchword of Labour* devoted half its front page to elaborating the head-
line 'a Catholic may be a Socialist'.[22]

Sinn Féin tended not to join in such attacks. There were exceptions, such as the occasion during the treaty when Countess Markievicz, having stressed her abstract republicanism, referred to
Connolly's ideal of a workers' republic and thereby provoked an
unnamed deputy to interrupt with the taunt 'Soviet Republic'.[23] But
in general there was no return to the earlier hostility which had
characterised relations between Griffith and Larkin before 1914 or
between the Volunteers and the Citizen Army before January 1916.
Problems still remained, and many Sinn Féin members were embarrassed by their party's association with Labour and the trade
unions. Their attitude tended to be apologetic. Michael Staines,
soon to be a Sinn Féin T.D., assured one Dublin audience that

> Connolly died as a brave Irish Catholic. It was true that Connolly was
> now dubbed a Socialist. The word was often used in a loose sense. He
> [Staines] had never heard of a Socialist, in the condemned sense of the
> word, preparing for death as Connolly did.

He went on to expound on Connolly's associations with the Capu-
chins.[24] Even Hanna Sheehy-Skeffington, one of the few social
radicals in Sinn Féin, felt obliged to stress that Pearse and Connolly
were in one grave in quicklime,[25] as if Connolly had expunged his

errors through posthumous proximity to a hero as untainted as Pearse.

Socialism's godless image made it easier for the Sinn Féin party to do what many of its supporters were inclined to do in any case: keep their distance. Even those sympathetic towards the Labour movement tended to regard it as a mere appendage, and Helena Molony of the Women Workers' Union warned Sinn Féin at the party convention in 1917 that it was inclined to dictate too much to Labour.[26] Sinn Féin accepted Labour's support as its due and offered nothing but platitudes in return. It would not commit itself to any of Labour's objectives except in the most generalised and innocuous terms.

Sinn Féin did contain a small radical element, prominent among which were Markievicz, the first minister for labour in the underground Dáil cabinet, and Hanna Sheehy-Skeffington, who turned down the offer of a seat in 1918 but later became the party's director of organisation. It was prepared to reinforce this group on an *ad hoc* basis, borrowing Richard Corish from the Labour stronghold of Wexford for the duration of the second Dáil, and returning him in time to win a seat for Labour in 1922.

But after Connolly's death Liam Mellows was the only republican of any significance who put forward a radical programme. His importance was limited, and lies more in his uniqueness than in his influence or achievements. He was in the United States from October 1916 to October 1920 and he spent much of the next year in Britain, smuggling arms into Ireland. His electoral record did not mark him out as a great popular leader. He was returned unopposed for Galway in 1918 and 1921. The 1922 election was the first occasion on which he faced opposition, and then he was the only one of eight candidates who failed to be elected.[27] For much of his career he was a conventional republican; in the treaty debates, for example, he referred to the Dáil's declaration of independence of January 1921 but not to the democratic programme which followed it.[28] It was only in his jail letters, written shortly before his execution, that he revealed himself as a social radical.

One of the few genuine social revolutionaries within Sinn Féin was Peadar O'Donnell, but his influence was slight and, at least in one case, transient. C. S. Andrews remembered how, after taking his leave of O'Donnell in Letterkenny in 1921, 'the vision he had evoked for me vanished. I reverted to the "Aisling" which Pearse had created for the nation'.[29] O'Donnell later lamented that his colleagues had frowned on 'radical demands that could have moved whole counties'.[30]

The formal statements of the republican movement contained little to disturb Irish capitalists. Connolly was probably responsible for the Easter Week proclamation's guarantee of equal rights and equal opportunities to all citizens, and for its promise to cherish all children of the nation equally. Thomas Johnson can claim credit for the Dáil's democratic programme which guaranteed improved conditions for the working class as well as the right of every citizen to an adequate share of the nation's labour. But these were little more than sops or gestures on what were otherwise nationalist occasions. Even after the democratic programme had been censored to meet Sinn Féin's needs there was opposition to its remaining radical elements, and within a few months de Valera was engaged in explaining it away. He declared that the programme, as adopted by Sinn Féin, contemplated a different situation from the one in which they found themselves. It could not be put into effect until 'the occupation of the foreigner' was ended. He went on to point out that he had never made any promise to Labour because, while the enemy was within the gates, the immediate problem was to get possession of the country.[31]

Sinn Féin gave innumerable examples of its caution and respectability. In August 1917, for example, not long after his release from Lewes Jail, de Valera assured an audience in Kilkenny that members of Sinn Féin were not anarchists and Jacobins.[32] A syndicated column, circulated by party headquarters, warned that 'Sinn Féin stands less for a party than for the Nation... it cannot, as such, have a programme for labour any more than it can have a programme for capital'. (It went on to point out sensibly that any programme which might satisfy labour would certainly not satisfy capital.)[33] At times its tone became sanctimonious, as in its claim 'that Sinn Féin will be just towards Labour no intelligent or impartial observer can doubt.... Sinn Féin suffers to-day for all classes of the Irish people, but particularly for the working class'. (The effect of this statement was lessened by what seemed like a vein of self-parody when it continued: 'if on the summit of its Calvary it is not dismayed by the surrounding gloom it is because it knows that the Resurrection Morn shall come, that the nation shall be saved'.)[34]

Sinn Féin was prepared to cooperate with Labour on the understanding that it represented the Irish people politically, that the Volunteers represented them militarily, and that the Labour and trade union movements were a worthy sectional interest whose views would be given serious consideration. The left was to form a pressure group, not a party. Labour could foster its members' interests provided that such interests would not damage those of the country. Sinn Féin would represent the country.

In the view of *The Times*, Ireland in 1919 presented the spectacle of a community on strike against its government.[35] Sinn Féin would have agreed wholeheartedly, and it was deeply and genuinely appreciative of those political strikes which reinforced such an impression. Non-political strikes, carried out for motives less worthy than the achievement of national independence, were unwelcome in so far as they distracted from the principal objective. To help prevent them the Dáil established a department of labour which, among other objectives, tried to settle disputes between employers and employees. Its achievements were modest, and other, more purely 'national', interests took up much of its attention. In May 1921, for instance, the department reported to the Dáil cabinet that almost all its efforts for the previous eight weeks had been devoted to enforcing the Belfast boycott.[36]

Sinn Féin's general attitude was summed up in the phrase 'Labour must wait'. Whether or not de Valera or any other Sinn Féin leader actually used these words they were an accurate summary of the party's views. At an institutional level the relationship between Sinn Féin and Labour, between the forces of revolutionary nationalism and of democratic radicalism, can best be illustrated by the pattern of the three general elections of 1918, 1921 and 1922. In the first two campaigns Labour *did* wait.

Elements in the Labour movement were anxious to contest the 1918 elections, even though as yet the party showed little sign of activity or organisation. It was still in effect an extension of the trade unions, and in the eyes of many trade unionists who were determined to vote Sinn Féin it was a redundant extension.

Sinn Féin wanted a straight fight against the Irish Parliamentary Party and it was alarmed by the prospect of opposition from Labour; in the words of one member of a delegation to the party's standing committee, Labour would be unable to win any seats but might deprive Sinn Féin of as many as twenty.[37] The standing committee was prepared to negotiate over the allocation of three Dublin seats, but Labour demanded more: four in Dublin, one each in Cork and Derry, and the prospect of contesting three others as well.[38] This was over-ambitious, and Labour's preparations for the campaign began to run into difficulties. Entries in William O'Brien's diary illustrate problems which the party faced. On 29 September he attended a conference on the general election with the

Meath Labour Union. It was decided not to run a candidate. On 1 October Louie Bennett withdrew. When O'Brien arrived in Cork on 19 October he found that a conference to select a Labour candidate would not take place.[39] From around the country there were discouraging reports, and in the end Labour was realistic in deciding to field only four candidates. But even such reduced ambitions provoked resentment. In Dublin, some of the Sinn Féin rank and file were alarmed by rumours of the party's secret negotiations with Labour and they opposed any compromise which would force their candidates to stand down. Their complaints to the Sinn Féin standing committee reinforced pressure on Labour from trade and labour councils throughout the country, and in the end the party decided not to run any candidates. A special conference in Dublin decided on withdrawal from the elections by the substantial margin of four to one, by 96 votes to 23. Thomas Johnson declared piously that Labour was the only party prepared to sacrifice itself in the interests of the nation. The very different reality was expressed by a delegate who warned that organised bodies of Labour supporters had declared they would vote Sinn Féin against any man.[40]

The significance of this decision has often been exaggerated, although recent studies claim that Labour had little choice and that withdrawal, however unpalatable, averted a worse disaster.[41] There is evidence to support the argument that abstention in 1918 did Labour no harm whatever.

In the urban and municipal elections in 1920 Sinn Féin, which had swept the country only a year before, performed badly and won only 422 seats to Labour's 324. The discrepancy between Sinn Féin's vote and Labour's was far greater in the rural elections five months later; the two parties worked as a team but Labour secured only 11 per cent of the seats won by the panel. By this stage the Transport Workers' Union had reached its peak in terms of membership, but there was little follow-through from union card to ballot paper. By this stage, too, with the Government of Ireland Bill half-way through parliament and the partition of Ireland apparently inevitable, Belfast trade unionists' restraints on Labour's nationalism were less marked than they had been before.

In the elections of May 1921 Labour made a formal but empty protest and then stood down again, allowing Sinn Féin to win every seat for the new southern Irish parliament apart from those reserved for Trinity College. Not until the treaty had been signed at the end of the year did the Labour Party begin to organise itself and play an active rather than a passive role in public affairs. It urged the rival factions in the Dáil and the I.R.A. to concentrate on solving social problems rather than on expounding their constitutional differences, and it took the lead in denouncing the drift towards violence.

The pattern of 1916 was repeated in 1922 in that Labour felt obliged once again to remain silent on the great issue of the day. The party leaders believed that to take one side or the other in the dispute over the treaty would antagonise a large section of their members. This time, however, its neutrality posed fewer problems and caused it no damage.

It was only by the surprisingly narrow margin of 115 votes to 82 that a special Labour conference decided to contest the forthcoming general election. A more full-blooded determination to end Labour's ten-year abstinence from effective politics might have been expected, all the more since this vote was taken only hours before a meeting of the Sinn Féin Árd Fheis which was widely, though wrongly, expected to result in the party's disintegration. One delegate warned that Labour could win only a handful of seats, two handfuls at most, and that they should postpone their efforts until the Sinn Féin factions had decided the question of the treaty.[42]

In the circumstances such a lack of self-confidence was hardly surprising. The *Voice of Labour* later commented that only Sinn Féin's decision to postpone elections for some months gave Labour any chance whatever of contesting more than those seats 'where there might be an irresistible local demand'.[43] In late 1921, after the truce, Sinn Féin members had been exhorted to revive their party's organisation. This was done, just in time for it to split in two over the treaty. In 1922 there were corresponding pleas for the *creation* of Labour's electoral machinery, and lamentations over the party's inexperience and disarray. One advantage which it enjoyed was the agreement by both sections of Sinn Féin that the principal topic of the day, the treaty, should not be an issue in the elections. To a greater extent than would have been possible in 1918 or 1921, Labour could fight on ground of its own choosing.

The Party selected only twenty-two candidates, and in the end four of them were not nominated. Despite the official blessing given to third parties by the rival wings of Sinn Féin, republicans tried to discourage Labour, farmers and independent candidates from standing, calculating rightly that their presence would weaken opponents of the treaty. Perhaps the clearest instance of this comes from Co. Clare. As the final minutes before the deadline for nominations ticked by, the Labour candidate, Patrick Hogan, was urged not to fight. He was told 'be either a man or a mouse', the clear implication being that withdrawal was the heroic course. Discussions continued. Time passed. Hogan began to speak and had just said 'Well, of course . . . .' when one of the republicans interrupted 'It is done! Withdraw first and make a speech afterwards!' He withdrew, and in his speech admitted that he had no mandate to stand down.[44] If he had run he would probably have been elected. A year later, under far less promising circumstances, he won a seat and then held it with only one break for the next forty-four years.

In the light of its previous almost non-existent record, Labour's success in 1922 was remarkable. Seventeen of its eighteen candidates were returned, and the eighteenth was defeated on the last count by only thirteen votes in a constituency where the circumstances were particularly unfavourable. The party's candidates headed the poll in five constituencies. In Wexford Labour won more first preferences than both Sinn Féin factions combined. Cathal O'Shannon came first in Louth–Meath with 14,000 votes, double the number won by his nearest rival and over double the quota. With 21 per cent of the first preferences Labour had secured, at its first test, a higher share of the vote than it was ever to achieve again. If one excludes Dan Breen, republican in sympathy but supported by both sides of Sinn Féin (although not supported by enough voters to be elected), Labour won more first preferences than the anti-treaty section of Sinn Féin. The unopposed election of thirty-four panel T.D.s reduced the vote which the rival Sinn Féin factions would otherwise have received, but on the other hand there can be no doubt that if Labour had shown more courage it could have won more votes and more seats.[45]

All this reinforces the argument that Labour's prospects had not been doomed irrevocably by its failure to fight in 1918. It does not prove that Ireland was in a socially radical mood in 1922, or that a left-wing party might easily have established itself as a major force in Irish politics. Labour gained sympathy on the rebound, as a result of widespread distaste for the feuding which had characterised Sinn Féin's activities during the six months since the treaty. It was able to win support by calling 'a plague on both your houses'. As well as mobilising its own followers, it could exploit the readiness of disillusioned Sinn Féin supporters and former Redmondites to vote for anyone other than a Sinn Féin candidate. Farmers and independents also benefited from this antipathy to Sinn Féin; they won a total of seventeen seats, four of them in Trinity College.

Non-nationalists benefited from an anti-nationalist mood.

It is ironic that while Labour's success in 1922 was brought about in large measure by fear of a civil war between forces ranged for and against the treaty, its subsequent failure resulted largely from the outbreak, course and legacy of this war. The bitterness of guerrilla warfare polarised loyalties and hatreds in a way in which the skirmishing during the first half of 1922 had failed to do. Just as the post-war recession of 1921 had halted the progress made by the Transport Workers' Union, so the civil war enhanced or restored the primacy of the 'national' question. Issues such as the choice between Free State or Republic, or of Ireland's relations with Britain, regained the hitherto-dominant role which, the 1922 election results seemed to indicate, they were in danger of losing. The civil war restored Irish normality, European abnormality, to independent Ireland. The revolution, nationalist as ever, crushed radicalism.

The 1923 elections confirmed this trend and reversed Labour's recent advance. Labour was now an established party, the official opposition in the Dáil, and in its short active history it had much to be proud of. It entered the campaign with high hopes, fielding forty-four candidates in twenty-seven of the thirty constituencies. But in some respects it was weaker than it had been a year earlier. Many radicals were alienated by Labour's respectability and moderation. The party was now divided into rival factions as Larkin, recently returned to Ireland, quarrelled bitterly with his successors. Unable to rule as he wished, he wrecked. It seemed as if Sinn Féin's lesson of the previous year had been ignored. Cosgrave's government campaigned with the slogan 'safety first', and it was able to dispute the role of peace party which Labour had enjoyed in 1922.

The membership of the Dáil had been increased by twenty-five and most parties increased their number of seats. Cumann na nGaedheal gained five, Sinn Féin eight, the farmers eight and independents seven. Labour lost three. Its share of first preferences was halved, falling to 11.5 per cent. It lost its few urban seats and became a rural party. Cathal O'Shannon, who had headed the poll so comfortably a year before, was the first to be eliminated in Louth. From being the second largest party in terms of votes in 1922, Labour was reduced to being the fourth party in the new Dáil in terms of seats. The Farmers won more, and there were even more independents than Labour deputies. The election of 1922 had been an aberration; that of 1923 relegated Labour to the minor role it has suffered ever since.

The new Irish government proved itself even more conservative than its British predecessor. This was a natural development. Long-ingrained habits made it second nature for nationalists to postpone dealing with radical demands, to regard them as a distraction and a threat. Even during the Anglo–Irish war, when they were on the run and operated from attics and cellars, the Sinn Féin administrators exuded the pomposity of experienced bureaucrats. A Dáil of July 1920 which prohibited emigration stated in its preamble:

> whereas it has come to our knowledge that a number of men of military age and other citizens of the Republic are leaving Ireland. And whereas Ireland cannot spare any of her children at the present juncture.... [46]

The tone and attitude were far more significant than any impact which the decree might have had on would-be emigrants. Long before independence, Sinn Féin was an establishment-in-waiting.

This conservatism was reinforced by the civil war. Supporters of the treaty tended to view social radicalism and republicanism as twin apparitions of anarchy. At the height of the civil war the former Redmondite M.P. Thomas Esmonde noted in his diary 'there was ambushing and bolshevism in many parts of the country',[47] and some months earlier the provisional government had referred to 'Bolshevism sheltering under the name of Republicanism'.[48] Supporters of the new *status quo* ignored the mutual independence, even hostility, of republicanism and social radicalism. They used each term to disparage the other.

During the civil war all the government's efforts were devoted to defeating the anti-treaty forces and to maintaining order. Then and later it was concerned with proving that it could administer the country with greater firmness and efficiency than the British had displayed, and it showed little inclination to experiment. The old habit of postponing social change was maintained intact. Kevin O'Higgins's remark 'we were probably the most conservative-minded revolutionaries that ever put through a successful revolution'[49] reflects accurately the mood and policy of the Cumann na nGaedheal government.

More surprising, at least at first glance, was the equal conservatism displayed by republican opponents of the treaty. Long before the 1922 elections gave them only 21 per cent of the first preference votes they realised that their views enjoyed little popularity outside the ranks of the I.R.A.; those who claimed most ardently to represent Ireland were under no illusion that they represented the Irish people. It might have seemed good tactics to seek support from other discontented elements, particularly the poor, the landless and the unemployed, and to forge a coalition of interests opposed not only to the treaty but to other grievances as well. With a few marginal exceptions this did not happen, and during the first half of 1922 the rival sections of the I.R.A. could blur their disagreements over the treaty by cooperating in a common hostility to strikers and pickets. In their social beliefs the most zealous revolutionaries remained conservative; their Republic was too sacred to be associated with class conflict.

The attitude of the minuscule Irish Communist Party was even more surprising, although of no more than symbolic importance. The party opposed the treaty, not because it had failed to advance a workers' or a soviet republic, but because it had betrayed the mystical Republic.[50]

Radicals might reasonably have expected that the Irish national-ist obsession might weaken after independence had been achieved and that attention might then be diverted to other questions. Any such hopes were disappointed as divisions over the treaty polarised southern Irish politics on nationalist rather than on class lines. After 1921 as before, social questions continued to be viewed as a distraction from what the bulk of the population believed to be the most urgent, exciting or feasible national objective.

Partition ensured that anti-British nationalism would survive and prosper, and, far more importantly, it divided the most industrial-ised part of Ireland from the rest of the country. In a united inde-pendent Ireland Belfast might have become a socialist stronghold, but partition consolidated the old hegemony of orange and green. Nationalists failed to secure a united Ireland but even their failure helped to stifle social radicalism.

In 1912 George A. Birmingham, in a novel about Ulster unionism, made one of his characters declare that

> nowadays, when the industrial proletariate is breaking free from all control, it is a splendid thing for us to have a cause in which we take the lead, which will bind our working class to us, and make them loyal to those who are after all their best friends and their natural leaders.[51]

The ideologies of unionism and nationalism appealed to Irishmen's imaginations, evoked loyalties which transcended class interests, and ensured that the middle class would continue to dominate Irish public life. Before, during and after the revolutionary years from 1916 to 1922, social change was a distraction from what both the political establishment and the electorate regarded as the most pressing issue of the day. Even during a period of upheaval nationalists were able to defeat radicals with remarkable ease. Labour waited.

Notes

1. Bulmer Hobson, *Defensive warfare* (Belfast, 1909), p. 9.
2. *Irish Freedom*, Apr. 1911.
3. *Nationality*, 24 Mar. 1917.
4. Griffith to Lily Williams, 29 Nov. 1916, N.L.I., MS 5943.
5. J. L. McCracken, *Representative government in Ireland* (Oxford, 1948), pp 33–4.
6. Dáil proclamation, 29 June 1920, Barton papers, N.L.I. MS 8786 (1).
7. Cabinet minutes, 31 May 1920, S.P.O., DE 1/2.
8. *Irish Labour Party and Trade Union Congress report*, 1918, p. 168 (hereafter cited as *Labour Party report*).
9. Arthur Mitchell, *Labour in Irish politics, 1890–1930* (Dublin, 1974), p. 18.
10. *Voice of Labour*, 7 Jan. 1922.
11. Sean O'Casey, *Drums under the windows* (London, 1945), p. 315.
12. See Michael Gallagher, 'Socialism and nationalist tradition in Ireland, 1798–1918' in *Eire–Ireland*, xii (1977), pp 91–2; Henry Patterson, *Class conflict and sectarianism* (Belfast, 1980), pp 84–5, 87.
13. C. Desmond Greaves, *The Irish Transport and General Workers' Union: the formative years, 1920–1923* (Dublin, 1982), pp 178, 206, 276.
14. For strikes see David Fitzpatrick, 'Strikes in Ireland, 1914–21' in *Saothar* 6 (1980), pp 26–39; D. R. O'C. Lysaght, 'Class struggle during the Irish war of independence and civil war, 1916–1924' (unpublished M.A. thesis, U.C.D., 1982).
15. *Voice of Labour*, 10 Dec. 1921, leader entitled 'Soviet eels in the Shannon'.
16. David Fitzpatrick, *Politics and Irish life, 1913–21* (Dublin, 1977), p. 255.
17. Lysaght, op. cit., p. 185.
18. *Labour Party report*, 1919, p. 31.
19. *Voice of Labour*, 17 Dec. 1921, leader.
20. *Irish Independent*, 3 Oct. 1919, leader.
21. Ibid., 30 Nov. 1918.
22. *Watchword of Labour*, 18 Oct. 1919.
23. *Debate on the treaty. Official report*, p. 182 (3 Jan. 1922).
24. *Irish Independent*, 9 Dec. 1918.
25. Ibid., 31 Oct. 1918.
26. *Report on the Sinn Féin convention*, 14 Nov. 1917, P.R.O., CO.904/23/5.
27. In his 400 page biography of Mellows C. Desmond Greaves finds no space to mention this defeat.
28. *Debates on the Treaty*, p. 228 (4 Jan. 1922).
29. C. S. Andrews, *Dublin made me* (Dublin, 1979), p. 200.
30. Michael McInerney, *Peadar O'Donnell, Irish social rebel* (Dublin, 1974), p. 42.
31. *Dáil debates, 1919–21*, p. 78 (11 Apr. 1919).
32. *Freeman's Journal*, 13 Aug. 1917.
33. *Kerryman*, 19 Oct. 1918.
34. *Irishman*, 12 Oct. 1918.
35. *Times*, 9 Dec. 1919.
36. Report by Joseph MacDonagh, acting minister for Labour, May 1921, S.P.O., DE 2/5.

37. Sinn Féin standing committee minutes, 7 Oct. 1918, N.L.I., MS P 3269.
38. Ibid., 23 Sept. 1918.
39. O'Brien papers, N.L.I., MS 15,705 (11).
40. *Labour Party report*, 1918, pp 104, 114.
41. See Fitzpatrick, *Politics* p. 257; Gallagher, 'Socialism' pp 101–2; Tom Garvin, *The evolution of Irish nationalist politics* (Dublin, 1981), p. 120.
42. *Labour Party report*, 1922, pp 71, 84.
43. *Voice of Labour*, 4 Mar. 1922.
44. *Clare Champion*, 10 June 1922.
45. On the results see Michael Gallagher, 'The pact election of 1922' in *I.H.S.*, xxi (1979), pp 404–21.
46. S.P.O., DE 2/8/27 (27 July 1920).
47. N.L.I. MS 3907 (16 Aug. 1922).
48. Cabinet minutes, 25 May 1922, S.P.O., G 1/1.
49. *Dáil debates*, ii, 1909 (1 Mar. 1923).
50. Lysaght, op. cit., p. 158.
51. George A. Birmingham, *The Red Hand of Ulster* (repr. Shannon, 1972), p. 58.

'We are with you':
solidarity and self-interest
in Soviet policy towards
Republican Spain, 1936–1939

Denis Smyth

On 3 August 1936, a crowd of around 150,000 people thronged Moscow's Red Square. It was a female worker from the 'Red Dawn' factory, E. Bystrova, who expressed the purpose of this gathering most eloquently:

> Our hearts are with those who at this moment are giving up their lives in the mountains and streets of Spain, defending the liberty of their people. We send our greeting of fraternal solidarity, our proletarian greeting to the Spanish men and women workers, to the Spanish wives and mothers, to all the Spanish people. We say to you: remember that you are not alone, that we are with you.[1]

Although the *Pravda* journalist Mijail 'Koltsov', maintained that the Muscovite manifestation had not been pre-planned, and had been organised at the shortest notice, foreign diplomatic observers did not doubt that it represented the official Soviet attitude, on that date, towards the recent military uprising against the Spanish Republic.[2] Indeed, Republican Spain's ambassador to the U.S.S.R., Dr Marcelino Pascua, reminded his government, on several occasions, during his accreditation to Moscow from October onwards, that Soviet 'public opinion' was so 'absolutely directed and controlled' that it could be viewed as a reliable guide to the Soviet régime's inclinations and intentions, at any given moment.[3] Moreover, there was no denying the official Soviet Communist inspiration behind the first practical expression of the allegedly spontaneous upwelling of Russian proletarian solidarity with the embattled Spanish Republic. Collections in aid of the 'Spanish fighters for the Republic' were organised in all Soviet factories by the All-Union

Central Council of Trade Unions. It was reported that so enthusiastic was the response of Soviet workers to this appeal for support for democracy in Spain that they voted unanimously, in every instance, a 'voluntary' contribution of an identical share of their wages, 0.5 per cent deductible at source. The levy yielded 12,145,000 roubles (*c*.£500,000 sterling) by 6 August, and amounted to 47,595,000 roubles by the end of October.[4] This financial resource was rapidly translated into humanitarian assistance to Spain: on 18 September, the first Soviet ship to sail for Republican Spain, the *Neva*, departed with a cargo of foodstuffs. Other Soviet ships followed in a sustained effort to deliver alimentary aid to the populous Republican zone of central and eastern Spain, an area deprived of its agrarian hinterland in the south and north of the country by the rapid advance of the military rebels on Madrid.[5]

However, Republican Spain needed more than the mere means to keep body and soul together in order to survive, as Franco's Army of Africa drove on the capital city in the autumn of 1936. Madrid was indeed, as Auden put it, 'the heart', but to keep beating it had to exercise the sinews of modern warfare.[6] Once again, the Soviet Union revealed itself to be willing to provide this vital form of help to the Spanish Republican civil war effort. During the autumn and winter of 1936–37, twenty-three Soviet merchant ships laden with military equipment, arms and ammunition left Black Sea ports for Spain, while other Russian munitions were smuggled over the Pyrenean frontier. Soviet aircraft and tank crews helped the new Republican Popular Army employ this *matériel* to such effect that Madrid was rescued, a defensive victory won at the Jarama in February, and the Italian Corpo Truppe Volontarie routed at Guadalajara in March 1937.[7] Moreover, the International Brigades recruited and trained, at Moscow's behest, by the Comintern and its 'front' organisations proved to be more than just proficient 'shock' troops in the battles that saved Madrid. They also seemed to be the very embodiment of the resolve of 'the fatherland of the working class of all countries' (as Stalin described the U.S.S.R. in January 1934) to honour its obligation to uphold the Spanish Popular Front against domestic reaction and foreign fascist intervention.[8] Indeed, Joseph Stalin, the general secretary of the Communist Party of the Soviet Union, claimed that it was precisely this international class consciousness which had prompted Russia to support the beleaguered Spanish Republicans. In a telegram addressed to José Díaz, the general secretary of the Partido Comunista de España (P.C.E.), published on 16 October 1936, Stalin made this declaration:

The working people of the Soviet Union are only doing their duty in rendering what aid they can to the revolutionary masses of Spain. They are fully aware that the liberation of Spain from the yoke of the fascist reactionaries is not a private concern of Spaniards, but the common cause of all forward-looking and progressive humanity.[9]

Nearly forty years later, the then chairperson of the P.C.E., Dolores Ibarruri, 'La Pasionaria', repeated Stalin's contention that it was a disinterested internationalism that had induced the U.S.S.R. to become engaged in the Spanish conflict: 'it declared from the very first hour of the struggle that the cause of the Spanish Republic was that of all progressive and forward-looking mankind'.[10]

Leaving aside, for the moment, La Pasionaria's analysis of the motives behind Soviet intervention in Spain, her memory is faulty on the question of its timing, for as late as 29 July 1936 (the military revolt against the Republic having broken out during the night of 17–18 July), she herself appealed to all countries to save Spanish democracy, by which date neither in word nor deed had the Soviet government come out in clear support of Republican Spain.[11] Indeed, on the very day of La Pasionaria's urgent plea for international help, the British ambassador in Moscow, Viscount Chilston, reported that the officially-controlled Soviet press had displayed a 'great' but only a 'non-commital interest' in the Spanish Civil War, since its outbreak. He also recorded a specific Soviet press refutation of a Francoist allegation that a Russian oil tanker had supported an attack by a unit of the Republican fleet on the rebel-held Spanish Moroccan coastline:

Spanish government has never asked Soviet Union for assistance and we are convinced that they will find in their own country sufficient forces to liquidate this mutiny of fascist generals acting on orders from foreign countries.[12]

Italy's ambassador in Moscow similarly reported home in early August 1936 that the Soviet government had 'made every effort to commit itself as little as possible' in the Spanish affair.[13]

Yet the events that were to produce an eventual *volte-face* in Soviet policy towards the Spanish Civil War also began on 29 July 1936. On that day, the first aircraft of a contingent of twenty German Junkers 52s arrived in Spanish Morocco, and set to work at once, transporting Franco's troops over the Strait of Gibraltar which was dominated by the Spanish Republican fleet. On 30 July, three of the twelve Savoia-Marchetti S.81 bombers sent by Mussolini to augment this air ferry crashed *en route*, two of them on to French Moroccan territory.[14] The news of fascist intervention in the Spanish conflict on the rebel side was out.[15] According to Chilston's dispatch of 10 August 1936 to the Foreign Office, it was 'the growing weight of evidence that the two principal "fascist" states were actively assisting the insurgents' that caused the Soviet government to abandon the 'correct and neutral' attitude it had maintained towards the Spanish Civil War during the first fifteen days after its outbreak.[16] The Moscow demonstration of 3 August, already mentioned, the similar meetings held across the Soviet Union and the collection of funds for Republican Spain were intended to signal the communist state's displeasure at the evidence of foreign fascist interference in the Spanish troubles. Yet the Soviet response was still cautious. For, though there were advocates of immediate, active Soviet and international communist support for Republican Spain within the Comintern, the French military attaché in Moscow, Lieutenant-Colonel Simon, informed Paris that there was also a 'moderate group', to which Stalin belonged, which wanted to avoid any intervention in the Spanish fight, 'so as not to provoke a reaction from Germany and Italy'.[17] Indeed, the Soviet government replied to the Anglo–French project for an international non-intervention agreement on Spain with alacrity, readily affirming its willingness to adhere to the principle of non-intervention in the internal affairs of Spain.[18] The Italian ambassador to the U.S.S.R. got the impression that 'the French proposal for a non-intervention agreement with regard to Spain was received with the greatest relief', since it absolved Moscow from making the difficult choice between abandoning the Spanish Left or risking precipitation of a European war.[19]

In subscribing, on 23 August 1936, to the international non-intervention agreement on Spain, which prohibited arms supplies to either of the Spanish contestants, the Soviet Union was lending its support to a scheme which denied the Republican Popular Front its right under international law, as the legitimate government of its country, to acquire the means abroad to supress the domestic rebellion against it.[20] Moreover, as the French chargé d'affaires, Payart, told the Quai d'Orsay on 3 September 1936, Soviet adherence to the non-intervention scheme was a victory for 'M. Stalin's currently constructive ideas'. Although it had provoked violent opposition at the heart of the Communist Party of the Soviet Union, Stalin's line of participation in the non-intervention agreement had prevailed. Inspired by 'the two principles of European solidarity and the peaceful coexistence of peoples', Stalin's 'positive policy' represented a deliberate dereliction by 'the fatherland of the working class of all countries' of its duty to help its proletarian progeny in time of need.[21]

Nor did the Soviet Union join the non-intervention powers all the better to render effective aid to its comrades in Spain for as long as possible, as did Fascist Italy and Nazi Germany. Some Soviet military experts and perhaps some limited amounts of Soviet small arms did find their way to Republican Spain during the days immediately following Soviet subscription to the non-intervention agreement. However, the first large-scale shipment of Soviet military supplies did not reach Spain until 15 October, when the *Komsomol* docked at Cartagena.[22] Moreover, this breach of promise occurred only after the Kremlin had warned the London-based Non-Intervention Committee, on 7 October 1936, that 'if violations of the agreement for Non-Intervention [were] not immediately stopped the Soviet Government [would] consider itself free from the obligations arising out of the agreement'.[23] An *Izvestiya* editorial of 26 August 1936 had explained Soviet participation in the non-intervention agreement on the grounds that the latter scheme was 'apparently directed towards the cessation of this [fascist] aid to the rebels and to the guaranteeing of the actual non-participation of other countries in Spanish affairs'.[24] If the non-intervention agreement proved effective the Soviet Union was prepared, seemingly, to uphold it. However, if the agreement failed to cut the Francoists off from their fascist providers, then Moscow would examine other ways and means of attaining its policy-goal in Spain.

The Italian ambassador in Moscow defined that Soviet policy-goal towards Spain in these terms on 13 August 1936: 'Soviet leaders have in the final analysis allowed their attitude to be dictated by the demands of peace, which is their principal aim'.[25] From the time of his arrival in Moscow, on 7 October 1936, the Spanish Republican representative, Pascua (who was afforded a privileged access to the Kremlin granted to no other western diplomat at this time) was able to accumulate direct evidence which led him to form an identical view of the predominant purpose of Soviet policy. Pascua informed his government in January 1937 that the Soviet leaders realized that they needed 'several years of peace which would permit the U.S.S.R. to develop its enormous domestic plans [which were] of such great importance for it and the socio-political world and to consolidate and perfect its still immature military power'. Pascua maintained that the Soviet Communists had relegated the fomenting of Marxist revolutions abroad to a subordinate role in their international strategy:

> The present policy of the U.S.S.R. is dominated by the idea of the socialist construction of this country... the socialist construction of the U.S.S.R. absolutely predominates over everything else not only as a current task, but also as decisive for the future of socialism. This is... the axis of the question as regards the Soviets.[26]

Pascua had perceived the essential nature of Stalinist foreign policy: the building of 'socialism in one country', the Soviet Union, was held to be in the overriding interest not only of Russian workers, but of the whole world's proletariat. Thus was the pre-eminence of *raison d'état* in Soviet foreign policy reconciled with revolutionary internationalism. To complete their massive socio-economic transformation of the U.S.S.R. through the Five-Year Plans, the Soviet Communists needed a quiet international existence, free from external distraction and foreign interruption. Peace and security were their principal international aims. The protection of their gigantic exercise in socio-economic engineering was, Pascua recognised, the factor which conditioned every foreign policy move made by the Soviet Government: 'all the political game is being subordinated to the colossal and essential task of the Soviet leaders'.[27] It was firmly within this hierarchy of policy priorities that the Spanish problem was evaluated by the Soviet government. Pascua even concluded that the Spanish war was in itself a minor matter in Moscow's international calculations.[28] The sole criterion of strategic significance apparently applied by the Kremlin in the mid-1930s to international affairs was the possible impact of a foreign development upon the security of the one land where socialism was under construction. This was the grand strategic perspective from which Soviet policy towards the Spanish Civil War was formulated.

The Soviet ambassador in London, Ivan Maisky, tried to impress this very point upon the British foreign secretary, Anthony Eden, on 3 November 1936. In a conversation with Eden, Maisky gave what he himself described as 'an exposition of the motives which had actuated the Soviet government in the Spanish conflict':

> He [Maisky] was emphatic that the Soviet government's admitted sym-pathy with the government in Spain was not due to their desire to set up a communist regime in that country. I [Eden] remarked that the ambassador could hardly be surprised if other people thought differently in view of the declared objective of the upholders of communism to make their method of government universal. The ambassador replied that it was quite true that this was their ultimate objective but it was a very distant one—nobody [in] Russia today thought that could be

achieved for instance in our lifetime—and the Soviet government's purpose in attempting to assist the Spanish government was far more
immediate than that... The Soviet government were convinced that if
General Franco were to win the encouragement given to Germany and
Italy would be such as to bring nearer the day when another active
aggression would be committed—this time perhaps in central or eastern
Europe. That was a state of affairs that Russia wished at all costs to
avoid and that was her main reason for wishing the Spanish government to win in this civil strife.[29]

The Foreign Office's Soviet expert, Laurence Collier, accepted
'Maisky's account of his government's motives' as 'substantially
accurate'.[30] Stalin's Spanish policy was an integrated part of Soviet
international strategy as a whole. It was the general strategic implications of fascist intervention in Spain which prompted Soviet concern over that country and their eventual engagement there.[31]

The Kremlin had been alarmed for some time at the seemingly
endemic antagonism of Nazi Germany towards the Soviet state and,
as Maisky had impressed upon Eden, Moscow wanted to thwart
any success for Hitler in Spain which might encourage him to under-
take military adventures eastwards. The Soviet Union had already
moved to counter the potential threat to its security, posed by the
developing bloc of right-wing states formed by Germany, Italy and
Japan, by altering its own ideological and diplomatic course during
1934–5. Forsaking political sectarianism and revolutionary isola-
tionism, Stalin had sought anti-fascist allies among the bourgeois
democratic parties and states.[32] The main result of the effort to
create a popular front at the international level was the Soviet-
French Treaty of Mutual Assistance of 2 May 1935, by which both
powers promised 'immediate' joint consultation if either were
'threatened with or in danger of aggression' and also pledged
'reciprocally' to render each other aid and assistance in case of 'an
unprovoked aggression on the part of a European state' on either
country.[33] Although right-wing reluctance in France to bind their
country to Communist Russia delayed the parliamentary ratification
of the treaty until March 1936, its confirmation then was followed
soon afterwards by the election victory of the French Popular Front
coalition under Léon Blum. This happy coincidence appears to have
reawakened the Soviet interest in concluding a military convention
with France that would develop their diplomatic association into an
effective military alliance. The Soviet leadership pursued this project especially actively from the early summer of 1936 until the
spring of 1937, the same period during which it had also to form its

basic line of foreign policy towards the Spanish Civil War. The hope that France might become Soviet Russia's military partner was the main positive influence (and, of course, it was clearly connected with the major negative influence on Soviet policy at that time, anxiety about Hitler's Germany) affecting Moscow's attitude towards the Spanish Civil War, during the crucial months of late 1936 and early 1937. It was only subsequent to the Soviet elaboration of a stable policy-line on Spain that the Kremlin's hopes for an alliance with France were to be definitively disappointed by opposition from within the French government and the army's general staff.[34]

It was, then, the Soviet preoccupation with protecting the strategic position of their potential ally, France, that produced the twists and turns in Russian policy towards Spain in the vital early phases of the Civil War there. Viscount Chilston realized that it was precisely this concern which had induced Moscow to abandon its initially aloof attitude towards the Spanish struggle. On 10 August 1936 the British ambassador relayed home Karl Radek's refutation, in *Izvestiya* of 4 August, of the Nazi charge that the Spanish war was Moscow' work:

> The louder the German fascists shout about Bolshevik or French intervention in Spain, the plainer it becomes that they are preparing for serious action not only against Spain but against France also.

Chilston emphasised the importance of this latter statement by commenting on it, thus:

> This last sentence reveals of course the kernel of the Soviet government's problem. Lenin prophesied long ago that Spain would be the first to follow in Russia's footsteps, but Spain and the world revolution can wait; meanwhile any danger to France is a danger to the Soviet Union.[35]

The Soviets were quick to grasp that the Spanish conflict might well result in acute danger for France. On 14 August 1936 *Pravda* editorialized in this vein:

> It is absolutely essential to submit to serious study the possible consequences of Spanish events 'for the future, for the independence and for the security of France'.[36]

A fascist regime in Spain, in alliance with Hitler or Mussolini, or both, could create a military threat along France's previously secure Pyrenean frontier and might even interrupt metropolitan lines of communication with French North Africa, where large-scale forces were stationed in time of European peace. As has been mentioned above, the Soviet government did sign the international non-intervention agreement on Spain, in late August 1936, in spite of its growing alarm about the possible repercussions of a fascist victory there. However, as the people's commissar for foreign affairs, Maxim Litvinov, declared at the League of Nations on 8 September 1936, 'the Soviet government has associated itself with the Declaration on Non-Intervention in Spanish affairs only because a friendly power (i.e., France) feared an international conflict if we did not do so'.[37] Recognising that Blum's Popular Front government was too divided on the issue of aid to the Spanish Republic to take practical steps to safeguard French strategic interests in Spain, the Soviets apparently rallied to the non-intervention agreement in the hope that the scheme would succeed in its purpose of localising the conflict by ending foreign fascist assistance to Franco. Yet, when continuing Italo–German aid brought the Spanish military rebels to the brink of victory in late September and early October 1936, the Soviet government resolved to intervene to save Republican Spain because it realised that the French government was too paralysed by internal dissent over Spain to take action to help itself.[38] Stalin was emphatic that this determination to defend France was the sole motive behind his intervention in Spain, when he discussed the matter with Pascua early in 1937:

> Spain, according to them [the Soviet leaders] is not suitable for communism, nor prepared to adopt it and [even] less to have it imposed on her, nor even if she adopted it or they imposed it on her, could it last, surrounded by hostile bourgeois régimes. In opposing the triumph of Italy and Germany, they are trying to prevent any weakening in France's power or military situation.[39]

Moreover, the final influence impelling the U.S.S.R. to become involved in the Spanish conflict must have been the awareness that not only would France, the linchpin of the embryonic Soviet defensive network, be defended, but that a collective security system might be extended to embrace other major democratic powers, particularly Britain. The defence of Republican Spain against fascist aggression might provide convenient ground for co-operation between the Soviet Union and the western democracies, a working partnership that could develop into a fully-fledged military alliance with Britain and France, thereby realising the Kremlin's general design for the protection of Communist Russia against Nazi Germany. The role of Soviet advisers and Spanish communists in restraining, reversing and even repressing the revolutionary process inside the

Republican zone of Spain seems explained, in part at least, by Stalin's determination that the régime there should present a moderate, bourgeois democratic image to capitalist politicians in Britain and France, who might be persuaded to mount a joint Anglo–French–Soviet rescue operation on its behalf. Stalin counselled Republican Spain's socialist premier, Francisco Largo Caballero, on this point in a letter of 21 December 1936:

> The urban petty and middle bourgeoisie must be attracted to the government side ... The leaders of the Republican party should not be repulsed; on the contrary they should be drawn in, brought close to the government, persuaded to get down to the job in harness with the government ... This is necessary in order to prevent the enemies of Spain from presenting it as a Communist Republic, and thus to avert their open intervention, which represents the greatest danger to Republican Spain.[40]

A radical Spanish republic, moreover, would frighten off conservatives in Britain and France whose co-operation the Soviets sought in joint action over the Civil War, with the immediate aim of saving Republican Spain, but with the more fundamental purpose of obtaining Anglo–French membership of an anti-Nazi bloc which would guarantee the strategic security of the U.S.S.R. Indeed, acute Spanish Republican observers discerned a clear Soviet unwillingness to help their cause on a scale greater than that which the British and French would complement or tolerate. Thus, the president of the Spanish Republic, Manuel Azaña, was sure, in August 1937, that the Soviet Union would avoid any action in support of Republican Spain that could injure seriously Moscow's relations with Britain or jeopardise its pursuit of 'western friendships'.[41] Again, Pascua informed his governent in January 1937 that Soviet support for the Spanish Republican cause was 'conditional on a clearer and more effective French attitude, doubtless subordinate to English solidarity'.[42]

It was in order to be able to project a credible image to Paris and London of the Spanish Republic as a moderate bourgeois democracy that the Soviets spearheaded a socio-economic counter-revolution inside Republican Spain. This process dismantled agrarian collectives, returned collectivised industries to private enterprise, destroyed (with admittedly sectarian ideological zeal) the 'Trotskyist' Partido Obrero de Unificación Marxista and disbanded the socialist and anarcho-syndicalist militia, absorbing their elements into a new regular formation, the Popular Army of the Republic.[43]

The inevitable result of this exercise in repression was the destruction of the popular *élan* of the masses of Republican Spain, whose very talent for spontaneous, direct action had saved the Republic in the first days of the military *pronunciamienta* against it, between 18 and 20 July 1936. Perhaps the people's energy had to be controlled and the revolutionary process channelled if the Civil War was to be won. However, the brutal communist suppression of Republican Spain's left-wing socialist and anarcho–syndicalist revolution deprived the Spanish Republic of its domestic power-base. Only foreign aid, the elusive intervention of Britain and France, could have saved the demoralised and divided Republic. However, the Soviet communist strategy failed to achieve its goal: British indifference and French indecision doomed Republican Spain.

However, Moscow continued to exercise a moderating influence on political and social developments within Republican Spain for the effective duration of the Spanish Civil War, in the hope of ultimate strategic association with the western democracies. This courtship of the capitalist powers in the Spanish cockpit was pursued notwithstanding its lack of return and the condemnation it drew on Spanish communists from other leftists. Indeed, a significant dissenting voice was raised even within the Spanish Communist Party as the fortunes of civil war turned against the Republic, with the progress of the Aragonese offensive launched by the Francoist forces with massive amounts of fascist equipment and German and Italian aircraft on 9 March 1938. As the outgunned Spanish Republicans retreated before this onslaught, the editors of the Communist Party paper, *Mundo Obrero*, who were based in Madrid and thus situated at some remove from direct control by the party leadership, which was located in Barcelona, expressed open opposition to the official communist line on the Civil War. *Mundo Obrero*'s issue for 23 March 1938 contained an article rejecting the view that the fate of Republican Spain depended on it so limiting its socio-political revolution as to ensure that its struggle remained one in defence of bourgeois democracy and national independence, war aims that might appeal to foreign democrats. This article dismissed the argument that 'the only solution for our war is for Spain to be neither Fascist nor Communist, because this is what France wants', and also contended that the Civil War would be won by the Spanish people 'despite the opposition of capitalism'.[44] The Communist Party's leadership moved at once to reimpose conformity with the Kremlin's policy towards the Spanish conflict and a letter to the editors of *Mundo Obrero*, signed by José Díaz, was published on 30 March. It confirmed the party line:

> You affirm that 'the Spanish people will win despite the opposition of capitalism'... but, politically, it corresponds neither to the situation nor to the policy, of our party and the Communist International. In my report to the November Plenum of our Central Committee, we affirmed:
>
>> That there is a terrain on which all democratic States can unite and act together. It is the terrain of defence of their own existence against the common aggressor: fascism; it is the terrain of defence against the war that threatens us all.
>
> When we spoke here of 'all the democratic states', we were not thinking only of the Soviet Union, where socialist democracy exists, but also of France, England, Czechoslovakia, of the United States, etc., which are democratic, but capitalist, countries. We want these states to aid us; we think that in aiding us they defend their own interest; we strive to make them understand this and ask for their aid.[45]

As Fernando Claudín notes, Díaz's revealing reference to a war 'that threatens us all' indicates that it was the Russian apprehension about a fascist attack on the U.S.S.R., not the actual war against Spanish democracy, which was the principal inspiration behind this reaffirmation of the official communist line and, indeed, of that Soviet policy itself.[46]

When the secretary general of France's foreign ministry, Alexis Léger, was told in October 1936 of the Soviets' decision to become involved in the Spanish Civil War, the French diplomat was 'somewhat puzzled by the sudden change in Russian policy'. Believing that 'Stalin had no ideals', that he was a 'realist and an opportunist', Léger could only speculate on the reasons for the *volte-face* in Soviet policy towards Spain. He imagined that 'the idealists in Russia, the followers of Lenin and Trotsky and the advocates of world war and revolution' had been able to force their view upon the reluctant Stalin.[47] Léger's opposite number in the British Foreign Office, Sir Robert Vansittart, was equally perplexed by this shift in Soviet policy, as is evident from his comment on receiving report of it:

> It is rather a surprising development seeing that the growth of the German danger in Europe had, since 1933, been until this summer steadily tending to cause Russia to make friends so far as possible with the western democracies and to go slower on the revolutionary doctrines.[48]

However, as has been explained above, Stalin's intervention in the Spanish Civil War was not due to a resurgence of revolutionary internationalism in Soviet foreign policy. On the contrary, Soviet engagement in Spain's civil conflict was meant to consolidate, and perhaps complete by military alliance, Moscow's *rapprochement* with the western powers, in the face of the common Nazi danger. Dr. Juan Negrín López, premier of Republican Spain in the later years of the Civil War, understood the rationale of Soviet policy towards his country, as his declaration before the United States Council on Foreign Relations in May 1939 demonstrates:

> Moscow tried to do for France and England what they should have done for themselves. The promise of Soviet aid to the Spanish Republic was that ultimately Paris and London would awake to the risks involved to themselves in an Italo–German victory in Spain and join the U.S.S.R. in supporting us. Munich, with its unnecessary surrender to the totalitarians, probably crushed this hope beyond repair. Moscow alone could not have saved us... France and England never acted as their imperial interests dictated.[49]

Stalin's foreign policy failure in Spain appears, therefore, to have stemmed from the 'objective correctness' of his assessment of the international issues at stake in the conflict there. Calculating carefully the common Spanish ground on which the bourgeois democracies could co-operate with the Soviet Union against the menace of fascism, Stalin underestimated the subjective factors militating against such a development. The instinctive anti-communism of British statesmen and the doctrinaire antipathy of many French policy-makers towards any Soviet connection were prominent amongst the influences which frustrated Stalin's design for an international alliance of anti-fascist powers. This must have seemed an ironical state of affairs to a communist politician like Stalin who was prepared to subordinate ideological imperatives to, or at least reconcile them with, the exigencies of *realpolitik*.

Notes

1. Mijail Koltsov, *Diario de la guerra española* (Madrid, 1978), pp 7–8; International Editorial Board, *International solidarity with the Spanish Republic* (Moscow, 1975), p. 300.
2. Koltsov, *Diario*, p. 7; W. N. Medlicott and Douglas Dakin (ed.), *Documents on British foreign policy, 1919–1939*, series 2 (hereafter cited as D.B.F.P.), xvii, *Western pact negotiations: outbreak of the Spanish Civil War, June 23, 1936– January 2, 1937*, (London, 1979), 83.
3. Angel Viñas, *El Oro de Moscú: Alfa y omega de un mito franquista* (Barcelona, 1979), p. 320.

4. D.B.F.P., xvii, 83–4; *International solidarity*, pp 301–2; Koltsov, *Diario*, p. 8.
5. *International solidarity*, p. 302.
6. W. H. Auden, 'Spain', in Valentine Cunningham (ed.), *The Penguin book of Spanish Civil War verse* (Harmondsworth, 1980), p. 99.
7. *International solidarity*, p. 315.
8. Fernando Claudín, *The Communist movement: From Comintern to Cominform* (Harmondsworth, 1975), pp 176–7.
9. Ivan Maisky, *Spanish notebooks* (London, 1966), p. 48; *International solidarity*, pp 303–4.
10. *International solidarity*, p. 7.
11. *Istoriya Vtoroi Mirovoi Voiny, 1939–1945*, ii, (Moscow, 1974), 52.
12. D.B.F.P., xvii, 36.
13. Cited by John F. Coverdale, *Italian intervention in the Spanish Civil War* (Princeton, 1975), p. 94.
14. Ibid., pp 3–4, 85–6.
15. Ibid., p. 4; D.B.F.P., xvii, 44.
16. D.B.F.P., xvii, 83.
17. Ministère des Affaires Étrangères, *Documents diplomatiques Français 1932–1939, 2e série* (hereafter cited as D.D.F.), iii, *19 Juillet–19 Novembre 1936*, (Paris, 1966), 208.
18. Ibid., 143.
19. Coverdale, *Italian intervention*, pp. 94–5.
20. D.D.F., iii, 271–2.
21. Ibid., 338.
22. Viñas, *El Oro de Moscú, p. 152; id.*, 'Gold, the Soviet Union and the Spanish Civil War' in *European Studies Review*, ix (1979), pp 110–11.
23. D.B.F.P., xvii, 367–9.
24. Quoted by David T. Cattell, *Soviet diplomacy and the Spanish Civil War* (Berkeley and Los Angeles, 1957), p. 19.
25. Cited by Coverdale, *Italian intervention*, p. 94.
26. Viñas, *El Oro de Moscú*, pp 320, 323.
27. Ibid., p. 321.
28. Manuel Azaña, *Obras completas*, iv, *Memorias políticas y de guerra* (Mexico, 1968), 734.
29. D.B.F.P., xvii, 495–6.
30. Ibid., 496.
31. See, e.g. *Dokumenty vneshnei politiki SSSR*, xix (Moscow, 1974), doc. 305.
32. Isaac Deutscher, *Stalin: A Political Biography* (revised ed., Harmondsworth, 1966), pp 407–12; Claudín, *Communist movement*, pp 174–9; E. H. Carr *The twilight of Comintern, 1930*–1935 (London, 1982), pp 116–55, 403–27.
33. J. A. S. Grenville, *The major international treaties, 1914–1973: a history and guide with texts* (London, 1974), pp 152–3.
34. John E. Dreifort, 'The French Popular Front and the Franco–Soviet Pact, 1936–37: a dilemma in foreign policy' in *Journal of Contemporary History*, xi (1976), pp 217–36; Robert J. Young, *In command of France: French foreign policy and military planning, 1933–1940* (Cambridge, Massachusetts, 1978), pp 145–50; Anthony Adamthwaite, *France and the coming of the second World War* (London, 1977), pp 47–50.
35. D.B.F.P., xvii, 84–5.
36. Cited by Cattell, *Soviet diplomacy*, p. 6.
37. Ibid., p. 39.

38. D.B.F.P., xvii, 475–6.
39. Azaña, *Obras completas*, iv, 618.
40. Cited by Claudín, *Communist movement*, p. 707.
41. Azaña, *Obras completas*, iv, 734.
42. Viñas, *El Oro de Moscú*, p. 322.
43. Burnett Bolloten, *The Spanish Revolution: The Left and the struggle for power during the Civil War* (Chapel Hill, 1979), pp 177–477.
44. José Díaz, *Tres años de lucha* (Paris, 1970), p. 557; Claudín, *Communist movement*, pp 234–5.
45. Díaz, *Tres años*, p. 559.
46. Claudín, *Communist movement*, p. 714.
47. D.B.F.P., xvii, 475–6. The German ambassador in Moscow, von Schulenburg, also attributed the Soviet decision to become involved in the Spanish war to the growing influence of forces emanating from 'the basically revolutionary orientation of the Soviet Union'. (U.S., British, French Board of Editors, *Documents on German foreign policy, 1918–1945, Series D (1937–1945)*, iii, *Germany and the Spanish Civil War* (London, 1951), 108).
48. D.B.F.P., xvii, 476.
49. Cited by Julio Álvarez del Vayo, *Freedom's battle* (London, 1940), pp 76–7.